Crisis Intervention
and
Crisis Management
Strategies That Work in
Schools and Communities

Rosemary A. Thompson, EdD, LPC, NCC, NCSC

BRUNNER-ROUTLEDGE

New York and Hove

Published in 2004 by
Brunner-Routledge
29 West 35th Street
New York, NY 10001
www.brunner-routledge.com

Published in Great Britain by
Brunner-Routledge
27 Church Road
Hove, East Sussex
BN3 2FA
www.brunner-routledge.co.uk

Brunner-Routledge is an imprint of the Taylor & Francis Group.
Printed in the United States of America on acid-free paper.

10 9 8 7 6 5 4 3 2

Library of Congress Cataloging-in-Publication Data

Thompson, Rosemary, 1950-
   Crisis intervention and crisis management : strategies that work in schools and
communities / Rosemary A. Thompson.
         p. ; cm.
Inlcudes bibliographical references and index.
   ISBN 0-415-94818-5 (hardback : alk. paper) — ISBN 0-415-94494-5 (pbk. : alk. paper)
   1. School crisis management—United States. 2. Crisis intervention (Mental
health services)—United States.
   [DNLM: 1. Crisis Intervention—organization & administration. 2. Disaster Planning—
organization & administration. 3. Crisis Intervention—methods. 4. Schools.
5. Terrorism. WA 295 T475c 2003] I. Title.
   LB2866.5.T46 2003
   363.11'9371—dc21

                                                                    2003012666

This book is dedicated to all the school counselors, teachers, and administrators across the nation and the world who have dedicated themselves to the well-being and safety of children.

Contents

Preface

Suicide or sudden loss, critical incidents, disasters, and terrorism have become major concerns for school counselors, teachers, parents, and helping professionals. The status of crisis management in schools nationwide varies. Some school districts with strong leadership have developed building-specific crisis plans, require lock-down and evacuation drills, and provide extensive training to the building response teams in conjunction with local police, mental health workers, and other community providers. Simulation drills that involve students, staff, and community providers further solidify their skills and preparedness. The terrorist attacks on September 11, 2001, have changed not only the landscape of America but also the ways that schools and communities respond to crises, critical incidents, and potential disasters. Schools and communities continue to maintain a heightened sense of alertness that has the entire country feeling more vulnerable and perhaps less secure than at any time in our nation's history.

Administrators, teachers, and counselors may be held personally liable if crises, critical incidents, or disaster situations are handled improperly, or, in the worst-case scenario, if there is a failure to act when action is clearly called for, in order to ensure safety. Relative to a single successful or even unsuccessful lawsuit, the cost of training individuals in crisis management is negligible. In times of crisis, schools will need to respond immediately to prevent or reduce the possibility of further accidents and tragedies. Schools are not immune to naturally occurring conditions like earthquakes and cannot avoid completely unwanted disturbances or intrusions; however, school personnel can prevent unnecessary confusion and turmoil if they plan certain steps to minimize the possibility of further accidents or tragedies on their school campus.

Planning for schoolwide crises, critical incidents, and crisis response can significantly reduce disruption during times of chaos. A structured response by a trained team of school or community staff members, or both, can facilitate the return to a normal school routine and precrisis equilibrium. Having crisis, critical incident, and disaster plans in place improves school morale, promotes safety and security, and enhances community respect and cohesiveness. Schools remain at the forefront as institutions of stability, continuity, and accountability. They are also viewed as resources of information, safety, and security whenever there is chaos or confusion.

An overall school safety plan requires a thoughtful process for identifying security needs, developing prevention and intervention techniques, evaluating physical facilities, and providing communication and professional development for school and community members. This book serves as a collective resource for schools and communities by providing practical techniques and the best practice strategies to restore safety and security and to maintain continuity and integrity.

Chapter 1 briefly examines international and domestic terrorism to provide a perspective on why it is so critical to have contingency plans, professional development, and the coordination of services between school and community agencies on an ongoing basis; that is, crisis, critical incident, and disaster plans are developed, reviewed, and practiced annually. Case managers may move to other jobs, community contacts may reorganize, and the school, the community, or both might change in terms of resources, experience, and commitment. Essentially, "plans are nothing, planning is everything"; this includes a concerted effort between the school and the community, students and families, educators and helping professionals. Chapter 2 differentiates between a crisis, a critical incident, and a disaster, which sets the stage for chapters 3, 4, and 5.

Chapter 2, "Crises, Critical Incidents, Disasters, and Terrorism: Fundamental Emotional Reactions From a Developmental Perspective," outlines the wide range of emotional, physical, and cognitive reactions that young people experience by age level. It differentiates between normal behavior and stressful behavior. The ramifications of post-traumatic stress disorder, acute stress disorder, general anxiety disorder, panic disorder, and agoraphobia are outlined, along with factors that increase the risk of lasting readjustment problems. Essentially, the school district and its surrounding community are a unique blend of individuals from numerous disciplines that can bring the school, the community, or both to its precrisis equilibrium.

Chapter 3, "Crisis Intervention and Crisis Management: First-Response Procedures," delineates roles and responsibilities of crisis team members and stresses the importance of having a comprehensive crisis communication contingency plan and first-response procedures. It delineates the roles and responsibilities of school administrators, teachers, and a school counselor as case manager, as well as staff duties. The importance of designating a care center for teachers and students is also outlined. The self-destructive behavior of students who may consider suicide is also examined, with a discussion of how to interview a student during a crisis, in addition to response and referral procedures.

Chapter 4, "Critical Incidents and First-Response Procedures," identifies 18 potential critical incidents, from student assaults to terrorist attacks, with procedures to follow for each incident. It lists the members of *Critical Incident Teams* and outlines the characteristics and the duties of team members. The chapter includes a *Critical Incident Faculty Survey* to identify faculty and staff members who have expertise in CPR, first aid, or emergency management.

Chapter 5, "Disasters and First-Response Procedures," provides an overview of tasks required for four distinct stages following a disaster: *rescue state, early inventory state, late inventory stage,* and *reconstruction stage.* This chapter addresses the special needs of children following a disaster, outlines nine typical disaster incidents, and concludes with a timely piece on homeland security.

Chapter 6, "Strategies for the Resolution of Grief and Loss," addresses ways to meet the needs of students and survivors in a physical, a cognitive, an emotional, and a behavioral context, which all interact interdependently. It outlines the states of nine stages of grief from shock and denial, to acceptance, hope, and resilience. Common signs of grieving children are outlined, as well as children's concept of death from a developmental perspective. This chapter also provides 47 specific practical ideas to deal with grief and loss, for example, "The only answer to grief is action."

Chapter 7, "Debriefing Survivors Following a Crisis, a Disaster, or a Critical Incident," provides an overview of what researchers are learning about trauma in children and adolescents; this includes the emotional effects of trauma and how these differentiate according to developmental age. Psychological debriefing is explained, as well as critical incident stress management, seven core components of critical incident stress management, critical incident stress debriefing, suggestions for leading a school group, and post-traumatic stress debriefing. All components of this particular chapter are *skills and tools,* indicating what to do in each particular situation.

Chapter 8, "Activities for Children and Adolescents to Process Grief and Loss," includes behavioral reactions that adults can expect from their children, such as increased fear and anxiety, poor academic performance, irritability, and depressed feelings. Also included are activities that classroom teachers can implement such as traumatic symptoms and therapeutic interventions. Activities include group projects, guided free play, stimulating discussions, creative writing, dramatic enactment of stories and metaphors, music, and bibliotherapy. The chapter concludes with *Structured Sensory Intervention for Traumatized Children, Adolescents, and Parents (SITCAP).*

Chapter 9, "Sample Policies to Prevent Legal Liabilities and to Use for Assessments and as Screening Instruments," addresses ethical policies and liabilities pertaining to school counselors, teachers, administrators, and all those who professionally interact with the school.

Chapter 10, "Compassion Fatigue: The Professional Consequences of Caring Too Much," examines the importance of debriefing the trauma team, taking care of emotional needs, and establishing boundaries in terms of caring for others and for oneself. Specific strategies for care and renewal are provided.

Acknowledgments

Many counselors and helping professionals have directly or indirectly contributed or influenced the development of this book. I would like to thank the students at Old Dominion University, Norfolk, Virginia, and my colleagues at Regent University, Virginia Beach, Virginia as well as the participants of the New England School Counselors Institute. I would be remiss if I did not credit Chesapeake Public Schools, Chesapeake, Virginia for both their leadership and insight by creating policies and procedures for crisis management two decades ago.

Another significant influence in the development of this book was steadfast support of the late Joseph Hollis who recognized my potential as a writer and offered me my first book contract in 1986. I am also grateful for the support and encouragement of Emily Epstein Loeb of Taylor and Francis Publishers (after 71 e-mails to each other, we finally have a book!). I also appreciate the vision of the staff at Brunner-Routledge for their commitment to growth and development of the school counseling profession.

Finally, I am most indebted to my family, my husband Charles and our two children Ryan and Jessica. Sometimes I feel they know more about the back of my head than the front of my face as I log long hours on the computer. They unconditionally give their love, patience, and support to make my writing interests a reality.

Chapter 1

Glimpse of Terrorist Acts Both International and Domestic

INTERNATIONAL THREATS

International terrorist acts committed in the United States are not unique to our recent past. Concern has grown, however, during the last 2 decades over increased terrorist activities in the Middle East, particularly suicide bombings, and the deep involvement of the United States in Middle East peace negotiations. That the United States has become a target for terrorists was tragically demonstrated by the bombing of the World Trade Center in 1993 and, again, when commercial airline planes that were hijacked by terrorists on September 11, 2001, destroyed its twin towers. These acts and the related hijacked plane crash into the Pentagon on the same day, as well as earlier attacks and attempted attacks on U.S. targets, demonstrate that the United States must take the security of its people more seriously. Terrorism will be the legacy of the twentieth century. This never-ending conflict will ultimately dominate the political landscape.

DOMESTIC THREATS

In addition, researchers from the U.S. Secret Service and the U.S. Department of Education have completed a detailed analysis of 37 school shootings. Official arrest data offer an obvious means of determining the extent of youth violence. Indeed, a surge in arrests for violent crimes marked what is now recognized as an epidemic of youth violence from 1983 to 1993. Arrests were driven largely by the rapid proliferation of firearm use by adolescents who engage in violent acts. These confrontations often produced serious or lethal injuries, resulting in more severe criminal charges.

Today, with fewer young people carrying weapons, including guns, to school and elsewhere than in the early 1990s, violent encounters are less likely to result in homicide and serious injury and therefore are less likely to draw the attention of police. By 1999, arrest rates for homicide, rape, and robbery had all dropped below 1983 rates. In contrast, arrest rates for aggravated assault remained higher than they were in 1983, having declined only 24% from the peak rates of 1994.

Confidential surveys find that 10 to 15% of high school seniors report having committed an act of serious violence in recent years. These acts typically do not come to the attention of police, in part because they are less likely to involve firearms than in previous years. Over the last 2 decades, self-reported violence by high school seniors increased nearly 50%, a trend similar to that found in arrests for violent crimes. But this percentage has not declined in the years since 1993—it remains at peak levels.

Childhood risk factors for violence in adolescence include involvement in serious (but not necessarily violent) criminal acts and substance use before puberty, being male, aggressiveness, low family socioeconomic status/poverty, and antisocial parents—all either individual or family risk factors. The influence of family is largely supplanted in adolescence by peer influences; thus, risk factors with the largest predictive effects in adolescence include having weak social ties, having ties to antisocial or delinquent peers, and belonging to a gang. Having committed serious (but not necessarily violent) criminal offenses is also an important risk factor in adolescence.

PREVENTION STRATEGIES

Early Warning, Timely Response: A Guide to Safe Schools (Dwyer, Osher & Warger, 1998) also includes a warning not to jump to conclusions about students who may fit a specific profile or who possess a set of early warning indicators. The document, which was written in part by the National Association of School Psychologists, calls for school officials to use the following principles to ensure that early warning signs are not misinterpreted:

- Do no harm. Get help for the child; don't use the early warning signs as a rationale to exclude, isolate, or punish. Instead, as federal law requires, qualified professionals must give individualized evaluations and make recommendations on how to deal with the troubled child.
- Understand violence and aggression within their context. Violent and aggressive behavior as an expression of emotion may have many antecedent factors, and certain environments can set it off. If a child does not have adequate coping skills, he or she may react with aggression.
- Avoid stereotypes. Race, socioeconomic status, cognitive or academic ability, or physical appearance is a false cue of how a child may act. In

fact, such stereotypes can unfairly harm children, especially when the school community acts upon them.

- View warning signs within a development context. Youths at different levels of development have different emotional and social capabilities. Know what is developmentally typical behavior so that those behaviors are not misinterpreted.
- Understand that children typically exhibit multiple warning signs. Research confirms that most children who are troubled and at risk for aggression exhibit more than one warning sign, with more intensity over time. Thus, it is important not to overreact to single signs, words, or actions.

Warning Signs

Dwyer, Osher, and Wagner (1998) maintain that it is not always possible to predict behavior that will lead to violence. And, they say, none of these signs alone is sufficient for predicting aggression and violence. The early warning signs are offered only as an aid in identifying and referring children who may need help. They are not equally significant, nor are they presented in the order of seriousness. However, they include

- Social withdrawal and an excessive feeling of isolation. Gradual and eventual complete withdrawal from social contacts can be an important indicator of a troubled child.
- Extreme feelings of rejection. Troubled children are often isolated from their peers. They may seek out aggressive friends who reinforce their violent tendencies.
- Being a victim of violence. Physical or sexual abuse may make some children at risk for becoming violent toward others.
- Feelings of being picked on and persecuted. Being constantly picked on, teased, bullied, or singled out for ridicule and humiliation may cause a youth to vent these feelings in inappropriate ways—including aggression or violence.
- Low school interest and poor academic performance. It is important to assess emotional and cognitive reasons for changes in academic performance to determine the true nature of the problem.
- Expression of violence in writings and drawings. Many children produce work about violent themes that for the most part is harmless when taken in context. But an overrepresentation of violence in writings and drawings directed consistently at specific individuals could signal emotional problems that could lead to violence. However, there is a real danger of misdiagnosing this type of sign, and professional guidance—such as from a school psychologist—would be needed in this situation.

- Uncontrolled anger. Anger that is expressed frequently and intensely in response to minor irritants may signal potential violent behavior.
- A history of discipline problems. Chronic behavioral and disciplinary problems in school and at home may suggest that underlying emotional needs are not being met. These problems could set the stage for aggressive behavior.
- A past history of violent and aggressive behavior. Unless provided with support and counseling, a youth who has a history of aggressive or violent behavior is likely to continue those behaviors. Children who engage in aggression and drug abuse before age 12, for example, are more likely to show violence later on, than are children who begin such behavior at an older age.
- Intolerance for differences and prejudicial attitudes that may lead to violence against those who are perceived to be different.
- Drug and alcohol use. These actions expose youths to violence, either as perpetrators or victims or both.
- Affiliation with gangs. Youths who join gangs or emulate their behavior may adopt violence-related values and react violently in certain situations.
- Inappropriate access to, possession of, and use of firearms. Children and youths who inappropriately possess or have access to firearms can have an increased risk for violence—and a higher probability of becoming victims.
- Serious threats of violence. Although idle threats are common responses to frustration, one of the most reliable indicators that a youth is likely to commit a dangerous act toward self or others is a detailed and specific threat to use violence. Recent incidents across the country clearly indicate that threats to commit violence against oneself or others should be taken very seriously. Steps must be taken to understand the nature of these threats and to prevent them from being carried out (Dwyer, Osher, & Warger, 1998).

The Final Report and Findings of the Safe School Initiative: Implications for the Prevention of School Attacks in the United States (2002) found the following characteristics of "school shooters":

Characteristics of Attacker

There is no accurate or useful "profile" of students who engaged in targeted school violence. The attackers came from a variety of family situations, ranging from intact families with numerous ties to the community to foster homes with histories of neglect.

Peer Relationships

Attackers also varied in the types of social relationships they had established, ranging from socially isolated to popular among their peers.

Disciplinary Problems

Attackers' histories of disciplinary problems at school varied. Some attackers had no observed behavioral problems, whereas others had multiple behaviors warranting reprimand and/or discipline.

Academic Performance

Most attackers showed no marked change in academic performance, friendship patterns, interests in school, or school disciplinary problems prior to their attack.

Bullying and Harassment

Many attackers felt bullied, picked on, persecuted, threatened, attacked, or injured by others prior to the incident.

Mental Well-Being

A history of having been the subject of a mental health evaluation, diagnosed with a mental disorder, or involved in substance abuse did not appear to be prevalent among attackers. However, some attackers showed some history of suicidal attempts or thoughts, or a history of feeling extreme depression or desperation.

Violence

Over half of the attackers demonstrated some interest in violence, through movies, video games, books, and other media. However, there was not one common type of interest in violence indicated. Instead, the attackers' interest in violent themes took various forms. Most attackers had no history of prior violent or criminal behavior.

Loss

Most attackers were known to have had difficulty coping with significant losses or personal failures. Moreover, many had considered or attempted suicide.

Planning

Incidents of targeted violence at school rarely are sudden, impulsive acts. Some attackers developed their plans on the day of their attack or only 1 or 2 days prior; others developed their plans between 6 and 8 months prior to the attack.

Revenge

Revenge was a motive for more than half of the attackers. Other motives included trying to solve a problem, suicide or desperation, and efforts to get attention or recognition. In addition, most attackers held some sort of grievance at the time of the attack, either against their target(s) or against someone else.

Prior Knowledge

Many attackers told other people about these grievances prior to the attacks. Prior to most incidents, other people knew about the attackers idea(s), plan to attack, or both. In most cases, other people knew about the attack before it took place. Some peers knew exactly what the attacker planned to do; others knew something "big" or "bad" was going to happen, and in several cases knew the time and date it was to occur.

No Prior Threats

Most attackers did not threaten their targets directly prior to advancing the attack. The majority of the attackers did not threaten their target(s) directly.

Complacent Concern

Most attackers engaged in some behavior prior to the incident that caused others concern or indicated a call for help. Almost all of the attackers engaged in some behavior prior to the attack that caused others, such as school officials, parents, teachers, police, and fellow students, to be concerned. In most cases, at least one adult was concerned by the attackers' behavior.

Peer Pressure

Many attackers were influenced or encouraged by others to engage in the attacks. Nearly half of the attackers were influenced by other individuals in deciding to mount an attack, dared or encouraged by others to attack, or both.

Intervention

Despite prompt law enforcement responses, most attacks were stopped by means other than law enforcement intervention. Most school-based attacks stopped through intervention by school adminstrators, educators, and students, or by the attacker stopping their own violent behavior.

All these characteristics have implications for school policy, campus security, school climate, and collective communication between schools and communities, children and families.

PREVENTION EFFORTS

Many school districts throughout the nation are training their teachers how to recognize and respond to early warning signs. Teachers and school personnel are also receiving instructions on how to react during a school crisis. These lessons range from calling 911 before calling the district superintendent, to learning how to disarm an intruder, to holding mock crises and drills, such as hostage-taking, to prepare for what could be the inevitable (Portner, 1998). Other schools and districts are using metal detectors, drug tests, dress codes, and uniforms; have taken out lockers; and insist that all book bags and backpacks be made of see-through material. Others have gone so far as to close faculty restrooms, which increases the presence of teachers in the students' restrooms. These are all punitive measures that make schools seem more like schools-as-institutions rather than schools-as-communities. Although many of these actions are controversial, providing violence-prevention programs, counseling for potentially violent students, and emotional support for survivors can only strengthen the nation's resolve to keep schools safe for our children.

PROGRAM SUMMARY:

Generally, this program requires that students in unsafe situations be allowed to transfer to other, safer, public schools. Specifically, transfers must be allowed for two reasons: (1) when a school is determined to be "persistently dangerous" and (2) when a student becomes the victim of a violent crime at a school.

To the extent possible, local educational agencies (LEAs) should allow transferring students to transfer to a school that is making adequate yearly progress and has not been identified as being in school improvement, corrective action, or restructuring. The LEA is encouraged to take into account the needs and preferences of the affected students and parents to the extent possible.

**PERSISTENTLY DANGEROUS SCHOOLS AND
THE SCHOOL CHOICE OPTION:**

The State, in consultation with a representative sampling of LEAs, should develop the criteria to be used in identifying unsafe schools.

Such criteria must be objective and could include data such as the number of times a firearm was brought into a school, the number of fights, etc.

The State should look for trends in the data or patterns of incidents within the current or most recent school year in determining if a school should be designated as persistently dangerous.

When a school has been identified as persistently dangerous, the LEA must inform parents of the designation within 10 days and offer the students the option to transfer to a safe public school within 20 days. Students should be allowed to transfer within 30 days.

CRIMINAL OFFENSES AND THE SCHOOL CHOICE OPTION:

If a student becomes the victim of a violent criminal offense at school, the LEA must allow the student to transfer to another public school.

The transfer is optional—the student is not required to transfer, but the offer for such a move must be made.

COMPLIANCE:

States must develop an USCO policy, and ESEA funding is contingent upon compliance with USCO.

The guidance document directs that States that have not fully complied with the USCO provisions qualify their certification by August 15, 2002, to include (1) what steps remain to be completed, and (2) a timetable for their completion. It also requires quarterly reporting to the Secretary on the State's progress in completion of these steps.

The timeline should provide for full compliance no later than July 1, 2003.

Source: The guidance document for the Unsafe Schools Choice Option is available at: http://www.ed.gov/offices/OESE/SDFS/unsafeschoolchoice.doc

FIGURE 1.1

Recent legislation from Congress entitled "No Child Left Behind" has furthered safe school initiatives with the Unsafe Schools Choice Option (USCO), which appears in Title IX, section 9532 of the Elementary and Secondary Education Act (ESEA). See Figure 1.1 for the essential language of the legislation.

This represents a serious mandate from the U.S. government to maintain schools and assure that they are safe havens for learning. Yet we must also find ways to help children and adolescents build meaningful relationships in their schools. This means more than improving the school climate; it cuts through the core of family, school, and community. All must be united to promote the well-being of children and adolescents in our society. Every behavior is a communication, and students today are communicating their pain through aggression, violence, suicide, homicide, self-mutilation, and depression. The onus of responsibility is on all adults who interact with the school and the community. A coalition of parents, teachers, administrators, counselors, support staff, police officers, the clergy, the courts, community leaders, and politicians (to name a few) is desperately needed. Schools cannot accomplish this alone, primarily because they cannot control what goes on in the community that is often brought to the school setting.

WHAT CONSTITUTES A CRITICAL INCIDENT

Each school will need to develop its own management plan to identify the nature and the range of critical incidents to which students and staff may be exposed. A critical incident is broadly defined as an event that causes disruption to an organization, creates significant danger or risk, and traumatically affects individuals within the organization. It can include:

- A bomb threat
- A break-in, accompanied by major acts of vandalism
- Copycat threats
- Destruction of the whole or part of the school or workplace
- An earthquake
- An explosion
- A fire
- A flood
- A gas or chemical hazard
- Hostage situations—students or staff members taken hostage
- An industrial or transport accident
- A natural or other major disaster in the community

- Students being lost or injured on an excursion
- Students or staff members witnessing a serious injury or death
- Unfavorable media attention
- Extremes in temperature or weather, such as wind storms, tornadoes, and hurricanes

An effective critical incident management plan will include each of the following six major areas:

1. Establishment of a Critical Incident/Crisis Response Team
2. Management of evacuation
3. Response planning
4. Recovery timeline
5. Evaluation of the management plan
6. Identifying people who may be affected by critical incidents. (This will be elaborated on in chapter 3: "Crisis Intervention and Crisis Management: First-Response Proceedings.")

WHAT CONSTITUTES A CRISIS

- Child sexual assault
- Date rape
- A child abducted by someone other than custodial parent
- Death of a student or a staff member
- Suicide of a student or a staff member
- Violence between students, or assault on a teacher or a student
- School shootings
- Hostage situations
- Lockdowns because of dangerous intruders

A crisis is perhaps the ultimate "teachable moment." As educators, our team members are uniquely qualified to promote opportunities for learning and growth. Three basic objectives in managing a crisis are

1. To plan and prepare the school and the community with the skills and the organization to respond in a crisis;
2. To come to the immediate aid of affected and vulnerable students, teachers, support staff, and community members; and
3. To vigorously advocate for children and school staff member in healing, rebuilding, and establishing their precrisis equilibrium.

WHAT CONSTITUTES TERRORISM

Terrorism or the threat of terrorism is the most insidious form of violence, both domestically and internationally. People become hostages in their own city, town, community, or country. Terrorism leaves members in a constant state of anticipation and anxiety, which in the long run affect daily living, occupational performance, and overall emotional well-being. Terrorism is defined as the systematic, illegitimate use of violence or threats of violence for political or religious purposes. Terrorism involves activities such as assassinations, bombings, random killings, hijackings, and skyjackings. It is used for political, not military, purposes, and by groups too weak to mount open assaults. Children in the United States today had never experienced an attack on the United States like the events that began on September 11, 2001, with planes crashing into the World Trade Center in New York City and the Pentagon in Virginia. Terrorism involves activities such as:

- Assassinations
- Bombings, random killings
- Skyjackings
- Hijackings
- Suicide bombers
- Hate crimes
- Ethnic cleansing
- Bioterrorism
- Forced protection training
- Weapons of mass destruction (WMD), that is, nuclear, biological, and chemical weapons
- Sniper shootings

EMOTIONAL RESPONSES TO TERRORISM, CRISES, CRITICAL INCIDENTS, OR DISASTERS

A universal sense of shock, fear, sadness, and compassion for those whose loved ones who have been affected directly will linger for weeks, months, and, for some, years, along with concerns for the well-being of children and adolescents. Emotional responses vary in nature and severity from child to child. Nonetheless, there are some common characteristics to how children (and adults) feel when their lives are impacted by acts of terrorism, critical incidents, or an unexpected crises.

- *Fear:* Fear may be the initial reaction—fear for the safety of all those involved. A child's or an adolescent's worries may seem unreasonable, but to that individual, they are quite possible. Children will hear rumors at school that foster destructive fantasy building. They may think the worst, however unrealistic it is. The threat of further terrorism or war may magnify their fears. Other fears may be experienced as a result of media coverage (radio, television, newspapers). Fears or concerns may be about friends or relatives in the immediate vicinity of the terrorism.
- *Loss of control:* Terrorist actions or critical life-threatening incidents are something over which children—and most adults—have no control. Lack of control can be overwhelming and confusing.
- *Anger and rage:* Anger is not an unusual reaction. After fear, the next most common reactions among children are sadness and anger. Unfortunately, anger is often expressed toward those with whom children feel most secure. Or, children and adolescents may be angry with people in other countries for their acts of terrorism or angry at a higher being because of a tornado, for example. Children should be allowed to express their feelings during this time.
- *Loss of stability and security:* Terrorism interrupts the natural order of things. It is very unsettling. Stability is gone, and this is very threatening. It can destroy trust and upset balance and a sense of security.
- *Uncertainty and anxiety:* Children who have relatives or friends living in areas of danger will worry whether their loved ones are safe. The lack of information during the days that follow the event will increase children's anxiety and uncertainty. If a child has suffered other losses or traumatic events, memories of those events may also surface.

HELPING CHILDREN PUT THEIR FEARS IN PERSPECTIVE

Children's ages and individual personalities influence their reactions to stories they hear and images they see about violent acts in the newspapers and on television. With respect to age, preschool-age children may be the most upset by what they see and hear. In addition to age and maturity, children's personalities, temperaments, and previous life experiences can influence their responses. Some children are naturally more prone to be fearful; thus, news of a threatening occurrence may heighten their feelings of anxiety. Some children or adolescents may be more sensitive to, or knowledgeable about, a war if they are of the same nationality as those who are fighting. Children who know someone living near a dangerous situation may be especially affected by events. Children and adolescents also tend to personalize the news they hear, relating it to events or issues in their own lives. Young children are usually most concerned about separation from parents, about good and bad, and about fear of punishment. They may ask questions about the children they see on the news who are alone or might bring up topics related to their own good and bad behavior. Middle-school children are in the midst of peer struggles and are developing a mature moral outlook. Concerns about fairness and punishment will be more prevalent among this age group. Teens consider larger issues related to ethics, politics, and even their own involvement in a potential response through the armed services. Teenagers, like adults, may become reflective about life, reexamining their priorities and interests.

- Help children and adolescents to feel personally and physically safe.
- Help children and adolescents understand that precautions are being taken to prevent terrorism and critical incidents (e.g., bomb-sniffing dogs, passport checks, heightened airport security), which might actually make them safer now than they were in the past.
- Try to maintain daily routines to provide a sense normality, stability, and security.
- Help children to feel a sense of control by taking some action. Students at one intermediate school sent notes and a quilt, as well as 2,000 pounds of books, to the students at P.S. 166 who had watched the planes fly into the World Trade Center from their classroom windows on September 11, 2001.
- Send letters, cookies, or magazines through relief agencies to those who have been impacted.
- If family members get called away, plan some special activities to make pictures, drawings, or linking objects that they can take with them.
- Gather with other families who are also missing a loved one, to help provide mutual support for both children and adults.
- Provide special parent-and-child time together to create an extra sense of security, which might be badly needed. Set aside a particular half-hour each day to play. Make the time as pleasant and child-centered as possible. Talk with adolescents as well. Cellular phones make it easier to talk, because adolescents often find it difficult to intimately discuss their fears and concerns.
- Involve children in planning how to cope. Control and ownership are fostered when children help to plan strategies for dealing with a situation. With critical incidents, for example, if you give them simple chores like filling water bottles and collecting candles and flashlights, this lessens their anxiety and fosters a sense of self-worth.
- Prepare for children having difficulties with going to sleep at night.
- Maintain regular bedtime routines, such as story time, to provide a sense of security. For younger children, special stuffed animals or blankets may be especially important.

- For a few nights, sit near your child until he or she falls asleep. Gradually withdraw this support by checking back in 2 minutes and continuing to lengthen this time until your child feels secure again.
- Be flexible with sleeping arrangements. A light may be needed in or near your child's room. Siblings may want to sleep in the same room until they feel more secure again.
- Don't let your children focus too much of their time and energy on news coverage of the terrorist attacks or the traumatic event. Limit media exposure. If children choose to watch media coverage for hours each evening, find other activities for them. You may also need to watch the news less intensely yourself and spend more time in alternative family activities.
- Use outside support services if your child has a severe reaction. Your school counselor, school social worker, or school psychologist can assist or provide names of other professionals trained to deal with children. Religious and community organizations and mental health providers are possible resources.
- Adults need to take time to process and try to deal with their own reactions to the situation as fully as possible. This, too, will help children.
- Always be honest with children and adolescents, and do not be afraid to talk to others about universal fears and concerns.
- Ask children or adolescents what their biggest fears are, and encourage them to talk about these. If they're having trouble articulating the fears, consider the following common fears after a disaster or a tragedy, and try to address these even if children don't mention them specifically:

  1. Will the event happen again?
  2. Will someone whom I care about be injured or killed?
  3. Will I be separated from my family?
  4. Will I be left alone?
  5. If my mother or father is deployed, will he or she be safe?
  6. Will I be safe at school?

- Keep in mind, too, that it's also common for children to express concern for people they don't know. Be supportive of these concerns.
- To help young children express their feelings, get on the floor and start playing—puppet shows, drawing pictures, and reading books can help small children process those emotions. For adolescents, writing letters to the editor of the paper or collecting funds for people in need may be helpful.
- Get back to the family routine as soon as possible. Children of all ages thrive on routine. It doesn't make sense to pretend that life is normal if the family has been deeply affected by large events, but the routine of children's daily lives—dinner, bath, reading time—can be tremendously reassuring to them.

- Use words and concepts that children can understand. Gear your explanations to the child's age, language, and developmental level.
- Give children honest answers and information. Children will usually know or will eventually find out if adults are "making things up." It may affect their ability to trust and impair their belief in your reassurances about the future.
- Be prepared to repeat information and explanations several times. Some information may be hard to accept or understand. Asking the same question over and over may also be a way for a child to ask for reassurance.
- Acknowledge and validate children's thoughts, feelings, and reactions. Let them know that their questions and concerns are important and appropriate.
- Children learn from watching their parents and teachers. Children are very interested in how grown-ups respond to events in the world. They also notice changes in routines, and they learn from listening to conversations between adults.
- Let children know how adults are feeling. It's okay for children to know that adults experience anxiety, confusion, and apprehension or become preoccupied. Children will usually pick it up anyway, and if they don't know the cause, they may think it's their fault. They may worry that they've done something wrong.
- Don't let children watch lots of TV with violent images. The repetition of frightening scenes or confusing information can be very disturbing to young children.
- Don't confront your child's defenses. If a child is reassured that things are happening "very far away," it's probably best not to argue or disagree. The child may be telling you that this is how he or she needs to think about things in order to feel safe.
- Children who have experienced trauma or losses in the past are particularly vulnerable to having prolonged or more intense reactions to the current situation. These children may need extra support and attention.
- Monitor for physical symptoms, including headaches and stomach aches. Many children express anxiety through physical aches and pains. An increase in such symptoms without apparent medical cause, may be a sign that a child is feeling anxious or overwhelmed.
- Let children know that it is okay to feel upset. Explain that all feelings are okay when a tragedy like this occurs. Let children talk about their feelings, and help put these into perspective. Even anger is okay, but children may need help and patience from adults to assist them in expressing these feelings appropriately.
- Observe children's emotional states. Depending on their age, children may not express their concerns verbally. Children will express their emotions differently. There is no right or wrong way to feel or to express grief or fear. Signs of heightened anxiety include:

1. Refusing to go to school and excessive "clinging"
2. Persistent fears related to the shootings
3. Worry that loved ones might get hurt
4. Sleep disturbances, such as nightmares, screaming during sleep, or bed-wetting
5. Irritability and loss of concentration
6. Increased agitation
7. Being easily startled and jumpy
8. New or unusual behavior problems
9. Physical complaints for which a physical cause cannot be found
10. Withdrawal from family and friends
11. Sadness, listlessness, or decreased activity
12. Preoccupation withdeath or violence

- Look for children at greater risk. Children who have had a past traumatic experience or a personal loss, who suffer from depression or another mental disorder, or that with special needs may be at greater risk than others for severe reactions. Be particularly observant of those who may be at risk of suicide. Seek the help of a mental health professional if you are at all concerned.
- Children who are constantly preoccupied with questions about snipers or terrorism should be evaluated by a trained, qualified mental health professional. Other signs that children may need additional help include ongoing trouble with sleeping; intrusive thoughts, images, or worries; or recurring fears about death, leaving their parents, or going to school. Ask your child's pediatrician, family practitioner, or school counselor to help arrange an appropriate referral. If a child continues to be distressed or shows persistent signs of anxiety, such as changes in behavior, increased aggression, nightmares, clinginess, headaches, stomach aches, shyness, poor concentration, loss of appetite, or trouble sleeping, consider an evaluation by a mental health professional who specializes in caring for children.
- Keep your explanations developmentally appropriate. *Early elementary school* children need brief, simple information, balanced with reassurances that the daily structures of their lives will not change. *Upper elementary and early middle school* children will be more vocal in asking questions about whether they truly are safe and what is being done at their school. They may need assistance in separating reality from fantasy. *Upper middle school and high school* students will have various strong opinions about the causes of violence and threats to safety in schools and society. They will share concrete suggestions about how to make school safer and how to prevent tragedies in society. They will be more committed to doing something to help the survivors and the affected

community. For all children, encourage them to verbalize their thoughts and feelings. Be a good listener!

- Traumatic events are not easy for anyone to comprehend or accept. Understandably, many children, as well as adults, feel confused, upset, and anxious. As parents, teachers, and caring adults, we can serve their needs by listening and responding in an honest, consistent, and supportive manner. Fortunately, most children, even those exposed to trauma, are quite resilient. Like most adults, they will get through this difficult time and go on with their lives. However, by our creating an open environment where they feel free to ask questions, the recovery and healing can help them cope and can reduce the risk of lasting emotional difficulties (Fassler & Dumas, 1998).

WHAT SCHOOLS CAN DO

Schools represent routine, structure, and predictability. Caring adults are also present, who can reaffirm efforts of parents or caregivers. For many children and adolescents, school is the one place where they can depend on receiving a meal, medical care, and supervision.

1. *Assure children that they are safe* and that schools are well prepared to take care of them at all times. Reiterate that the lockdown procedures help keep students and staff members safe.
2. *Maintain structure and stability within the schools.* It may be best, however, not to have tests or major projects during this time if students seem especially unsettled. Allow parents to help determine whether their children need special arrangements.
3. *Have your crisis response plan in place.* Review procedures with your Crisis-Response Team. Confirm procedures with community agencies and law enforcement. Inform teachers and parents of protocols, resources, and so on.
4. *Provide teachers and parents with information* about what to say and do for children in school and at home. Reassure parents that their children are safe in school and should stay there if possible.
5. *Have teachers provide information directly to their students,* not during the public address announcements.
6. *Have school psychologists and counselors available* to talk to students and staff members who may need or want extra support.
7. *Be aware of students who may have recently experienced a personal tragedy* or a have personal connection to survivors or their families. Even a child who frequently goes or recently went to one of the sites may have a strong reaction. Provide these students with extra support and leniency, if necessary.

8. *Know what community resources are available* for children who may need extra counseling. School psychologists can be very helpful in directing families to the right community resources.
9. *Allow time for age-appropriate classroom discussions and activities,* if students need to talk. Do not expect teachers to provide all of the answers. They should ask questions and guide the discussion but not dominate it. Other activities can include art and writing projects, play therapy, and physical activity.
10. *Refer children who exhibit extreme anxiety, fear, or anger to mental health counselors* in the school. Inform their parents. Mental health professionals in the schools can help to recommend or can facilitate referrals to community resources, as requested or needed.
11. *Provide an outlet for students' desire to help.* Consider making get-well cards or sending letters to the families and survivors, or writing thank-you letters to emergency rescue workers and police officers.
12. *Monitor or restrict viewing* scenes of the events, as well as of the aftermath.

Source: This material is adapted from information posted on the NASP website, September 2001. For more information on helping children and youths cope with crises, contact NASP at (301) 657-0270 or visit NASP's website at www.nasponline.org. Specific crisis materials are located at http://www.nasponline.org/NEAT/resources.htm. This material may be adapted, reproduced, reprinted, or linked to on websites without specific permission, as long as the integrity of the content is maintained and NASP is given proper credit. Source: National Association of School Psychologists.

CONCLUSION

A sudden, accidental, unexpected, or traumatic death, whether it is a homicide or a terrorist attack, shatters the world as we know it. It is often a loss that does not make sense. We realize that life is not always fair and that sometimes bad things happen to good people. The sudden death leaves us feeling apprehensive, remorseful, anxious, and vulnerable. The grief response following sudden loss is often intensified because there is no opportunity to prepare for the loss, say good-bye, bring closure to unfinished business, or prepare for bereavement. Families and friends are forced to face the loss of a loved one instantaneously and without warning. This type of loss can generate intense grief responses, such as shock, anger, guilt, sudden depression, despair, and hopelessness.

Chapter 2

Crises, Critical Incidents, Disasters, and Terrorism Fundamental Emotional Reactions From a Developmental Perspective

INTRODUCTION

Each year, children, adolescents, and adults are affected by natural disasters and their after effects—loss of limb or life, as well as of shelter, possessions, safety and security, and financial certainty; collateral damage; debilitating disease; and injury. Survivors experience various levels of stress that may later manifest in distinct behavioral, emotional, and social readjustment problems. The National Organization for Victim Assistance provides an excellent typology of disasters, breaking them down by elements and by natural, industrial, and human causes.

Following a disaster, a crisis, or a critical incident, counselors, teachers, and administrators should assess students and survivors from three perspectives:

1. What psychological problems result from the traumatic experiences?
2. What factors increase the risk of readjustment problems?
3. What can students and those affected do to reduce the risk of negative psychological consequences and to best recover from trauma and stress, whether it is a crisis, a critical incident, a traumatic event, or a disaster?

TABLE 2.1
A Typology of Disasters

Elements	Causes		
	Natural	**Industrial**	**Human**
Earth:	Avalanches	Dam failures	Ecological irresponsibility
	Earthquakes	Ecological neglect	Road and train accidents
	Erosions	Outer-space debris fallout	
	Eruptions	Radioactive pollution	
	Toxic mineral deposits	Town waste disposal	
	Volcanoes		
	Landslides		
Air:	Blizzards	Acid rain	Aircraft accidents
	Cyclones	Chemical pollution	Hijacking
	Dust storms	Explosions above and below ground	Spacecraft accidents
	Hurricanes	Radioactive clouds and soot	
	Meteorite and planetary activity	Urban smog	
	Thermal shifts		
	Tornadoes		
Fire:	Lightning	Boiling liquid/expanding vapor accidents	Fire-setting
		Electrical fires	
		Hazardous chemicals	
	Tsunamis	Spontaneous combustion	
Water:	Drought	Effluent contamination	Maritime accidents
	Floods	Oil spills	
	Storms	Waste disposal	
People:	Endemic disease	Construction accidents	Civil strife
	Epidemics	Design flaws	Criminal violence
	Famine	Equipment problems	Guerrilla warfare/terrorism
	Overpopulation	Illicit drug making	Sports crowd violence
	Plague	Plant accidents	Warfare

It is now understood by many, especially by school personnel, that most children and adolescent bystanders or survivors experience normal stress reactions for several days after a traumatic event, such the following emotional, cognitive, physical, and interpersonal relationship difficulties:

- **Emotional reactions** include temporary feelings (i.e., for several days to a couple of weeks) of shock, fear, anxiety, grief, anger, resentment, guilt, shame, helplessness, hopelessness, emotional numbness (difficulty in feeling love and intimacy), uncontrollable emotions, unresolved issues from past losses or trauma, lack of interest and satisfaction in daily activities, or feelings of isolation and loneliness.
- **Cognitive reactions** include confusion, disorientation, indecisiveness, worry, shortened attention span, inability to focus, difficulty in concentrating, inability to problem solve, memory loss, unpleasant memories, intrusive images of the event, self-blame, and searching for answers or seeking vengeance.
- **Physical reactions** include tension; fatigue; edginess; nervousness; difficulty in sleeping, falling asleep, or staying asleep; hyperarousal; bodily aches or pain; increased startle reaction; racing heartbeat; nausea; change in appetite; headaches; rashes; and trembling.
- **Interpersonal reactions** include impaired relationships at school, in friendships, and in the family; feelings of distrust, separation anxiety, irritability, conflict, withdrawal, or isolation; feeling rejected or abandoned; being judgmental or overcontrolling; or clinging behavior.

Most children and adolescents may experience only mild stress reactions to a crisis, a trauma, or a critical incident, depending on their previous life experiences and their support systems. In many incidents, if handled appropriately by adults, these experiences may even promote personal growth, enhance coping skills, and strengthen relationships between children, adolescents, and adults. However, as many as one in three survivors or bystanders experience some severe stress symptoms, which may lead to lasting post-traumatic stress disorder (PTSD), anxiety disorders, or depression. If the duration of symptoms is less than 3 months, it is considered *acute*. If the duration of symptoms is 3 months or more, it is considered chronic. Finally, if the onset of symptoms is at least 6 months after the stressor, it is considered *delayed onset* (*DSM-IV-TR*, 2000, p. 468). The vulnerability of children to traumatic events arises from such factors as (1) their immature ability to understand the nature of events; (2) their relative limitations in ways that they can cope with such events; (3) their lack of experience in enduring painful life events; (4) their relative intolerance for painful life events, such that they avoid dealing directly with their thoughts and feelings; and (5) their dependence on others to identify their needs and to seek help when necessary. Therefore, children need special attention to prevent long-term debilitating behaviors, in order to help them endure the crisis.

WHAT DO RESEARCHERS AND PRACTITIONERS KNOW ABOUT HOW CHILDREN RESPOND TO A CRISIS, A TRAUMA, OR TERRORISM FROM A DEVELOPMENTAL PERSPECTIVE?

Children and adolescents respond with a wide range of emotional, physical, and cognitive reactions, depending on their previous life experiences, their support systems, and the nature and the intensity of the incident. From previous research, it is acknowledged that more severe reactions are associated with a higher degree of exposure; closer proximity to the disaster; a history of prior trauma, such as sexual abuse; being female; inadequate parental response; and family dysfunction or psychopathology.

Findings from a study after the Oklahoma City bombing and the World Trade Center attack indicate that more severe reactions are related to being female (perhaps because emotions are more easily expressed and accepted by society than if one were male), knowing someone who was injured or killed, and bomb-related television viewing and media exposure (Pfefferbaum & Doughty, 2001; Pfefferbaum, Seale, McDonald, Brandt, Rainwater, Maynard, Meierhoefer, & Miller, 2001). Following are some common reactions that children and adolescents may manifest from a developmental perspective, according to some researchers (DeWolfe, 2001; Pynoos & Nader, 1993):

Pre-K to First Grade Children (1–5 years)
- Thumb sucking
- Speech difficulties
- Decrease or increase in appetite
- Helplessness and passivity; lack of usual responsiveness
- Generalized fear (fear of the dark)
- Heightened arousal and confusion
- Cognitive confusion
- Difficulty talking about event; lack of verbalization
- Difficulty in identifying feelings
- Nightmares and other sleep disturbances
- Separation anxiety and clinging to caregivers
- Regressive symptoms (e.g., bed-wetting, loss of acquired speech and motor skills)
- Inability to understand death as permanent
- Anxieties about death
- Grief related to abandonment by caregiver

- Somatic symptoms (e.g., stomach aches, headaches)
- Startle response to loud or unusual noises
- "Freezing" (sudden immobility of body)
- Fussiness, uncharacteristic crying, and neediness
- Avoidance of, or alarm response to, specific trauma-related reminders involving sights and physical sensations
- Infants and early toddlers live in a world of senses, feelings, and immediate interactions. They need warmth and reassurance in simple, direct form; for example, being held, having a constant caregiver, and maintaining a routine, such as reading books and singing songs, are helpful responses to meet infant and toddler needs.
- This is the age of "magical thinking." Death is seen as a temporary departure or an absence and, as a result, reversible. The child may exhibit a belief that it is possible to come back to life.
- Behavioral reactions such as giggling, joking, and attracting attention may indicate the children's need to distance themselves from their pain over the loss.
- Children need adult's time and compassion. Use real terms. Repeat. Clarify. Ask children about their understanding if they show a desire to communicate. Listen to words and feelings.

Elementary School-Aged Children (6–8 years)
Children have a deeper understanding of death in the concrete sense. They may exhibit:
- Sadness and crying
- School avoidance
- Attention-seeking behavior
- Feelings of responsibility and guilt
- Repetitious traumatic play and retelling
- Feeling disturbed by reminders of the event
- Nightmares and other sleep disturbances
- Concerns about safety and preoccupation with danger
- Aggressive behavior and angry outbursts
- Fear of feelings and trauma reactions
- Close attention to parents' anxieties
- School avoidance
- Worry and concern for others
- Changes in behavior, mood, and personality
- Somatic symptoms (complaints about bodily aches and pains)
- Obvious anxiety and fearfulness
- Withdrawal/social isolation
- Specific trauma-related fears; general fearfulness
- Regression (behaving like a younger child)

- Separation anxiety
- Loss of interest in activities
- Confusion and inadequate understanding of traumatic events (more evident in play than in discussion)
- Unclear understanding of death and the causes of "bad" events
- Giving magical explanations to fill in gaps in understanding
- Loss of ability to concentrate at school, with lowering of performance
- "Spacey" or distractible behavior
- They still associate misdeeds or bad thoughts with causing death and can feel intense guilt and responsibility for the event. However, because of their higher cognitive abilities, they respond well to logical explanations and can comprehend the figurative meaning of words more than younger children can.
- Children may develop a fantasy relationship with the deceased person, in an attempt to keep that individual alive; they may also identify with the deceased and try to be like that person as a way of keeping him or her alive
- Concerns arise about the consequences of death that affect the living. Children may be overly concerned about their parents' health and well-being.

Preadolescents (Middle School) and Adolescents (12–18 years)
Preteens and adolescents may exhibit the following behaviors:

- Withdrawal/isolation from peers
- Self-consciousness
- Life-threatening reenactment
- Rebellion at home or school
- Abrupt shift in relationships
- Depression and social withdrawal
- Decline in school performance
- Trauma-driven acting out, such as with sexual activity and reckless risk taking
- Effort to distance oneself from feelings of shame, guilt, and humiliation
- Excessive activity and involvement with others, or retreat from others in order to manage inner turmoil
- Accident-proneness
- Wish for revenge and action-oriented responses to trauma
- Increased self-focusing and withdrawal
- Eating and sleeping disturbances, including nightmares
- Death comes to be recognized as a final and irrevocable biological event, yet due to adolescent egocentricity, it is accompanied by disbelief in the possibility of one's personal death.

- Adolescents can have much difficulty coping with death. They are least likely to accept the cessation of life. Their rejection of death is understandable developmentally because the developmental task of adolescence is to establish an identity by finding out who they are, what their purpose in life is, and where they belong.
- Adolescents strive for group acceptance and independence from parental constraints. As a result, they rely on the norms of their peers and beliefs for personal direction, and they reject opposing parental demands. Should they feel isolated from their peer group because "death" has made them feel "different," they may feel and be very alone.
- Although some teenagers are able to cope with death by expressing appropriate emotions, talking about loss, and resolving their grief, others may appear disturbed by the event, feel extremely angry, or be unusually silent and withdrawn. Denial, delayed reaction, the repression of feelings, depression, and somatic symptoms are not uncommon when death enters the adolescent's life space.
- Interactions with adolescents should be structured to allow for their sense of self-control and independence. The interactions should convey the adults' true concern for the adolescents' physical and emotional welfare.
- Adolescents' questions should be answered honestly; adults should treat them as mature individuals and should respect their solitude and personal expressions of emotions such as anger, sadness, and fear.

MORE PERVASIVE SYMPTOMS THAT MAY RESULT FROM A CRISIS, A TRAUMA, OR A CRITICAL INCIDENT

Post-Traumatic Stress Disorder

Children, adolescents, and adults with post-traumatic stress disorder often describe painful feelings of guilt, especially about surviving when others, such as close friends did not. They often are unable to concentrate, have intrusive dreams about the traumatic event, and experience other physical symptoms, such as heart palpitations, anxiety, trembling, decreased appetite, and the inability to fall or stay asleep. The following constellations of symptoms may occur and are more commonly seen in association with an interpersonal stressor: impaired affective adjustment; self-destructive and impulsive behavior; acute tendency to distance, detach, or disconnect from others; somatic complaints; feelings of ineffectiveness, shame, despair, or hopelessness; feeling permanently damaged; loss of previously sustained beliefs; hostility; impaired relationships with others; or a change from the child's, the adolescent's or the adult's previous personality characteristics (adapted from the *DSM-IV-TR*, 2000, p. 465).

TABLE 2.2
Normal Behavior Versus Stressful Behavior

	Normal Development	Possible Stressful Reactions	Consider Referral for Professional Assistance
Preschool (1–5)	thumb sucking, bed-wetting	uncontrollable crying	excessive withdrawal
	lack self-control, no sense of time, want to exhibit indepen- dence (2+)	trembling with fright, immobile	does not respond to special attention
	fear of the dark or of animals, night terror	running aimlessly	
	clinging to parents	excessive clinging, fear of being left alone	
	curious, explorative loss of bladder/bowel control	regressive behavior marked sensitivity to loud noises, weather	
	speech difficulties	confusion, irritability	
	changes in appetite	eating problems	
Middle Childhood (5–11)	irritability	marked regressive behaviors	
	whining	sleep problems	
	clinging	weather fears	
	aggression, questioning of authority, try new behaviors for "fit"	headache, nausea, visual or hearing problems	
	overt competition with siblings for parents' attention	irrational fears	
	school avoidance	refusal to go to school, distractibility, fighting	
	nightmares, fear of the dark	poor performance	
	withdrawal from peers		
	loss of interest/ concentration in school		

TABLE 2.2
Continued

	Normal Development	Possible Stressful Reactions	Consider Referral for Professional Assistance
Early Adolescence (11–14)	sleep disturbance	withdrawal, isolation depression	disoriented, has memory gaps
	appetite disturbance	depression, sadness, suicidal ideation	severely depressed, withdrawn
	rebellion in the home/ refusal to do chores	aggressive behaviors	substance abuser
	physical problems (skin, bowels, aches and pains)	depression	unable to care for self (eat, drink, bathe)
Adolescence (14–18)	psychosomatic problems (rash, bowels, asthma)	confusion	much the same as middle childhood
	headache/tension, hypochondrias	withdrawal, isolation	hallucinates, afraid will kill self or others
	appetite and sleep disturbance	antisocial behavior, such as, stealing, aggression, acting out	cannot make simple decisions
	begin to identify with peers, have a need for alone time, may isolate self from family on occasion	withdrawal into heavy sleep *or* night frights	excessively preoccupied with one thought
	agitation, apathy	depression	
	irresponsible behavior		
	poor concentration		

Source: http://www.disasterrelief.org/Library/Prepare/chilcope.html
Reprinted with permission.

TABLE 2.3
Post-Traumatic Stress Disorder

Diagnostic Criteria for 309.81 Post-Traumatic Stress Disorder

A. The person has been exposed to a traumatic event in which both of the following were present:
   (1) The person experienced, witnessed, or was confronted with an event or events that involved actual or threatened death or serious injury, or threat to the physical integrity of self or others.
   (2) The person's response involved intense fear, helplessness, or horror. **Note:** In children, this may be expressed instead by disorganized or agitated behavior.
B. The traumatic event is persistently reexperienced in one (or more) of the following ways:
   (1) Recurrent and intrusive distressing recollections of the event, including images, thoughts, or perceptions. **Note:** In young children, repetitive play may occur, in which themes or aspects of the trauma are expressed.
   (2) Recurrent distressing dreams of the event. **Note:** In children, there may be frightening dreams without recognizable content.
   (3) Acting or feeling as if the traumatic event were recurring (includes a sense of reliving the experience, illusions, hallucinations, and dissociative flashback episodes, including those that occur on awakening or when intoxicated). **Note:** In young children, traumatic-specific reenactment may occur.
   (4) Intense psychological distress at exposure to internal or external cues that symbolize or resemble an aspect of the traumatic event.
C. Persistent avoidance of stimuli associated with the trauma and numbing of general responsiveness (not present before the trauma), as indicated by three (or more) of the following:
   (1) Efforts to avoid thoughts, feelings, or conversations associated with the trauma
   (2) Efforts to avoid activities, places, or people that arouse recollections of the trauma
   (3) Inability to recall an important aspect of the trauma
   (4) Markedly diminished interest or participation in significant activities
   (5) Feeling of detachment or estrangement from others
   (6) Restricted range of affect (e.g., unable to have loving feelings)
   (7) Sense of a foreshortened future (e.g., does not expect to have a career, marriage, children, or a normal life span)
D. Persistent symptoms of increased arousal (not present before the trauma), as indicated by two (or more) of the following:
   (1) Difficulty falling or staying asleep
   (2) Irritability or outbursts of anger
   (3) Difficulty concentrating
   (4) Hypervigilance (persistent overarousal; watchfulness)
   (5) Exaggerated startle response
E. Duration of the disturbance is more than 1 month.
F. The disturbance causes clinically significant distress or impairment in social, occupational, or interpersonal functioning.

Source: Diagnostic and Statistical Manual (DSM-IV-TR), 2000, pp. 467–468.
Reprinted with permission.

Acute Stress Disorder (ASD)

Acute stress disorder exhibits distinct characteristics of anxiety; a tendency to distance, detach, and disconnect from others; and other acute symptoms that usually occur within 1 month after exposure to an extreme traumatic stressor. Children, adolescents, and adults may manifest ASD by finding it difficult to impossible to enjoy previously pleasurable activities; they frequently feel guilty about pursuing routine life responsibilities. Children, adolescents, and adults may experience difficulty in concentrating, may feel detached from their bodies, may experience the world as surreal or illusory, or might have a hard time recalling specific details of the traumatic event.

TABLE 2.4
Acute Stress Disorder

Diagnostic Criteria for 308.3 Acute Stress Disorder

A. The person has been exposed to a traumatic event in which both of the following were present:
  (1) The person experienced, witnessed, or was confronted with an event or events that involved actual or threatened death or serious injury, or threat to the physical integrity of self or others.
  (2) The person's response involved intense fear, helplessness, or horror.
B. Either while experiencing or after experiencing the distressing event, the individual has three (or more) of the following dissociative symptoms:
  (1) A subjective sense of numbing, detachment, or absence of emotional responsiveness
  (2) A reduction in awareness of his or her surroundings (e.g., "being in a daze")
  (3) Derealization
  (4) Depersonalization
  (5) Dissociative amnesia (i.e., inability to recall an important aspect of the trauma)
C. The traumatic event is persistently reexperienced in at least one of the following ways: recurrent images, thoughts, dreams, illusions, flashback episodes, or a sense of reliving the experience; or distress on exposure to reminders of the traumatic event.
D. Marked avoidance of stimuli that arouse recollections of the trauma (e.g., thoughts, feelings, conversations, activities, places, or people).
E. Marked symptoms of anxiety or increased arousal (e.g., difficulty sleeping, irritability, poor concentration, hypervigilance, exaggerated startle response, motor restlessness.

(Continued)

TABLE 2.4
Continued

F. The disturbance causes clinically significant distress or impairment in social, occupational, or other important areas of functioning or impairs the individual's ability to pursue some necessary task, such as obtaining necessary assistance or mobilizing personal resources by telling family members about the traumatic experience.
G. The disturbance lasts for a minimum of 2 days and a maximum of 4 weeks and occurs within 4 weeks of the traumatic event.
H. The disturbance is not due the direct physiological effects of a substance (e.g., a drug of abuse, a medication) or a general medical condition.

Source: Diagnostic and Statistical Manual (DSM-IV-TR), 2000, pp. 467–468.
Reprinted with permission.

Generalized Anxiety Disorder

The essential characteristics of generalized anxiety disorder are excessive apprehension, anxiety, and worry about traumatic events or activities, occurring for a period of at least 6 months. Victims report subjective distress due to constant anxiety and worry and have difficulty controlling the worry which eventually impairs personal, social, and school-related activities, as well as other important areas of functioning. People with this disorder find it hard to keep worrisome thoughts from interfering with their attention to daily routine and have difficulty in stopping the worrying. Children and adolescents with generalized anxiety disorder tend to worry excessively about their own competence or the quality of their performance. Testing anxiety, public speaking, or other public performances are extremely perplexing and disturbing to children with this kind of disorder. It often causes sleep disturbances, panic attacks, diarrhea, nausea, vomiting, skin breakouts, and hives.

Panic Disorder

The fundamental characteristic of a panic disorder is the presence of recurrent, unexpected panic attacks, followed by at least 1 month of persistent concern about having another panic attack, worry about the possible implications or consequences of the panic attacks, or a significant behavioral change related to the attacks.

> The essential feature of a Panic Attack is a discrete period of intense fear or discomfort in the absence of real danger that is accompanied by at

Table 2.5
Generalized Anxiety Disorder

Diagnostic Criteria for 300.02 Generalized Anxiety Disorder

A. Excessive anxiety and worry (apprehensive expectation), occurring more days than not for at least 6 months, about a number of events or activities (such as work or school performance).
B. The person finds it difficult to control the worry.
C. The anxiety and worry are associated with three (or more) of the following six symptoms present for more days than not for the past 6 months). **Note:** Only one item is required in children.
   (1) Restlessness or feeling keyed up or on edge
   (2) Being easily fatigued
   (3) Difficulty concentrating or mind going blank
   (4) Irritability
   (5) Muscle tension
   (6) Sleep disturbance (difficulty falling or staying asleep or restless, unsatisfying sleep)
D. The focus of the anxiety and worry is not confined to features of an Axis 1 disorder, for example, the anxiety or worry is not about having a Panic Attack (as in Panic Disorder) being embarrassed in public (as in Social Phobia), being contaminated (as in Obsessive-Compulsive Disorder), being away from home or from close relatives (as in Separation Anxiety Disorder), gaining weight (as in Anorexia Nervosa), having multiple physical complaints (as in a Somatic Disorder), or having a serious illness (as in a Hypochondria), and the anxiety and worry do not occur exclusively during Post-traumatic Stress Disorder.
E. The anxiety, worry, or physical symptoms cause clinically significant distress or impairment in social, occupational, or other important areas of functioning.
F. The disturbance is not due to the direct physiological effects of a substance (e.g., a drug of abuse, a medication) or general medical condition (e.g., hyperthyroidism) and does not occur exclusively during a Mood Disorder, a Psychotic Disorder, or a Pervasive Developmental Disorder.

Source: Diagnostic and Statistical Manual (DSM-IV-TR), 2000, p. 476.
Reprinted with permission.

least 4 to 13 somatic or cognitive symptoms. Symptoms can be somatic (physical complaints) or cognitive (thinking) in nature and include palpitations, sweating, trembling, or shaking, sensations of shortness of breath or smothering, feeling of choking, chest pain or discomfort, nausea or abdominal distress, dizziness or lightheadedness, derealization or depersonalization, fear of losing control or "going crazy," fear of dying, paresthesias (impaired skin sensations, such as burning, prickling, itching or tingling), and chills or hot flashes. The attack has a sudden onset and builds to a peak rapidly (usually in 10 minutes or less) and is often accompanied by a sense of imminent danger or impending doom and an urge to escape. (*DSM-IV-TR*, 2000, p. 430)

TABLE 2.6
Panic Disorder

Diagnostic Criteria for 300.01 Panic Disorder

A. Both (1) and (2):
   (1) Recurrent, unexpected Panic Attacks
   (2) At least one of the attacks has been followed by 1 month (or more) of one
      (or more) of the following:
      (a) Persistent concern about having additional attacks
      (b) Worry about the implications of the attack or its consequences (e.g.,
         losing control, having a heart attack, "going crazy")
      (c) A significant change in behavior related to the attacks
B. Absence of Agoraphobia
C. The Panic Attacks are not due to the direct physiological effects of a substance
   (e.g., a drug abuse, a medication) or a general medical condition (hyperthyroidism).
D. The Panic Attacks are not better accounted for by another mental disorder, such
   as Social Phobia (e.g., occurring on exposure to feared social situations), Specific Phobia (e.g., on exposure to a specific phobic situation), Obsessive-Compulsive Disorder (e.g., on exposure to dirt in someone with an obsession about
   contamination), Post-traumatic Stress Disorder (e.g., in embarrassing (e.g., loss
   of bowel or bladder control, vomiting in public, or fainting.

Source: Diagnostic and Statistical Manual (DSM-IV-TR), 2000, p. 400.
Reprinted with permission.

Many children, adolescents, and adults become discouraged, ashamed and despondent about the difficulties of carrying out their normal routines. They often attribute their panic disorder to a lack of "strength" or "charac-ter." As a result, children and adolescents may frequently be absent from school and eventually drop out of school altogether.

Agoraphobia

Agoraphobia is an anxiety disorder that involves multiple, intense fears of crowds, public places (especially places that remind one of a traumatic event or incident), and other situations that require separation from secu-rity, such as the home. The "panic-like symptoms" include any of the 13 symptoms listed for panic attack (or other symptoms that may be incapaci-tating or in response to stimuli associated with a severe stressor) or separa-tion anxiety disorder (e.g., in response to being away from home or close relatives).

These selected descriptive diagnoses, given in by the *Diagnostic and Statistical Manual of Mental Disorders, Fourth Edition (DSM-IV-TR)* and pro-

TABLE 2.7
Criteria for Panic Attack

Criteria for Panic Attack

Note: A Panic Attack is not a codable disorder. Code the specific diagnosis in which the Panic Attack occurs.

A discrete period of intense fear or discomfort, in which four (or more) of the following symptoms developed abruptly and reached a peak within 10 minutes:

(1) Palpitations, pounding heart, or accelerated heart rate
(2) Sweating
(3) Trembling or shaking
(4) Sensations of shortness of breath or smothering
(5) Feeling of choking
(6) Chest pain or discomfort
(7) Nausea or abdominal distress
(8) Feeling dizzy, unsteady, lightheaded, or faint
(9) Derealization (feelings of unreality) or depersonalization (being detached from oneself
(10) Fear of losing control or "going crazy"
(11) Fear of dying
(12) Paresthesias (numbing or tingling sensations)
(13) Chills or hot flushes

Source: Diagnostic and Statistical Manual (DSM-IV-TR), 2000, p. 432.
Reprinted with permission.

vided by the American Psychiatric Association (2000), are especially important for counselors, teachers, administrators, and support staff. The diagnoses unlock and demystify the *DSM-IV-TR,* which often creates a therapeutic distance that prevents individuals from seeking further help, because of fear that they may have a mental illness, when in reality they are experiencing a normal reaction to a stressful, traumatic event. In many cases, the diagnoses explain a normal reaction to an acute emotional or traumatic event. They cover, unfortunately, reactions that have become a common occurrence in our society, from the trauma of witnessing a homicide, to experiencing a threat of suicide, a disaster, a critical incident, or the traumatic experience of a child who has been sexually, physically, or emotionally abused and has lost the innocence of childhood. The list of disorders is also provided because the heightened risk of terrorism necessitates our being aware of the emotional and psychological effects that these events have on victims. The effects manifest as symptoms that range from anxiety disorders to school phobia—not attending to school or eventually dropping out, the greatest travesty of all.

TABLE 2.8
Comparison of Disorders

Acute Stress Disorder	Generalized Anxiety Disorder	Panic Disorder	Agoraphobia
Occurs within 4 weeks of traumatic incident	Not incident-specific	Recurrent, unexpected attacks (at least two) followed by 1 month of persistent worry about another attack occurring	Not a codable disorder
Disturbance lasts for minimum of 2 days	Anxiety/worry present for 6 months	No identifiable situational trigger	Occurs within a specific disorder, such as panic disorder with agoraphobia
All other reactions found in PTSD	Restlessness	Significant change in behavior related to attacks	Fear of being in places/situations in which escape might be difficult
	Easily fatigued	Worry about consequences of attack (having heart attacks, going crazy, etc.)	Avoidance of places, people, situations that may trigger reactions (panic attack reactions)
	Difficulty in concentrating	Four or more of the following are present: palpitations, pounding heart, or accelerated heart rate; sweating; trembling or shaking; sensations of shortness of breath or smothering; feeling of choking; chest pain or discomfort, nausea or abdominal distress; feeling dizzy, unsteady, light-headed, or faint, derealization (feelings of unreality) or depersonalization (being detached from oneself); fear of losing control or going crazy; fear of dying; parethesias (numbing or tingling sensations); chills or hot flashes.	

Irritability

Muscle tension

Sleep disturbance

Focus of anxiety/worry not specific to any one situation or concern

Significant distress or impairment in social, occupational, or other areas of functioning

Source: The National Institute on Trauma and Loss in Children, www.tlcinst.org (2003). Reprinted with permission.

WHAT FACTORS INCREASE THE RISK
OF LASTING READJUSTMENT PROBLEMS

Children and adolescents are at the greatest risk for experiencing severe
stress symptoms and lasting readjustment problems if any of the following
are either directly experienced or witnessed:

- Life-threatening danger or physical harm (especially to children)
- Exposure to gruesome death, bodily injury, bodies, or the death of animals
- Extreme environmental or human violence or destruction, such as the
terror and tragedy of September 11, 2001, when the World Trade Center
in New York City was destroyed
- Loss of home, valued possessions, neighborhood, or community
- Loss of communication with or support from close relationships
- Intense emotional demands (such as those faced by rescue personnel—
firemen, policemen, emergency medical technicians, Red Cross workers,
clergy, counselors, mental health workers, and health workers)
- Extreme fatigue, extreme weather exposure, hunger, sleep deprivation,
lack of physical or human resources
- Extended exposure to danger, loss, and emotional or physical strain or
both
- Exposure to toxic contamination (such as gas or fumes, chemicals, radio-
activity, bioweapons)

Studies also show that some individuals have a higher than typical risk
for severe stress symptoms and lasting PTSD, such as those with a history
of:

1. Exposure to other traumas (such as severe accidents, witnessing the death
of a someone, abuse, assault, combat, rescue work, or random terrorism)
2. Chronic medical illness, psychological disorders, or other debilitating
disorders, such as chronic poverty, homelessness, helplessness, hopelessness, unemployment, or discrimination because of race, religion,
ethnicity, or culture
3. Recent or subsequent major life stressors or emotional distress (such as
single parenting; skip-generation parenting; or dealing with courts, the
juvenile justice system, the foster-care system, or the neighborhood drug
trade)

Trauma, critical incidents, or traumatic stress may revive memories of
prior traumas, as well as possibly intensify preexisting social, economic,
spiritual, psychological, or medical problems.

COUNSELORS, MENTAL HEALTH WORKERS, AND OTHER HELPING PROFESSIONALS NEED TO ASSIMILATE A NUMBER OF PRIORITIES AND ROLES IN THEIR HELPING PROCESS

Helping professionals need to possess in common a similar demeanor and set of skills and attitudes. They must be prepared for the worst, yet hope for the best possible resolution to the crisis. Significant personality characteristics include sensitivity, assertiveness, responsiveness, intuitiveness, resourcefulness, creativity, flexibility, common sense, and the ability to maintain a calm demeanor.

- First, counselors and helping professionals must work as a team and respect the chain of command within the school and the community, having the essential mission of providing basic care, open communication, a sense of security, and comfort.
- Second, counselors and helping professionals must make personal contact in a genuine way with those affected. They must listen without giving advice and assess people's needs, whether it is food, a phone call, or a safe place to wait.
- Third, they must help victims, survivors and bystanders "defuse their experience" by encouraging them to tell their story and asking relevant questions, such as
  1. *"Have you ever been through something like this before?"* (Rationale: This assesses the person's previous life experience.)
  2. *"Is there anyone you need or want to get in touch with?"* (Rationale: This identifies whether they have a reliable or a fragmented support system.)
  3. *"What do you find yourself remembering most since all this happened?"* (Rationale: This identifies acute stressors that the person is experiencing.)
  4. *"What are your top three main concerns for the next few hours or days?"* (Rationale: This helps the counselor meet immediate survival needs.)
  5. *"In the past month, have you had repeated dreams or nightmares about theses experiences?"* (Rationale: This helps the counselor assess acute stress disorder.)
  6. *"Have you tried not to think about these experiences or avoided situations, conversations, people, or feelings that reminded you of the event?"* (Rationale: This helps the counselor to assess acute stressors).
  7. *"Have you often felt extremely unsafe, anxious, jumpy, or easily startled when you didn't need to be?"* (Rationale: This helps the counselor to assess for acute stressors).

The goal of mental health care in the wake of a crisis, traumatic, or terrorist event is to

First, protect: Help preserve the safety, privacy, health, self-esteem, and emotional well-being of survivors, and bystanders, as well as those of counselors and helping professionals.

Second, direct: Get people where they belong; help them to organize, prioritize, plan, and follow through.

Third, connect: Help school and community personnel communicate supportively with students, teachers, administrators, family, peers, and service providers.

Fourth, identify: Screen, triage, and provide crisis care to those who appear at risk for severe problems as the result of a traumatic event.

Fifth, refer: Have a network in place to refer those affected to medical, mental health, and financial services, as well as to shelters and care centers.

Sixth, assess: Use formal and informal educational assessments to affirm the normalcy and value of each person's emotional reactions, personal concerns, coping skills, and outlook for the future.

(Adapted from the National Center for Post-Traumatic Stress Disorder, 2003. Reprinted with permission.)

ASSESSING WHEN A CHILD OR AN ADOLESCENT NEEDS MORE INDIVIDUALIZED ASSESSMENT AND MORE THERAPEUTIC INTERVENTIONS

With the systematic responsiveness of the school and the community, as well as communication with family members and the support of friends, most students will be able to recover from a traumatic event and return to their precrisis equilibrium. They will have developed more coping skills, will have had a tremendous opportunity for learning, and will be able to meet the demands of their school and community environments. However, some students, because of their psychological vulnerability, past trauma, lack of coping skills, and poor social support, will continue to experience difficulties that interfere with daily functioning. These students will need further attention and more therapeutic interventions. The following guidelines for identifying these students are provided by the American Academy of Experts in Traumatic Stress (1999):

1. Students who cannot engage adequately in classroom assignments and activities after a sufficient amount of time has passed since the crisis and after a most of their peers are able to do so
2. Students who continue to exhibit high levels of emotional responsiveness (e.g., crying, tearfulness) after most of their peers have discontinued to do so
3. Students who appear depressed, withdrawn, and uncommunicative
4. Students who continue to exhibit poor academic performance and decreased concentration
5. Students who express suicidal or homicidal ideation or students who intentionally hurt themselves (e.g., self-mutilation or cutting themselves)
6. Students who exhibit an apparent increased usage of alcohol or drugs
7. Students who gain or lose a significant amount of weight in a short period of time
8. Students who exhibit significant behavioral changes
9. Students who discontinue attending to their hygienic needs

These kinds of behaviors demonstrate that the child or the adolescent is unable to concentrate, focus on routine tasks, and interact with others.

CONCLUSION

A crisis, a critical incident, a disaster, or a terrorist event is unpredictable and deeply unsettling. It typically leaves all those involved with feelings of shock, numbness, denial, confusion, disorganization, anxiety, vulnerability, and distrust. A school district and its surrounding community are a unique blend of individuals of all ages, professions, and disciplines, which can bring the school and community to their precrisis equilibrium. The reader has been provided with the developmental responses of children and adolescents to crises, traumas, and terrorism, as well as with five more pervasive symptoms that may result from these events. The goal is to demystify the diagnostic categories that directly affect children and adolescents, in order to prevent long-term debilitating effects. Essentially, an effective response to a crisis situation magnifies and strengthens the resources within the school and the community environments. By involving administrators, teachers, support personnel, students, and their families, in collaboration with clergy, mental health professionals, and such agencies as the American Red Cross, and public safety, health, and social services, a crisis can be responded to in a unified manner that can alter its aftermath and strengthen the community in the future. Unfortunately, this comprehensive need for preparedness has become the legacy of the twenty-first century.

Chapter 3

Crisis Intervention and Crisis Management First-Response Procedures

CRISIS INTERVENTION AND CRISIS MANAGEMENT STRATEGIES FOR SCHOOL-BASED RESPONSE TEAMS

Walking in the morning
he returns home
no longer confused
just battered
and
empty.
Sent to school
and directed
to a room without windows
he waits.
The counselor
late in arriving
switches on a small lamp
and together
they begin
to take the light in slowly.

Nicholas Mazza
Reprinted with permission

INTRODUCTION

Within 2 decades: Gooddard, Kansas (1985); Lewiston, Montana (1986); DeKalb, Missouri (1987); Virginia Beach, Virginia (1988); Orange County, California (1989); Olivehurst, California (1992); Napa, California (1992); Great Barrington, Massachusetts (1992); Grayson, Kentucky (1993); Wauwatosa, Wisconsin (1993); Union, Kentucky (1994); Greensboro, North Carolina (1994); Manchester, Iowa (1994); Redlands, California (1995); Blacksville, South Carolina (1995); Lynnville, Tennessee (1995); Moses Lake, Washington (1996); Patterson, Missouri (1996); Scottsdale, Georgia (1996); Bethel, Arkansas (1997); Pearl, Mississippi (1997); West Paducah, Kentucky (1997); Stamps, Arkansas (1997); Bethel, Alaska (1997); Fayetteville, Tennessee (1998); Jonesboro, Arkansas (1998); Edinboro, Pennsylvania (1998); Springfield, Oregon (1998); Littleton, Colorado (1999); Mount Morris Township, Michigan (1999); Notus, Idaho (1999); Conyers, Georgia (1999); Deming, New Mexico (1999); Fort Gibson, Oklahoma (1999); Lake Worth, Florida (2000)—Bullied, teased, taunted, often misfits, these young men were driven to suicide, homicide, and random acts of violence. Thirty-four reported incidents are recorded here. These students didn't just "snap." All acts were planned and many bystanders knew beforehand. Bullying and tormenting often led to revenge.

Suicide, homicide, and sudden unexpected death have become reoccurring crises for today's schools. Today families, schools, and communities have to help youths; even very young children, confront death, grief, and loss on a routine basis. The sudden or unexpected loss resulting from such occurrences affects everyone involved and requires an immediate and effective response by school personnel. In most cases, an appropriate response is critical in order to prevent further harm and additional stress. Collectively, crises that significantly impact schools include the following: completed suicides, suicide threats, natural and accidental deaths, medical emergencies, terminal illnesses, fires, natural disasters, and gang violence.

All can occur suddenly and in such a way as to have a rippling effect that permeates the entire interpersonal system of a school and a community. Suicide or sudden loss among student populations has become a major concern for school counselors, teachers, administrators, and support personnel, as well as for all who interact with the school and community. Within the context of the school and the community, sudden loss due to suicide, homicide, or other acts of violence can create a crisis of ambiguous proportions.

CRISIS INTERVENTION AND CRISIS MANAGEMENT: A THEORETICAL PERSPECTIVE

The development of a crisis theory and a practice has evolved from an eclectic collection of processes and procedures from the social sciences and health and human services. Helping people in crisis is a complex, interdisciplinary endeavor. Because human beings encompass physical, emotional, social, religious, and spiritual belief systems, no one theory is adequate to explain the crisis experience or the most effective approach to helping people. What holds true, however, is that all who are affected can come through a crisis enriched and stronger, or they can stagnate and feel hopeless. Individuals can gain new insights and coping skills or lose emotional and physical well-being.

Crisis is usually defined as a variant of stress so severe that the individual becomes disorganized and unable to function effectively. Crisis intervention differs from traditional counseling interventions in a number of ways. Slaikeu (1984) defined crisis intervention as a "helping process to assist an individual or group to survive an unsettling event so that the probability of debilitating effects (e.g., emotional trauma, post-traumatic stress or physical harm) is minimized, and the probability of growth (e.g., new coping skills, new perspectives on life, or more options in living) is identified and maximized" (p. 5).

Crisis intervention and counseling are considered much more directive, with the counselor taking an active role in giving information, educating about typical post-traumatic stress reactions, and offering strategies for coping with a crisis situation. A temporary dependency on the counselor (which is discouraged in traditional counseling) is often required to restore equilibrium. The therapeutic relationship has curative powers for most counselees, and in many cases, the therapeutic relationship itself permeates all current approaches of solution-focused or brief therapy.

Crises often fall into two major categories: (1) developmental crises that are universal and are often experienced while negotiating developmental tasks (as presented in chapter 2); and (2) situational crises such as injury, disaster, random acts of violence, homicide, suicide, death, divorce, or terminal illness. In an extensive study, Sandler and Ramsey (1980) found that loss events (e.g., death of a parent, sibling, or friend; divorce; and separation) were the main precursors of crisis reactions in children and adolescence, followed by family troubles (e.g., abuse, neglect, parent's loss of job). Lower on the scale were primary environmental changes (e.g., moving, attending a new school, or the mother reentering a full-time career), sibling difficulties, physical harm (e.g., illness, accidents, and violence), and disasters (e.g., fire, floods, hurricanes, earthquakes, and tornadoes).

PSYCHOLOGICAL DISEQUALIBRIUM

A stressful event alone does not constitute a crisis; rather, a crisis is determined by the individual's view of the event and response to it. If the individual sees the event as significant and threatening, has exhausted all of his or her usual coping strategies without effect, and is unaware of or unable to pursue alternatives, then the precipitating event may push the individual toward psychological disequilibrium, a state of crisis (Smead, 1988).

Psychological disequilibrium may be characterized by feelings of anxiety, helplessness, fear, inadequacy, confusion, agitation, and disorganization (Smead, 1988). At this point, the individual experiencing this disequalilbrium may be most receptive to outside assistance that will provide an opportunity for behavioral change and a return to balance. Inherently, a crisis results from a person's negative perception of a situation.

Helping professionals provide direct intervention by identifying alternative coping skills. A helping professional's primary goals in a crisis are to identify, assess, and intervene; to return the individual to his or her prior level of functioning as quickly as possible; and to lessen any negative impact on future mental health. It is important to focus on the event's significance in the person's present environment and the person's current functioning.

Assess the degree to which the person's functioning is impaired. Physical signs include changes in overall health, energy levels, and eating or sleeping patterns. Emotional signs include increased tension or fatigue and changes in temperament, such angry outbursts or depression. Behavioral signs include such symptoms as the inability to concentrate, social withdrawal, or obsessive thoughts (Greenstone & Leviton, 1993).

Sandoval (1985) maintained that the goal of crisis counseling is "to restore the counselee to equilibrium," with the number of counseling sessions ranging from one to eight. A secondary therapeutic role involves "taking action rather than listening and allowing the client to take responsibility and control over his/her decision making and understanding" (p. 260). For individuals, crisis reactions often become cycles of mounting tension, anxiety, and ineffective coping. Often, the ability to think clearly, to plan decisively, and to act responsibly becomes impaired.

As a primary prevention and early intervention initiative, counselors need to provide children and adolescents with coping skills before and when a crisis occurs. Such skills include (1) an understanding of what constitutes a crisis event; (2) an awareness of feelings, thoughts, or unfinished or unresolved issues in the past that can be reactivated by a crisis; (3) changes in feelings and thoughts that occur over time; and (4) coping strategies and behaviors that are useful in a time of crisis (Thompson, 1995).

STUDENTS' REACTIONS TO THE DEATH OF A PEER

The death of a peer affects his or her family and members of the school, including administrators, teachers, and support personnel, as well as members of the community. The ramifications of loss and the causes of death among children and youth are multifaceted:

- The most frequent cause of death among the 15- to 24-year-old age group is *accidents*. They may be auto-related, recreational (hunting, boating, skiing), or other unintended fatal injuries. Frequently, such accidents are unacknowledged or undetected suicide attempts. For example, a single-car accident may have been a suicide attempt.
- *Illness* is another leading cause of death among young people. It often seems so "unfair" to see a strong young body waste away from cancer or other terminal illnesses. Survivors often need help in coping with an untimely death that seemingly lacks concrete answers.
- *Catastrophic events,* such as homicides, fires, and natural disasters, also claim young lives. Teenagers are in the highest risk group to be victims of violent crimes. Youth gangs are on the rise, in which drive-by shootings are popular gang crimes. In this circumstance, grief is coupled with a volatile combination of *anger* and *revenge* when crime claims a young life.
- *Suicide* is an increasingly common cause of death among children and adolescents. The willful taking of one's own life is often the ultimate expression of despair. Survivors are left with intense feelings of loss and guilt.

MEETING THE EMOTIONAL NEEDS OF STUDENTS AND SURVIVORS

Balk (1983) identified acute emotional responses of students after the death of a peer. He revealed that although peer support and chances to talk with friends about the death at such a time of loss were important aids in coping with death, many peers feel uncomfortable talking about death. They frequently avoid the survivors, to decrease their own discomfort of not knowing what to say or how to say it. Young people sometimes hide their feelings of grief because such feelings often are not considered acceptable in public. As a result, youths are frequently confused about the source of their recurring grief reactions.

Furthermore, young people often take cues about how to react from the adults around them, more than from the event itself. It is crucial that counselors, teachers, administrators, and support personnel process the emotional needs of survivors. Structured opportunities to talk about the loss enhance coping skills. Validation of feelings as a perceptual check is particularly important to children and adolescents. Talking about the death and related anxieties in a secure environment that fosters trust provides a means to "work through" the loss experience. It also serves to prevent *destructive fantasy building*, which often occurs when young people cannot test their unprecedented perceptions and feelings against present reality.

Hawton (1986) and Perrone (1987) found that peers of adolescents who attempted suicide are more vulnerable because the rate of suicide is higher

- Among people with unstable social relationships;
- When a population is self-contained
- When imitative behavior is common
- When the element of bravado exists; and
- When the act is sure to be noticed.

Teachers and staff also need help in understanding and handling young people's normal, yet often inappropriate, reactions to death. A paramount need is for counselors, teachers, and other support personnel to process the emotional needs of survivors. Students often key into the behavioral clues provided by adults who are around them and allow these clues to give direction to their own reactions.

With adequate preparation, counselors, teachers, administrators, and other helping professionals can provide the curative environment that fosters a responsive and healing process. Collective efforts to provide structured programs and secure environments to work through significant losses are critical. Furthermore, all schools should have a detailed **Crisis Communication Contingency Plan.** Fundamentally, schools need plans that include steps to take to prevent further harm and a referral network for students and their families who are in need of long-term mental health counseling (Sheeley & Herily, 1989).

Without an available plan of action, normal coping mechanisms for many students (and staff) will break down, and disorganization will occur, causing destructive fantasy building, assigning inappropriate blame, and instilling guilt. Furthermore, if students are not led to discover a balanced resolution to the traumatic event, survivors will become vulnerable to developmental crises or overidentification with the deceased. Overidentification with the deceased has the potential of promoting copycat suicides. Therefore, it is paramount to process the emotional needs of survivors.

CRISIS MANAGEMENT RESPONSE TEAM:
ROLES AND RESPONSIBILITIES

Each school should organize a **Crisis Response Team.** Members should include school administrators, school counselors, identified teachers, the school psychologist, the school social worker, the school nurse, and other significant adults, depending on each school's skills, resources, and limitations. All local teams should be collectively assembled on a regular basis for training in crisis-intervention and crisis-management skills. The school crisis team's primary responsibility would be to mobilize school and community resources and to follow specific procedures in the event of a crisis.

Crisis team members can also include clergy or community agencies, such as the health department or the community services board. In combination, members should have *strong individual or group facilitation skills or both, knowledge of how the school and the community function, and experience with crisis intervention and management procedures.* Members need to be able to project multiple scenarios with all possible consequences and think clearly under stress. They also need to be familiar with the uniqueness of the school and the specific needs of the community.

Crisis-management strategies over a 2- to 3-day period may encompass the following procedures:

☑

❑ The building maintains its regular schedule and, in addition to the school counseling office, a **care center** may need to be established *away* from the central office to help small groups cope with the crisis. Students who need help and support or who are too upset to be in class are permitted to spend debriefing time in the care center.

Crisis Response Team members should:

☑

❑ Address concerns individually with faculty members or with the entire faculty at staff meetings. A care center can also be established in the building for support staff members, as they try to handle their classes during the crisis.
❑ Be prepared to cover classes for those teachers who seem especially upset or who need time to recover from the shock of the stressful news.
❑ Help teachers review debriefing strategies for dealing with death and dying issues in the classroom.
❑ Talk with individuals who have unresolved grief issues from the past.
❑ Help the building administrator develop a press release and a strategy for dealing with the media (when necessary).

❑ Recognize the importance of knowing how, when, and where to appropriately refer students whose concerns fall beyond the counselor's or helping professional's area of knowledge or skills.

❑ Maintain a network of mental health professionals to confer with and consult.

❑ Undergo training or reeducation for crisis prevention and intervention skills. Obtain adequate supervision and develop *a crisis team approach* to facilitate intervention and prevention efforts.

INTERVIEWING A STUDENT IN CRISIS

Assisting, interviewing, and counseling a suicidal youth ultimately involves mobilizing the **School Counselor Action Plan**. *Giving a student a crisis hotline number is inappropriate.* Nondirective approaches to intervention should be avoided during the initial stages of intervention. Essentially, nondirective approaches lack the control that school personnel will need to navigate the youth through the crisis. A high degree of perceptiveness on the part of the interviewer is necessary to confirm the emotional state of the student's crisis and to intervene adequately. The interviewer's approach should focus on resolving the immediate problem by mobilizing personal, educational, social, and environmental resources.

The primary outcome is to explore more concrete and positive alternatives to help the student reestablish a feeling of control over his or her life. Crisis intervention focuses on resolving the immediate problem through the use of the student's personal, social, and emotional resources, as well as his or her support network.

In Interviewing a Suicidal Student,
Six Crucial Steps Should Guide the Process:

1. Establish a therapeutic student-centered relationship; strive to convey an atmosphere of acceptance, support, and calm confidence about the future.

2. Obtain necessary information such as the *frequency, intensity, and duration* (FID) of suicidal ideation. Directly question the student's perception of the crisis, the frequency and the sequence of events, and his or her feelings and history of attempts to deal with the stressful situation. While supporting and empathizing with the student, avoid using the phrase "I understand," to allow the full and open expression of feelings and emotions.

3. Clarify the nature of the stress and the presenting problem. Also, clarify the incident and acknowledge any social and cultural factors that may relate to the crisis, to develop an awareness of the significance of the crisis from the student's point of view.

4. Evaluate suicidal potential and assess the student's present strengths and resources.
5. Document information and initiate the School Counselor Action Plan.
6. Inform the administration and notify the parent or the guardian, as well as identify referral resources such as members of the **Regional Crisis Response Team** and school psychologists and school social workers.

CRISIS MANAGEMENT: RESTORING EQUILIBRIUM

When managing a crisis, helping professionals need to know what to do and how to restore the school, the community, or both, to their precrisis equilibrium. A critical period of up to 3 or 4 weeks generally exists. After a suicide, however, some students may experience difficulties many months after the crisis has occurred. *Every school needs a plan, which includes steps to be taken to prevent panic and a referral network for students and their families in need of services.*

The ultimate goal of the crisis team should be to create a **Crisis Management Plan** before a crisis occurs. A *specific plan* should outline all the agreed-upon steps to be implemented that will effectively resolve the crisis situation. During the initial phases of the crisis, it is too difficult to think clearly through all necessary details, in order to manage and contain the crisis. Therefore, a **First Response Procedures File** should be housed in both the counseling and the administrative offices and made available to the Crisis Response Team.

Included in this First Response Procedures File should be:

☑
- ❑ A phone tree with emergency numbers for all faculty and crisis-response team members (as well as regional social workers and school psychologists) who have been identified and assigned to the building
- ❑ A school map with the location of school phones and designated meeting rooms or "care centers"
- ❑ Keys to all doors in the school facility and access to security personnel (Note: Security personnel should be included on the Crisis Team when possible)
- ❑ The bell schedule (It may be necessary to adjust the bell schedule.)
- ❑ The bus schedule and bus numbers
- ❑ An updated master schedule and a list of students enrolled in the school
- ❑ A laptop computer with attendance lists on disk
- ❑ In-house crisis management procedures (i.e., Who is responsible for what?)
- ❑ Resource telephone numbers of mental health counselors in the community

❑ Sign-in sheets for Crisis Team and school/community resource people in the community
❑ Name badges for Crisis Team members
❑ A sample letter from the principal informing parents of the crisis, and the procedures, or both
❑ A sample statement informing the faculty of the crisis, the procedures, or both
❑ Sample announcements for classroom or schoolwide communication
❑ Telephone numbers for community resources.
❑ Home and work telephone numbers of parent networks, school volunteers, clergy, and other previously identified resource people
❑ Walkie-talkies
❑ Cellular phones
❑ Fire extinguishers
❑ The location of emergency cut-off sources for gas, water, sprinklers, electricity, alarms, and so on
❑ Lockdown procedures
❑ A first aid kit and a first aid book
❑ A back-up supply of special medications for students (e.g., diabetic, epileptic, etc.)

Also included in this file should be the following: initial crisis-response sample statements for the media; a sample informing letter to the parents; a sample informing letter to the faculty; sample announcements for classroom or school-wide communication; and, finally, a sample outline of roles and responsibilities for administrators, counselors, and teachers.

In combination, members of the Crisis Response Team should have strong individual and group facilitation skills, knowledge of how the school and community functions, and experience with crisis-intervention and crisis-management procedures. Finally, all the interventions used should be guided by the principle of *focusing on strengths and constructive behaviors*. (Note: There should be several back-up copies for key personnel (e.g., principal, assistant principal, lead counselor, nurse, youth service officer).

☑ Be Prepared To:
❑ Verify the death.
❑ Activate the telephone tree to meet and inform faculty and staff to arrange for an early morning meeting to activate the **Crisis Management Plan**.
❑ Contain the information to prevent rumors.
❑ Convene the **School Crisis Response Team**.
❑ Meet with faculty members to provide accurate information and to review the school's Crisis Management Plan.
❑ Designate the lead school counselor to serve as a case manager.

❑ Call on citywide Crisis Response Teams or support services if needed.
❑ Identify Crisis Response Team Member(s) who will follow the deceased student's class schedule to meet with teachers and classmates and to work the hallways following the crisis.
❑ Contact resources in the community.
❑ Respond to the concerns of parents.
❑ Minimize the possibility that other students may imitate the behavior and take their own lives or seek revenge for the deceased person.
❑ Make counselors, support staff, or both available to students and faculty.
❑ Identify students about whom faculty and staff are concerned.
❑ Provide rooms for students to meet in small groups.
❑ Set up information and evening education programs for parents and the community.

Critical Questions to Consider
☑
❑ How and when should the students be informed?
❑ What specific information will be shared about the tragedy with the teachers and the staff?
❑ How will the school protect the family's privacy?
❑ Who is the spokesperson for the school and what information will be released to the media? What will staff members be told to say if contacted by the media?
❑ How should the personal possessions of the student be handled?
❑ If feeder schools are affected by the crisis, how should they be included in the overall interventional efforts?
❑ Will there be a care center for those students who are upset? Where will the care center be located? Who will supervise the care center? How will students be identified to come to the "care center"? How many days will the care center be in existence?
❑ Which available staff will be utilized from the Regional Crisis Response Team?
❑ How will teachers who are emotionally upset be assisted?
❑ Who will be the designated mental health professional to focus on and process the loss with those students in the deceased person's classes?
❑ Who will be assigned the responsibility of being the "floater" (i.e., the person who moves through the halls and facilitates communication between the care center, the counseling office, the crisis communication center, the administration, or the classrooms)?
❑ Who will be assigned the responsibility of being the "logger" (i.e., the person who records activities, contacts, and student or staff contacts)?
❑ Who will institute sign-in sheets to help monitor students who are in need of attention?

❑ Who will be designated as "security personnel" to control access to crisis areas and keep order within them?
❑ How will the school handle releasing students for the funeral or the memorial service? Will the school have a memorial service? How will the memorial service be handled? Don't release high-risk students during the school day until the parent or guardian has been contacted to pick them up and to provide full supervision.

Other Important Considerations
☑
❑ After school (possibly between the hours of 5:00 P.M. and 7:00 P.M.), it may be helpful to leave the school open for students, parents, or other community members who need assistance in responding to the crisis. Counselors, school psychologists, school social workers, and other direct service providers can be available for consultation.
❑ The Crisis Response Team should follow up specifically on the faculty or school staff members who were directly involved in the crisis. Custodians, cafeteria personnel, secretaries, bus drivers, teachers, counselors, and administrators may all need to be involved in a relatively intense "debriefing session" if they were directly involved in the crisis.
❑ It is important not to glamorize the death. Doing something in memoriam for the deceased can be appropriate for allowing students to express their feelings. A one-time event is frequently used, such as writing a song or a poem, planting a tree, or putting together a memory book of collected photos.
❑ The need for intervention efforts exists beyond the days immediately following a crisis, particularly in the event of a suicide. A critical period of up to 3 or 4 weeks generally exists. After a suicide, however, some students may experience difficulties many months after the crisis has occurred.

CHECKLIST OF RESPONSIBILITIES
FOR THE SCHOOL ADMINISTRATOR

A number of crucial roles must be performed by well-prepared key personnel who have the stamina to put in place critical plans for uncertain situations. Each participant has his or her own unique history with regard to crisis, trauma, and loss. It is not unusual for unresolved grief or past issues to resurface. Each student should also be given permission to feel his or her full range of emotions. There is no right or wrong way to feel, nor is there a time limit on the length of intense feelings. Typically, administrators, teachers, support staff, students, and their families will experience a sequence of emotional reactions following a trauma or a crisis: (1) extreme anxiety, (2) confusion, (3) denial, (4) anger, (5) remorse, (6) grief, and (7) reconciliation. Everyone will move through these emotional reactions at his or her own pace, based on the intensity and closeness to the one who was lost. A checklist of responsibilities includes the following:

☑

❑ Direct the intervention efforts.
❑ Inform the superintendent and his or her staff.
❑ Be visible, available (24 hours, if necessary), and supportive, to empower the staff members to carry out their difficult responsibilities.
❑ Verify the facts. Attempt to define the type and the extent of the crisis as soon as possible.
❑ Consult with the deceased student's or staff member's family before making any statement if the crisis is a death. Explain the school system policy and assure the family that confidential information is being protected.
❑ Delay releasing information until the facts are verified and the school's position about the crisis is clear.
❑ Activate the phone tree to *alert the School Crisis Response Team and the Regional Response Teams,* as well as others (police, rescue, fire department), if necessary.
❑ Activate the phone tree to alert faculty members of a debriefing meeting before or after school, depending on the time of the incident.
❑ Cancel scheduled activities, if necessary. Provide direction to teachers about how much to set aside the regular curriculum. Tests may have to be postponed in some classes.
❑ Set the tone and the direction for crisis management procedures (i.e., *an expedient and positive resolution*).
❑ Contact the superintendent's staff members at the school administration building and inform them of the crisis on an ongoing basis. Contact the appropriate administrator or designee to inform him or her of the current situation and emerging developments and to clarify information.
❑ Maintain a unified position and a uniform message when communicating with the media. Keep messages concise, clear, and consistent. Frame the message to each target group with accuracy and sensitivity.
❑ Prepare a written statement for the faculty to give to students, if appropriate.
❑ Prepare a general announcement for students. A straightforward, sympathetic announcement of a loss, with a simple statement of condolence, is recommended. Also, a statement that more information will be forthcoming, when it is verified, can be reassuring to the students, teachers, and support staff.
❑ Prepare a written statement for the media; designate a spokesperson, if applicable; or notify the public information officer.

❑ Remind employees that only designated spokespersons are authorized to talk with news media.

❑ Advise the school staff of media procedures. Advise students of the media policy. Let them know that they do not have to talk to the media and that they can say, "no."

❑ Designate a central area as a **Crisis Communications Center** and choose one person to manage and disseminate information. There will be inquiries from many sources (e.g., the media, parents, feeder schools, community leaders, school board members, and concerned citizens). The center could be located in the main office, the attendance office, or a designated office in the counseling suite. The person responsible will manage the center to ensure consistency and accuracy of information and to provide a timely response, in order to prevent destructive rumors.

❑ Prepare fact sheets and update information on the school's website.
  • Instruct all employees to refer all information and questions to the communication center.
  • Assign sufficient staff members to handle the phones and to seek additional information.
  • Keep a log of all incoming and outgoing calls and personal contacts. (This is for accountability and legal purposes.)

❑ Designate the lead school counselor as the case manager.

❑ Designate security personnel to control access to the crisis areas.

❑ Identify the faculty and staff in need of counseling.

❑ Inform the staff and students about funeral arrangements and identify the procedure for obtaining excused absences for students attending a funeral off campus.

❑ Keep the staff updated with daily debriefings after school.

❑ Ensure that memorials are appropriate.

❑ Follow up specifically with the faculty or the school staff members who were directly involved in the crisis. They need to attend a relatively intense "debriefing session" if they were directly involved in the crisis.

❑ Remain highly visible and accessible to others, especially to parents.

❑ Relieve key people from their normal duties so that they may focus on the crisis.

❑ Express appreciation to all people who helped bring the crisis *to an expedient and positive resolution.*

A CHECKLIST OF SCHOOL COUNSELOR
CASE MANAGER RESPONSIBILITIES

The school counselor who becomes the case manager is usually the director of the school counseling services. He or she usually has rapport with and the respect of administrators, teachers, and support personnel, as well as students, their families, and members of the community. The role of the school counselor has changed tremendously in the last 2 decades, with greater job demands and the need for critical helping skills.

☑

❑ Be available and visible. Have counseling staff members roam the areas where students hang out and bring them to a **care center** away from the main office to process and talk.
❑ Cancel other activities for the day.
❑ Announce the event to students; clarify facts to eliminate rumors.
❑ Activate previously identified community resources that will provide counseling assistance. These may consist of prepared school psychologists, school social workers, and trusted mental health professionals in the community.
❑ Follow the schedule of the deceased and visit the classrooms of his or her close friends.
❑ Lead a class discussion and generate activities to reduce the impact of the trauma (not discussing a loss with students can send a very powerful message, i.e., that someone's life is meaningless and expendable).
❑ Identify students in need of counseling and refer them to the counseling suite or care center. Contact parents of affected students and make suggestions for support and further referral, if needed.
❑ Notify the counseling office of students who want counseling.
❑ Postpone testing; restructure or shorten assignments.
❑ Keep the administration, counselors, and members of the Crisis Response Team informed of concerns or problems.
❑ If appropriate, ask the class members what they wish to do with the deceased's desk.
❑ In the event of a teacher's death, members of the department should rotate by planning who will cover the class for the first week following the loss. On the elementary school level, assign a staff member whom the students know. Students need the availability of a teacher, not a stranger, to cover the class. It sends a message of caring and shared loss.
❑ Prepare both students and teachers for funeral attendance, especially if they are asked to make a brief statement or deliver a eulogy. They may also need assistance with the religious customs or rituals of the deceased. Maintain the traditional ethnic and cultural mores regarding the procedures and the protocols of students from different cultural or ethnic backgrounds. The cultural diversity in school settings cannot be ignored. Education and responsiveness to different roles and rituals will help diffuse the rigidity and the expectations of other ethnic groups for the deceased. *This can be a powerful learning experience.*

❑ Coordinate counseling activities:
  • Identify a **floater** who will be available throughout the building to roam the halls and facilitate communication between the care center, the counseling office, administrative offices, and the communication center.
  • Identify a **logger** to record activities, school and community contacts, parent/teacher contacts, and others.
  • Seek additional community services and helping professional support if necessary.
❑ The lead school counselor should plan the logistics of crisis counseling:
  • Who will meet with individual students?
  • Who will meet with groups of students?
  • Who will meet with the faculty and staff?
  • Who will meet with parents?
  • Who will meet with school/community support services (i.e., school psychologists, community mental health counselors)?
  (Note: It is important that the lead counselor delegate tasks to others to maintain personal well-being and shared responsibility; for example, an explanation of the funeral service protocol can be given by a local member of the clergy.)
❑ Designate a **care center** away from the office for students who need additional time to cope with the situation or to meet with peers.
❑ Provide sign-in sheets to help monitor students who are in need of attention.
❑ Debrief the counseling staff at the beginning and the end of each day.
❑ Contact feeder or receiver schools so that they can provide support for students affected in their schools.
❑ Call the parents of counseled students to provide continued support for students who are very distressed. Provide information to parents; setting up a hotline number is very helpful.
❑ Focus on the needs of survivors. Initiate groups for the deceased's friends and conduct post-traumatic loss debriefings.
❑ Provide support personnel to be available for emergency counseling with students or faculty after hours.
❑ Communicate with faculty and enlist the help of teacher advisers, sponsors, and coaches to nurture and support their particular population of students.
❑ Identify students who attended the funeral and may need additional support for dealing with their grief and loss experiences.
❑ Provide information and seek assistance from students who are peer helpers. They are frequently the **first finders** of students in distress.
❑ Plan for the transition and the return of a student who attempted suicide or who was hospitalized due to illness or violence.

❑ Stop notifications of student activities (e.g., scholarship information, testing, and placement, failure, and attendance notices) from being sent to
   the home of a family whose child has died.
❑ Remove personal items from desk(s) and locker(s), and save them for
   parents.
❑ Prepare students who were chosen to participate in the memorial service.
❑ Keep records of affected students and provide follow-up services
❑ Acknowledge and thank all those on the team for their work and support.
❑ Plan some debriefing time toward the end of the day or the week to take
   care of one another and to share experiences.

A CHECKLIST OF FACULTY AND
SUPPORT STAFF RESPONSIBILITIES

☑

❑ Announce the event to students; clarify the facts to eliminate rumors;
   provide accurate information to students.
❑ Lead a class discussion and generate activities to reduce the impact of
   the trauma (not discussing a loss with students can send a very powerful
   message, i.e., that someone's life is expendable).
❑ Identify students in need of counseling and refer them to the counseling
   suite or the care center.
❑ Notify the counseling office of students who want counseling.
❑ Answer questions without providing unnecessary details or personal
   opinions.
❑ Recognize the various religious beliefs held by students.
❑ Model an appropriate response.
❑ Give permission for a wide range of emotions.
❑ Postpone testing; restructure or shorten assignments.
❑ Keep the administration, counselors, and members of the Crisis Response
   Team department informed of concerns or problems.
❑ If appropriate, ask the class members what they wish to do with the
   deceased's desk.
❑ Discuss and prepare both students and teachers for funeral attendance,
   especially if they are asked to make a brief statement or deliver a eulogy,
   and if they are unfamiliar with the religious customs or rituals of the
   deceased. Maintain the traditional ethnic and cultural mores regarding
   the procedures and the protocols of students from different cultural or
   ethnic backgrounds. The cultural diversity in school settings cannot be
   ignored. Education and responsiveness to different roles and rituals will

help diffuse the rigidity and the expectations of other ethnic groups for the deceased. This can be a powerful learning experience.
❑ Provide activities to reduce trauma, such as artwork, music, and writing.

WHAT TO DO IF A STUDENT IS SUICIDAL

Every year, 30,000 Americans take their own lives by committing suicide. At least 15% of people with depression complete the act of suicide, but an even higher proportion will attempt it. Although depression is one of the most treatable mental disorders, it is also one of the most underdiagnosed and underrecognized.

One of the distressing emotional experiences that children and adolescents can have is to experience a severe form of depression. Over one in five Americans can expect to get some form of depression during their lifetimes. Over one in 20 Americans have a depressive disorder every year. Depression is one of the most common and most serious mental health problems facing people today. However, much more is known now about the causes and the treatment of this mental health problem. Research has revealed that there are biological and psychological components to every depression and that the best form of treatment is a combination of medication and psychotherapy. Contrary to the popular misconceptions about depression today, it is not a purely biochemical or medical disorder.

HANDLING A SUICIDAL STUDENT

1. Be yourself. "The right words" are unimportant. If you are concerned, your voice and manner will show it.
2. Listen. Let the child or the adolescent unload despair and ventilate anger. If given an opportunity to do this, he or she will feel better by the end of the talk. No matter how negative the situation seems, the fact that it exists is a positive sign, a cry for help.
3. Be sympathetic, nonjudgmental, patient, calm, and accepting. Assure the child or the adolescent that he or she has done the right thing by getting in touch with another person.
4. If the child or the adolescent is saying, "I'm so depressed, I can't go on," ask THE QUESTION: "Are you having thoughts of suicide?" This is not putting ideas into his or her head; it is doing what is best for the child. It shows the child that you are concerned, that you take the child seriously, and that it is okay for the child to share his or her pain with you.
5. If the answer is "yes," you can begin asking a series of further questions: Have you thought about how you would do it? (PLAN); Have you got what you need? (MEANS); Have you thought about when you would do it? (TIME

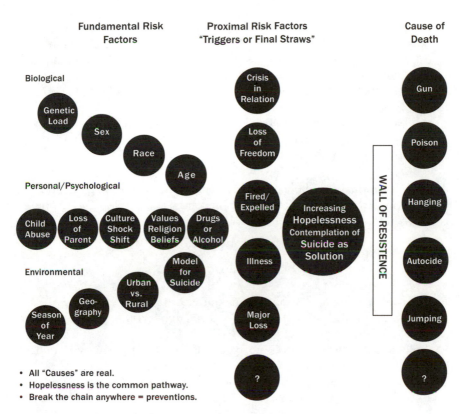

FIGURE 3.1
The many paths to suicide.
Source: Paul Quinnett, PhD, director, QPR Institute, P.O. Box 2867, Spokane, WA 99220, QPR Institute.com Reprinted with permission.

SET). At some point in this series, 95% of all suicidal children or adolescent will answer "no" or indicate that the time is set for some date in the future. This will be a relief for both of you.

6. Simply talking about their problems for a length of time will give suicidal people relief from their loneliness and pent-up feelings, make them aware that another person cares, and let them feel understood. Often they are also tired—their body chemistry changes, due to their agitated state. These conversations will take the edge off their anxiety so that so that they can get the help they need.

7. Avoid arguments, problem solving, advice giving, quick referrals, belittling, and making the child or the adolescent feel that he or she has to justify the suicidal feelings. It is not how bad the problem is, but how badly it's hurting the child or the adolescent who has it.

8. If the child or the adolescent is ingesting drugs, get the details (what, how much, alcohol, other medications, last meal, general health) and call Poison Control at _____. If Poison Control recommends immediate medical assistance, call 911 and the child's parents. Remember that the suicidal threat is still a cry for help and stay with the child in a sympathetic and nonjudgmental way.
9. Finally, Quinnett (1995) recommends **QPR**—Question . . . a person about suicide; Persuade . . . someone to get help, and Refer . . . someone to the appropriate resource.

At the first national conference on suicide prevention, a set of guidelines for helping potential suicide victims was presented. The following responses could be therapeutic when talking with a trouble student:

- "I am here for you."
- "I want to hear what's bothering you."
- "I really care about you."
- "Let's talk and figure out how to make things better."
- "Things are tough now, but they will change—you've got to hang in there, and I'm here to help you."
- "I would feel horrible if you hurt yourself, and I don't want you to die."
- "If I can't help you, I'll find someone who can help."
- "No one and nothing is worth taking your life for" (Peach & Reddick, 1991, p. 109).

WARNING SIGNS

Conditions Associated with Increased Risk of Suicide

- Death or terminal illness of a relative or a friend
- Divorce, separation, broken relationship, stress on family
- Loss of health (real or imaginary)
- Loss of job, home, money, status, self-esteem, personal security
- Alcohol or drug abuse
- Depression. In the young, depression may be masked by hyperactivity or acting-out behavior. In the elderly, it may be incorrectly attributed to the natural effects of aging. Depression that seems to quickly disappear for no apparent reason is cause for concern. The early stages of recovery from depression can be a high-risk period. Recent studies have associated anxiety disorders with an increased risk for attempted suicide.

Emotional and Behavioral Changes Associated with Suicide

- Overwhelming pain: pain that threatens to exceed the person's coping capacities. Suicidal feelings are often the result of long-standing problems that have been exacerbated by recent precipitating events. The precipitating factors may be new pain or the loss of pain-coping resources.
- Hopelessness: the feeling that the pain will continue or get worse; things will never get better.
- Powerlessness: the feeling that one's resources for reducing pain are exhausted.
- Feelings of worthlessness, of shame, of guilt, of self-hatred, "no one cares." Fears of losing control, of harming self or others.
- The person becomes sad, withdrawn, tired, apathetic, anxious, irritable, or prone to angry outbursts.
- Declining performance in school, work, or other activities. (Occasionally the reverse: people who volunteer for extra duties because they need to fill up their time.)
- Social isolation or association with a group that has different moral standards than those of the family.
- Declining interest in sex, friends, or activities previously enjoyed.
- Neglect of personal welfare, deteriorating physical appearance.
- Alterations in either direction in sleeping or eating habits.
- (Particularly in the elderly) Self-starvation, dietary mismanagement, disobeying medical instructions.
- Difficult times: holidays, anniversaries, and the first week after discharge from a hospital; just before and just after the diagnosis of a major illness; just before and during disciplinary proceedings.

Suicidal Behavior

- Previous suicide attempts, "mini-attempts."
- Explicit statements of suicidal ideation or feelings
- Development of a suicidal plan, acquiring the means, "rehearsal" behavior, setting a time for the attempt.
- Self-inflicted injuries, such as cuts, burns, or head banging.
- Reckless behavior. (Besides suicide, other leading causes of death among young people in New York City are homicide, accidents, drug overdose, and AIDS.) Unexplained accidents among children and the elderly.
- Making out a will or giving away favorite possessions.
- Inappropriately saying good-bye.
- Verbal behavior that is ambiguous or indirect: "I'm going away on a real long trip"; "You won't have to worry about me anymore"; "I want to go to

sleep and never wake up"; "I'm so depressed, I just can't go on"; "Does God punish someone who suicides?"; "Voices are telling me to do bad things"; requests for euthanasia information; inappropriate joking; stories or essays on morbid themes.

SUICIDE INTERVENTION PLAN

When intervening with a high-risk student, it is paramount that the safety and the best interest of the student be first and foremost. McKee, Jones, and Barbe (1993) provide the following guidelines for school staff members who encounter students in need of crisis services:

Step 1: Stabilize

1. Under no circumstances should a potentially suicidal youth be left alone.
2. Calmly talk to the student to determine if the student possesses any life-threatening instruments or substances on or near his or her person (i.e., a gun, a knife, drugs, or other controlled substances).
3. If possible, calmly remove any life-threatening instruments or substances from the student or the immediate environment (e.g., locker or car). *Do not struggle with the student if you meet resistance.*
4. Inform the school administration and the closest Crisis Response Team member of the situation and your location.
5. Calmly move the student to a prearranged, nonthreatening place, away from other students, where there is access to a telephone.
6. A Crisis Response Team member should assume responsibility for the crisis interview. If a teacher or another staff member who began the process wishes to remain with the student, this should be allowed.

Step 2: Assess Risk

The Crisis Intervention Team member should calmly talk to the student in order to assess the risk that the student will harm himself or herself.

1. If the student will not give up life-threatening instruments, follow *extreme risk procedures.*
2. If the student gives up the dangerous device but is still in imminent danger of harming himself or herself, follow *severe risk procedures.*
3. If the student is in no imminent danger of harming himself or herself, follow *moderate risk procedures.*

Step 3: Determine Services

Extreme Risk Procedures

1. Call an ambulance in the event of an overdose or an injury requiring medical attention.
2. Call the police if there is an immediate threat to the safety of the student or others.
3. Call the parents or caregivers to inform them of the situation and the action taken.
4. Calm the student by talking and reassuring the individual of his or her best interest until the police arrive.
5. Try to have the student relinquish the means of harming himself or herself.

Severe Risk Procedures

1. Determine whether the student's distress appears to be the result of parent or caretaker abuse, neglect, or exploitation. Determine whether further internal referral is necessary before proceeding with the interview (e.g., Does the school social worker or the counselor need to come in to check out allegations of abuse or neglect?). If allegations are validated, refer to Child Protective Services.
2. If distress is apparently not related to abuse, neglect, or exploitation, referral should be made to parent(s) or primary caregiver(s). The parent(s) or primary caregiver(s) should be strongly encouraged to have the child evaluated. A list of referral sources and telephone numbers should be provided. Actions taken by the school should be documented that the event the parent or the primary caregiver fails to follow through.
3. If neither the parents, Child Protective Services, nor the police can or will intervene before the end of the school day, the student should be taken to the nearest hospital emergency room.
4. In all interventions, attention should be focused on the safety and the best interest of the child.

Moderate Risk Procedure

1. Determine whether the student's distress appears to be the result of parent or caretaker abuse, neglect, or exploitation. Determine whether further internal referral is necessary before proceeding with the interview (e.g., Does the school social worker or the counselor need to come in to check out allegations of abuse or neglect?). If allegations are validated, refer to Child Protective Services.
2. If distress is apparently not related to abuse, neglect, or exploitation, referral should be made to parent(s) or primary caregivers. The parent(s)

or primary caregivers should be strongly encouraged to have the child evaluated. A list of referral sources and telephone numbers should be provided. Actions taken by the school should be documented in the event the parent or the primary caregiver fails to follow through.

Step 4: Inform

1. Inform appropriate members of the administration, other Crisis Response Team members, teachers, and counselors of the facts and of the action taken.
2. Inform close friends and sibling(s) of the student of the facts and of the action taken. Be mindful that feeder schools may have students or personnel who will be affected. The Crisis Response Team at those schools should be notified.

Step 5: Follow-Up

1. Determine whether emergency or short-term procedures were followed through.
2. Determine whether long-term services have been arranged.
3. If emergency, short-term, or long-term services have not been satisfactorily pursued, contact Child Protective Services.
4. Continue to monitor the student.
5. Call a debriefing meeting of the Crisis Response Team to critique the handling of the situation.

AFTER A DEATH BY SUICIDE

After a death by suicide, the grief process is characterized from the beginning by unique characteristics, which both survivors and helping professionals should recognize (The Bereavement Association, St. John's, Newfoundland, Canada, 2003):

1. Denial and Repression: Suicide survivors experience shock not only because the death has occurred but also because it deviates from normal behavior. We expect people to die but not to take their own lives. As a result, initial denial and repression may occur. Some survivors refuse to discuss the death at all or refuse to believe that a suicide has occurred, rather insisting that it was an accident, in an attempt to hide the facts. Often people have greater difficulty in accepting the death weeks or even months later than they would in accepting a death by other causes.

2. Search for Meaning: Survivors experience a desperate need to find a reason for the death. In the case of illness or an accident—even though the death may have been untimely or tragic—the cause is known, but with suicide (even when a note is found) the rationale for the behavior is never understood. There is also a nagging question about the degree of one's own involvement.

3. Grief Process: Some people shut out all talk or interpretation of the event, whereas others replay the event over and over, searching for an answer to the question. The task of this aspect of the grief process is to reach an acceptable understanding of the experience before one can properly begin to cope with the loss or to progress through the "grief work." Survivors need to remove the aura of shame and restore a sense of dignity to the memory of the person, as well as to repair their own shattered sense of self-worth and self-esteem. This needs to be resolved, or it may result in incomplete mourning

4. Incomplete Mourning: When the search for meaning is compounded with denial, guilt, shame, anger, concealment, evasion, withdrawal of social and family support, subtle accusations, stigma and taboo, and the absence of a chance to share one's grief with others, the grief work can become severely crippled, if not altogether destroyed. Survivors may then become subject to the destructive effects and results of unresolved grief.

5. Depression and Self-Destruction: Manifestations of self-hatred, apathy, withdrawal, sadness, despair, rage, and self-blame can lead to depression. This self-destructiveness stems from unmet yearnings and unresolved grief. Implied disapproval and lack of empathetic understanding may lead to deeper depression or turn into a pattern of self-destructive behavior, such abuse of alcohol or other drugs, or high-risk actions, including suicidal behavior.

6. Increased Anger: Survivors struggle with anger: (1) at themselves, for having played a part in bringing about their own misery; (2) at the person who committed suicide, for having deliberately left the survivor alone and burdened with this sense of guilt, rejection, and desertion; and (3) at others, for the social stigma and isolation. Survivors feel angry at not having been given a chance to intervene, angry because they are now forced to face both old and new problems alone and to build a new life that was never anticipated or wanted. This anger is very intense, but there is no socially acceptable way to express it.

7. Identification with the Person Who Committed Suicide: Survivors may experience an intrusive intuition about the deceased's thoughts or feelings, believing that they knew exactly what the deceased thought or felt just prior to death. This overidentification may go as far as an imitation of the suicide act. Some survivors feel that they can atone for their neglect of the deceased by copying the suicidal behavior. This identification may be greatly intensified if there were conflicts or disturbed relationships prior to the death, or if the survivor depended upon the deceased for his or her own sense of identity. Many disturbed adolescents are particularly prone to committing copycat suicides.

8. Importance of Anniversaries: Suicide family survivors place greater emphasis on suicide-death anniversaries. They may dread or look forward to the date as a day of mourning. Especially crucial are anniversaries for each of the first 6 months, 1 year, 18 months, and, for some, the 2nd year. People strongly identifying with the deceased may choose to take their own lives on the anniversary of the death of the person they lost.

9. Withdrawal from Social Life: Mingled with doubt and distrust is the need to be with people. There is a hunger to be welcomed—included—but conversation and activities simply take too much energy. Fearful of closeness, survivors may withdraw, playing out object separation, that is, "the repetitive need to reenact separations, drive loved objects away, and replay experiences of estrangement and reunion." The resulting withdrawal of others completes the isolation and repeats the act of loss, reinforcing a possible concept of worthlessness, of being eternally unsure of self or others. Survivors lose emotional and social support when it is most needed, and continued isolation (even implicit accusation) is common. Widows often refuse to remarry, feeling that they are somehow eternally scarred.

10. Profound Sense of Shame: Survivors feel emotionally vulnerable and experience a tremendous about of shame; in other words, the deceased preferred death to living with the survivor. They are also often sensitive to the self-perception of others, that is, are they being judged as a less than worthy person or a failure? This leaves the survivor with a self-concept and diminished sense of well-being. An acute sense of worthlessness compounds the feeling of abandonment, because the other person chose to leave.

11. Memories: Many survivors are haunted by the vivid intrusive recollection of finding the body or of scenes of violence, mingled with confusion or conflict prior to the death. Perhaps there were agonizing hours of waiting, on the chance that the person attempting suicide might still live. Many resent the seemingly cold, accusing attitude of investigating officers and medical or emergency teams. These memories are relived and replayed through the survivor's conscious and unconscious, often leading to the most devastating of all aftereffects a suicide, that is, extreme guilt.

12. Guilt: Again, blame enters the picture. Survivors search for someone or something to blame. "Could it have been a debilitating illness, a fractured relationship, or an unsatisfactory career?" Survivors may remember all they said and did, and conflicting thoughts consume their inner dialogue: "Why didn't I know?" "I should have known." "I could have prevented it, but I didn't." There's a feeling that others should acknowledge and share in the blame. Dissension may occur within a family, as members attempt to establish a scapegoat in order to pass on the burden of blame.

Crises can occur in all students, regardless of age. Most frequently, the student in crisis may attempt or commit suicide. Some significant indicators of a student in crisis may include one or more of the following:

Significant Indicators

Suicide threat

Verbal indicators of self-destructive behavior, e.g., life would be better if the student didn't exist

Preoccupation with thoughts of suicide or death

Previous suicide attempt

Family member or close friend has attempted or completed suicide

Making final arrangements; giving away prized possessions; extreme cheerfulness after prolonged depression

Keeping guns, knives, or lethal medicines

Breakup with boyfriend or girlfriend and withdrawal from other friendships

School Indicators

Drop in grades

Difficulty concentrating on schoolwork

Loss of interest in extracurricular activities

Social isolation

New to school

Frequent referrals to office because of behavior, tardiness, or truancy

Significant Times of Danger/Rites of Passage

Graduation

Completion of parental divorce

Anniversaries of unhappy events (parent or sibling death)

Change of season

Custody disagreement

Family Indicators

Anniversary of loss of family member through death, separation, or divorce

Rejection by family members

Financial change or job loss

Recent household move

Family discord, change in immediate family or household membership

Alcoholism or drug use in the family

Student experiences sudden physical, sexual, or emotional abuse

Running away from home

Family history of emotional disturbance

(Continued)

FIGURE 3.2
Some Significant Indicators of Crisis in Students

Social or Emotional Indicators or Both
Noted personality change
Depression, feelings of sadness
Withdrawal; does not interact with others
Agitation, aggression, rebellion
Sexual problem (promiscuity, homosexuality, unintended pregnancy)
Feelings of despair, hopelessness, helplessness
Feeling a need to be punished
Unexplained accidents; reckless behavior
Recent involvement with the law

Physical Indicators
Changes in eating or sleeping patterns
Weight gain or loss
Neglect of personal appearance
Lethargy, listlessness
Frequent physical complaints
Pregnancy
Prolonged or terminal illness
Drug or alcohol abuse

FIGURE 3.2
Continued

This is a common occurrence in "suicidogenic families." Some people feel guilt because they don't feel guilty but rather are relieved that the troublesome concerns of the deceased have ceased. More often, parents, children, and spouses feel directly responsible. Guilt compounds itself, and often what are actually feelings of regret may be interpreted as guilt. Guilt may complicate all stages of the grief process; resolution of guilt is paramount to healthy recovery from grief.

CONCLUSION

According to the Surgeon General's *Call to Action to Prevent Suicide* (1999), (1) many fail to realize that far more Americans die from suicide than from homicide; (2) each year in the United States, approximately 500,000 people require emergency room treatment as a result of attempted suicide; (3) from 1980 to 1996, the rate of suicide among people ages 15 to 19 years old increased by 14% and among people ages 10 to 14 years old by 100%; and (4) more teenagers and young adults die from suicide than from cancer, heart disease, AIDS, birth defects, stroke, pneumonia, influenza, and chronic lung disease combined (p. 3).

A workable referral system, using resources within a school (school counselors, social workers, school psychologists) and within the community (mental health counselors, agency personnel), becomes very important in order to achieve a positive resolution of the crisis that usually develops when a sudden death or a suicide occurs. When managing a crisis, school counselors and helping professionals need to know what to do and must have the mechanisms to restore the school and community to their precrisis equilibrium. The intent of this chapter is to provide a general overview of such crisis situations and specific information pertinent to developing an effective crisis intervention and management plan. Schools need plans that include steps to be take to prevent panic and to assist school personnel in establishing guidelines for dealing with shock, grief, and the healing process that follow an untimely death, a suicide, or a homicide.

CLARIFICATION OF ISSUES TO THE MEDIA

A statement should be made as soon as the crisis occurs to show that school officials are perceptive and responsive to community and school needs. Remind faculty and staff that only designated spokespeople are authorized to talk with news media. The school should (a) decide what to say, define the ground rules, issue a statement, and answer questions within the limits of confidentiality; (b) advise students of the media policy and affirm that

A fight between a group of high school students occurred three blocks from campus Friday night after the football game. The incident resulted in the fatal shooting of one of our students. Police are investigating the incident and no further information is known at this time. Our school's crisis plan went into action immediately following the incident. The actions already taken:

- The school/community crisis team met last night. A parent telephone hotline has been established; the number is_____.

- School/community resources have been mobilized to help restore equilibrium.

- Counseling for students and faculty will be provided.

- Review and reinforcement of our weapons policy and safe schools plan are also underway.

FIGURE 3.3
Sample Statement for the Media

they have the right to decline interviews; and (c) if the crisis is a death, consult with the family before making any statement. Explain the school system policy and assure the family that confidential information will be protected. Also, have the following public relations plan for the school:

- Get to know the reporter(s) who are likely to cover school issues early every academic year.
- Respond to all media inquiries or telephone calls promptly.
- When asked to react to a statement or event, ask if you can return the reporter's call momentarily; write down the reporter's question, make notes for your answers, and then return the call.
- Periodically provide the media with contact people, resources, and services that are both routine and unique to your school.
- Write appreciation letters to staff writers when they portray a difficult or sensitive assignment well, and forward a copy to their editor.
- Be aware of reporters' deadlines and assist them in their information gathering with any written information about a prevention and intervention program.

Perhaps one of the most subtle defenses against the occurrence of a future suicide is for a school official to be firm and assertive with information given to the media. News reporters can influence the public's perceptions about a school, people, events, and decisions. The excitement, the lurid and romantic depiction of a student's suicide, seems to attract troubled youths, and to reinforce the act as a viable alternative. Displaying a student's death on the front page of the local newspaper (complete with picture and quotes from the grieving family or classmates) gives the deceased a "fame-in-death" that he or she may not have achieved in life. Perceiving the deceased as a hero or a martyr, many youths may personalize the act and see themselves in place of the deceased. A number of precautions should be sensitively heeded and routinely revisited:

- Don't put suicide stories on the front page of the newspaper; placing the story on the inside page may reduce the "copycat" phenomena.
- Don't use the word *suicide* in the headline.
- Don't use photographs or intimate descriptions of the deceased's life because this often promotes overidentification with the deceased.
- Don't fail to mention possible alternative causes of death. If suicide is the only alternative mentioned, it serves to exclusively advertise this self-destructive method.

Note: The statement shows accountability and responsiveness. It provides evidence of a plan of action that involves offering information to parents. A statement about weapons (if relevant) and safe school initiatives should be emphasized and services to students and their family outlined. It is important to take the initiative with the news media and to stress the positive actions taken by the school.

Dear Parents,

This morning, prior to school, there was an accident involving a school bus and an automobile. There were known injuries to the passengers of the car. The children on Bus #_____, substituting for Bus #_____, witnessed the aftermath of the accident but were not directly involved in it.

School counselors and administration took the children from the bus to the library. The children were asked if they were injured in any way, and their parents were then contacted. Your child may show a delayed reaction to the accident. Please be alert to symptoms over the next several days indicative of this, including:

- ❑ A desire to be alone; being unusually quiet
- ❑ Loss of appetite
- ❑ Problems with sleeping, nightmares
- ❑ Difficulty with concentration
- ❑ Crying
- ❑ Angry outbursts, short temper
- ❑ Headaches, upset stomach
- ❑ Depression, sadness

Your child may also exhibit some physical complaints. Please contact the principal to fill out an accident report. The school will be offering support services for students who need help dealing with the accident. We will also provide counseling services to parents in helping their children to cope. Please don't hesitate to call if you have any questions or concerns.

Sincerely,

Principal of the School

FIGURE 3.4
Sample Letter to Parents

Dear Parents,

Yesterday, we learned that one of our first graders, _____,
died while in the hospital. _____ had his/her appendix removed
over the past weekend. Complications set in after his/her parents took him/
her home and he/she had to return to the hospital. The doctors were trying
to help him/her when he/she died yesterday afternoon.

Today, at school, each teacher read a short message about_____ to (his/
her) class. We discussed what happened and how _____
died. We also stressed that many people have their appendix out every day
and have no problems with it. Our school counselors and our school psychologist were available throughout the day to talk with any student who
may have had a particularly difficult time dealing with the news.

Any death is difficult for children to understand. _____'s death is
particularly difficult due to (his/her) young age and its unexpectedness. The
fact that _____ died while at the hospital and the fact that it was related
to having (his/her) appendix out may also be frightening for children, especially those who may need to have their own appendixes out in the future.

We recommend that you take some time to discuss _____'s
death with your child. We suggest allowing your child to talk about how (he/
she) feels and any fears or concerns (he/she) may have as a result of hearing
this news. We are enclosing a list of suggestions to help you talk with your
child about _____'s death, about the death of any loved one, or both.

If you feel that your child would benefit from talking with our school counselor or our school psychologist about _____'s death or
about a related matter, please call us at the school and share your concerns.

The faculty, staff, and students extend our heartfelt sympathies to the family
and to all their friends. We at the school will miss _____very
much. (He/she) was our friend and we loved (him/her).

Sincerely,

School Principal

FIGURE 3.5
Sample Informing Letter for Elementary School

CONFIDENTIAL

We need your help in discussing the suicide of one of our students with your class during homeroom. Some students will already be aware of his suicide from the news on television or from this morning's paper. Others will be learning about the death from you.

It would be beneficial to give your class the opportunity to hear the necessary facts from you, to ask questions, to dispel rumors, and to discuss feelings and reactions. You can expect some students to be sad and upset, as well as angry.

The crisis team will be available throughout the day, this evening, and over the weekend. If you need some assistance in discussing this death with your class, a team member will be available to come to your classroom. A crisis team member will be in the teachers' lounge if you wish to talk further about this tragedy. Please identify any student whom you think needs further help dealing with this loss and send him or her to the counseling office or the care center, which is set up adjacent to the cafeteria.

Students may be excused from classes to attend the student's funeral if they bring a written excuse from home. Funeral arrangements are still pending. We will give you that information when we receive it.

FIGURE 3.6
Sample Informing Letter to the Faculty

Classroom Loss: We have something very tragic and very sad to tell you today. Melissa, our co-captain, was driving home after basketball practice last night in the rain. The streets were slick and it was foggy. There was a car accident and she was killed as a result. This is a tragic loss for all of us.

We will be around to talk with you all day. We will keep you updated about the funeral arrangements. We will also be open to any suggestions of activities that you might want to do in her memory.

Schoolwide Loss: Our school has had a tragic loss. As many of you know, Mrs. Smith, the school nurse, has been ill for many months. We just received word that she died this morning. We will be commemorating Mrs. Smith's contributions to our school. I would also like each class to discuss ways it would like to commemorate the life work of Mrs. Smith.

FIGURE 3.7
Sample Announcements for Classroom or Schoolwide Communication

Chapter 4

Critical Incidents and First-Response Procedures

INTRODUCTION: WHAT CONSTITUTES A CRITICAL INCIDENT

Critical incidents can create strong emotional responses in both students and staff. Symptoms of the impact may vary with people from diverse cultural backgrounds. In this emotionally charged climate following a critical incident, the existence of well-established plans for dealing with the situation can reduce confusion and ensure that decisions are reasoned and thorough.

- Established plans that list guidelines for providing support can speed up responses when timing is crucial.
- Schools must take steps to ensure that one critical incident does not lead to further crisis reactions in the school community or create harmful conflict among school personnel who are trying to make decisions under stress.
- The district and the school are subject to close scrutiny, based on their response to a crisis. Children and their families should be reassured by the school's actions that the incident is being competently managed.

Children proceed through a variety of stages following a trauma. The following stages have been identified as stages one might expect following a disaster:

- **Terror**—Exhibited in children through crying, vomiting or bodily discharge, becoming mute, loss of temper, or running away
- **Rage, anger**—Adrenaline release, tense muscles, heart rate increases
- **Denial**—Adults may exhibit denial differently than children. Some behaviors include feeling numb, blocking off pain and emotion, dreaming,

feeling removed from experiences, or having no feelings at all. Children may withdraw into uncustomary behavior patterns. Behaviors may appear nonresponsive and be overlooked.
- **Unresolved grief**—Unresolved grief could move into deep depression or major character changes to adjust to unresolved demands of grief and trauma. A child may stay sad or angry, be passive or resistant.
- **Shame and guilt**—Children do not believe in randomness and may even feel at fault after a disaster. Shame is one's public exposure of vulnerabilities. Guilt is private. There is a need to resolve these feelings, regain a sense of control, gain a new sense of independence, and feel capable.

Each school will need to develop its own Critical Incident Management Plan, which identifies the nature and the range of critical incidents to which students and staff may be exposed. A critical incident is broadly defined as an event that causes disruption to an organization, creates significant danger or risk, and traumatically affects individuals within the organization. A **Critical Incident Management Plan** ensures that all people affected by a serious incident receive the proper care and support. A critical incident can include one or more of the following:

- Bomb threat
- Break-in, accompanied by serious vandalism
- Copycat threats
- Criminal or terrorist activity
- Death of students or staff members
- Destruction of the whole, or part of the, school
- Discovery of suspected illegal drugs or substances
- Earthquake
- Explosion
- Extremes in temperature or weather, such as wind storms, tornadoes, hurricanes
- Fire
- Flood
- Gas or chemical hazards
- Hostage situations—students or staff members taken hostage
- Industrial or transport accidents
- Natural or other major disasters in the community
- Students lost or injured on an excursion
- Students or staff members witnessing serious injury or death
- Threats to the safety of students or the staff, including intruders who behave in a dangerous or threatening manner
- Unfavorable media or community attention, including major complaints or criticism of the school district, training activities, programs, or curriculum
- Violence between students or assault on a student or a staff member

The safety of the students and the staff should be the number one consideration in developing emergency procedures. Other key issues to be considered in the planning include:

- How to assess the severity of the situation
- The method to be used to call for assistance
- Procedures for defusing and controlling the crisis and accessing further help
- The role of experts and when to hand over the incident to outside experts (police, mental health professionals, etc.)
- Debriefing by the Critical Incident Team to decide what further action to take and whether response plans should be mobilized

An effective **Critical Incident Management Plan** will include each of the following six (6) major areas:

1. Establishing a Critical Incident Team/Crisis Response Team
2. Risk assessment (i.e., adequate assessment of hazards and situations that may require emergency action);
3. Incident prevention (i.e., management strategies are developed to prevent or minimize the impact of a critical incident)
4. Response planning (including evacuation support and management of evacuation with community agencies)
5. Recovery timeline
6. Procedures for the evaluation of the Critical Incident Management Plan

ESTABLISHING A CRITICAL INCIDENT COMMITTEE

Critical incidents and emergencies involve threats of harm to students, personnel, facilities, or any combination of these and require immediate and effective responses. Virtually every adult in the building, along with community agencies, will be involved in some way when there is a critical incident.

A **Critical Incident Committee** should be established to assist the principal in the prevention and management of critical incidents at the school. (Although the principal is normally responsible, the **Critical Incident Committee** must be prepared to assist the principal with all aspects of implementing the management plan.) One person should be appointed as the **Critical Incidents' Team Leader.** The committee may consist of any member of the school or the local community but should include the principal and the staff, including the school counselor, who may have to respond during a critical incident.

Characteristics of Critical incident Team Members

What might be of prime importance is the individual's own "emotional makeup" to handle the tasks of critical incident management. Wilson and Sigman (1996) suggest that mental health staff members must have the knowledge and the skills to be effective in crisis situations. Characteristics to consider when selecting **Critical Incident Team Members** include the following:

- Have the ability to handle stress with a minimum of other stressors present in their personal lives
- Are able to remain focused
- Can function well in confused, chaotic environments
- "Think on their feet" and have a commonsense, practical, flexible, and often improvisational approach to problem solving
- Are comfortable with changing situations and are able to function with role ambiguity, unclear lines of authority, and in minimal structure
- See problems as challenges, rather than as burdens
- Exhibit initiative and stamina, as well as self-awareness
- Monitor and manage their own stress
- Work cooperatively in a liaison capacity
- Are aware of and are comfortable with value systems and life experiences other than their own
- Eagerly reach out and explore the community to find people who need help, instead of taking a "wait and treat" attitude
- Enjoy people and do not seem lacking in confidence
- Comfortably initiate a conversation in any community setting
- Have special skills to match the needs of the population, that is, special expertise in working with children and the local schools
- Show sensitivity to cultural issues and are familiar and comfortable with the culture of the groups affected by the disaster
- Provide services that are culturally appropriate. Ideally, mental health workers will include individuals indigenous to specific cultural groups affected by the disaster.
- Are fluent in the languages of non–English-speaking groups that are affected and are able to establish rapport quickly with people of diverse backgrounds
- Show patience, perseverance, and an ability to function without seeing immediate results; are multidisciplinary and multiskilled
- Are able to remain calm when others are upset and emotional
- Can to follow instructions and work well with a team
- Are flexible
- Are willing to accept responsibility

- Are familiar with the community or are able to establish rapport quickly and meaningfully
- Are willing and able to "be with" survivors who may be experiencing tragedy and enormous loss, without being compelled to "fix" the situation
- Are knowledgeable about the functioning and the organization of a school and the association
- Have experience in psychiatric triage, first aid, crisis intervention, and brief treatment
- Understand crisis, post-traumatic stress, and grief reactions
- Are available. All team members must be able to set aside other duties and responsibilities to join the Critical Incident Team as quickly as possible.
- Other characteristics include:
  - Compassion, friendliness, and approachability
  - Leadership and decision-making ability;
  - Ability to follow through with decisions
  - Effective listening skills
  - Respect for confidentiality
  - Clarity about the way to take care of oneself during and after the crisis

Members of the Critical Incident Team Should Include the Following:

1. Principal
2. Assistant principal
3. Nurse
4. Youth service officer (police officer)
5. Lead counselor and counseling staff
6. Lead secretary
7. Lead custodian
8. Selected teachers and coaches
9. School psychologist
10. School social worker
11. Members of the clergy or spiritual leaders
12. Member of the Health Department
13. Member of emergency responders (e.g., EMT, firefighters, HAZMAT team)
14. Representative from the Armed Services (This is especially critical when the community is military-intensive, such as Norfolk, Virginia.)
15. The Coroner's Office
16. The Prosecutor's Office
17. The Information Office for the school system or district

Outside resources may be needed when:

1. There is a national interest in the tragedy;
2. There are multiple deaths or many serious injuries;
3. Many caregivers on the **Critical Incident Response Team** are also directly affected by the tragedy;
4. It is expected that the tragedy will continue to affect people for a long time;
5. Caregivers do not feel ready to do group crisis intervention or debriefing sessions for the local population because they have not had recent experience; or
6. The media are causing additional grief for the community (NOVA, 2001).

The duties of the committee will include

1. Adequate assessment of hazards and situations that may require emergency action;
2. Analysis of requirements to address these hazards; establishment of liaisons with all relevant emergency services; development of an effective management plan;
3. Dissemination of planned procedures;
4. Organization of practice drills to test the plan; regular review of the management plan;
5. Assisting the principal with all aspects of implementating of the management plan;
6. Arranging staff development activities, where necessary;
7. Developing, in consultation with the staff and community agencies, an effective Critical Incident Management Plan;
8. Advising the staff and the students of planned procedures, such as emergency evacuation plans and critical code words that have been preestablished, such as "*All transcripts are due in the counseling office today,*" or for middle school "*Dues for the honor society are due to the counseling office today.*" (Some statement that is true, yet innocuous to outside intruders);
9. Undertaking risk assessment; (e.g., vulnerable areas in the building and outside the building, such as portable classrooms, parking lots, and adjacent areas);
10. Assessing situations that may require emergency action;
11. Analyzing requirements to address these situations (e.g., clearing the front parking area of the school so that there is always emergency access);
12. Coordinating with all relevant community emergency services;
13. Facilitating the provision of counseling services to students, parents, and staff if necessary;

14. Ensuring that all staff members understand the **Critical Incident Management Plan**;
15. Ensuring that all emergency numbers are displayed in prominent locations (e.g., secretaries' station, principal's, and assistant principal's office, nurse's office, faculty lounge, cafeteria, workroom, the counseling offices, and on custodian's closet or room, youth service officer's station);
16. Organizing practice drills to test the **Critical Incident Management Plan** (note: These have been around since the 1950s. It's time for their resurrection.);
17. Assisting the principal with the implementation of the **Critical Incident Management Plan**, including distribution and communication of the plan to new and current staff members;
18. Arranging relevant training and development activities for the staff, when necessary; and
19. Regularly evaluating the **Critical Incident Management Plan**, including evaluating the plan after each serious incident or evacuation exercise by assessing how the plan worked each critical time.

The Need for Interagency Agreements

The school district should enter into agreements with various county government agencies, including mental health, police, and fire departments. The agreements specify the type of communications and services provided by one agency to another. The agreements also make school division personnel available beyond the school setting in the event of a disaster or a traumatic event taking place in the community.

TELEPHONE TREE

Once it is verified that a critical incident exists, the building administrator or the designee sets the phone tree in motion. When a critical incident occurs during weekends or vacation periods, or when a large number of staff members are away from school, it will be necessary to transmit information via a phone tree. At other times, if crises occur when school is in session, only the people outside the school building need to be contacted via telephone.

Checklist to Be Used in the Development of a Critical Incidents Management Plan

1. Is there an existing Critical Incident Team?
2. Have emergency plans been discussed with staff, students, and parents?

TABLE 4.1
Telephone Tree

Administrator or designee

Police liaison, as appropriate — Superintendent

CRT chair or contact person — Media liaison

Police, as appropriate

Team member

Team member

Team member — Community resource

Team member — Special program coordinator — Division-specific appointee

Team member — Feeder school contact — Feeder school — Community resource

Team member — Community resource contact

Community resource

3. Have the threats to the school been determined?
4. Are the school's emergency evacuation plans clearly understood by all students, staff, and parents? Are they publicized on the school's website?
5. Have emergency duties been assigned to members of the administrative staff, teachers, and other employees?
6. Have emergency shut-down and opening procedures been developed for gas, water, and electricity? Is the custodial staff aware and prepared?
7. Staff and students should be aware about emergency lockdown warnings; for example, the principal could announce over the P.A. system, *"Send all majorette applications to the guidance office today."* (The school does not have a majorette team).
8. Have plans been checked by relevant authorities, (e.g., police, fire, HAZMAT teams) before implementation?
9. Are there plans for reviewing and evaluating the Critical Incident Management Plan?

THE NEED FOR VARIOUS FORMS OF COMMUNICATION

Technology

Technology can be very effective for communicating during a crisis. Some common tools that may be used include the following:

1. **Telephone**—Although the telephone is the most commonly used communications tool in schools, most schools do not have enough lines and, worse, service is typically lost when electricity is lost. In preparing for crises, it is recommended that
   • Schools should have at least one line with an unpublished number.
   • The telephone company should be consulted in pre-planning; there may be unused lines in the school's control panel that can be activated if needed.
   • Use standard jacks and mark them clearly so that emergency service personnel can find them; the school floor plan should be part of the school's "emergency toolkit" and should have the location of jacks clearly marked.
2. **Intercom systems**—Most schools have such a system; systems that include teacher-initiated communications with the office and that use a handset, rather than a wall-mounted speaker, are most useful in an emergency. Instructions for using of the intercom system should be posted near the controls in the office area. In addition, students should be taught to use the intercom system—the teacher may have a medical emergency or be otherwise unable to operate the system.

3. **Bullhorns and megaphones**—Often used at pep rallies and on field days, battery-powered bullhorns or megaphones can also be very effective tools for communicating during an emergency and should be part of the school's "emergency toolbox."
4. **Walkie-talkies**—Routinely used in many schools, walkie-talkies provide a reliable method of communication between rooms and buildings at a single site. All staff members need to know how to operate the walkie-talkie (even those who don't routinely carry them).
5. **Computer telecommunications**—Though computers are a relatively new tool, their potential capability to be used for communication, both within the school and to other sites, needs to be assessed as part of the pre-planning process. E-mail or electronic bulletin boards may be useful tool for updating information for the staff, the central office, other schools in the affected area, and possibly other community agencies.
6. **Fax machines**—The fax machine is a potentially valuable tool for both sending and receiving information in an emergency. In the case of off-campus accidents, for example, lists of students and staff members involved, their locations, and needed telephone numbers can be quickly and accurately communicated. Medical information, release forms, and medical authorizations can be faxed, signed, and returned in emergencies.
7. **Cellular telephones**—Increasingly available and affordable, cellular telephones as a communications tool need to be carefully assessed. They may be the only tool working when electric service is out, and they are a particularly useful link to staff members who may be en route to or from the site of an accident or another emergency. They are increasingly being used to link the multiple vehicles transporting students and staff on off-campus trips.
8. **"Panic buttons"**—Some schools have installed "panic buttons" connected directly to the police or other emergency services. In some communities, there is an immediate response; in others, the police or fire department calls the school to confirm the emergency.
9. **Alarm systems**—Bells or buzzers may be sounded in different ways to signal different types of emergencies—for example, fire, tornado, or special alert (with instructions to follow).

Voice and Hand Signals

Although not involving "technology," voice and hand signals (and training staff and students to recognize these) are important instruments of communication in an emergency. Some signals that may be used include:

1. **Waving arms**—Waving arms back and forth overhead means to follow in the direction led by the teacher.
2. **Palms down**—Moving arms up and down with palms toward the ground will signal students to get down on the ground, wherever they are at the time.
3. **Palms out**—Pushing palms out, moving arms forward and back, will signal the students to stop where they are and to stand absolutely still.
4. **Waving arms side-to-side**—Moving arms side to side in front of the body will signal students to move away from the center of the playground and to take shelter toward the edges of the playground.

Using Code Messages

Some schools have established code words or phrases to notify the staff of certain emergencies—particularly those requiring quick action. These are most appropriate for extreme emergencies, such as an armed intruder, a sniper, hostage situations, or tornado warnings. Codes may signify certain levels of alert that require specific actions such as locking classroom doors, keeping students away from windows, or evacuation. It is important that all staff members—including substitutes—know the codes.

IDENTIFYING AND RESPONDING TO IMMINENT WARNING SIGNS

Imminent warning signs indicate that a student is very close to behaving in a way that is potentially dangerous to self, to others, or both. Imminent warning signs require an immediate response. No single warning sign can predict that a dangerous act will occur. Rather, imminent warning signs usually are presented as a sequence of overt, serious, hostile behaviors or threats directed at peers, teachers, administrators, support staff, or other individuals. Usually, imminent warning signs are evident to more than one staff member—as well as to the child's family.

Imminent warning signs may include

- Serious physical fighting with peers or family members
- Severe destruction of property
- Severe rage for seemingly minor reasons
- Detailed threats of lethal violence
- Possession, use, or both of firearms and other weapons
- Other self-injurious behaviors or threats of suicide

When warning signs indicate that danger is imminent, safety must always be the first and foremost consideration. Action must be taken immediately. Immediate intervention by school authorities and law enforcement officers is needed when a child:

- Has presented a detailed plan (time, place, method) to harm or kill others—particularly if the child has a history of aggression or has attempted to carry out threats in the past.
- Is carrying a weapon, particularly a firearm, and has threatened to use it.

In situations where students present other threatening behaviors, parents should be informed of the concerns immediately. School communities also have the responsibility to seek assistance from appropriate agencies, such as child and family services and community mental health professionals (Dwyer, Osher, & Warger, 1998).

SCHOOL THREAT ASSESSMENT RESPONSE PROTOCOL

The purpose of this protocol is to provide a mechanism to ensure that threats of violence in a school environment are addressed, whenever possible, before they occur. The protocol is intended to identify credible threats of violence and address those threats and the individual making the threats before these are carried out. *NOTE: This protocol is applicable during any school-sponsored event or the function, whether the event or function is on school property or not.*

The Process of Responding to a Critical Incident Involves Ten Distinct Steps
School Critical Incident Response Plan

  Step 1: Gathering the Facts
  Step 2: Contacting the Community and the District
  Step 3: Activating the School Team
  Step 4: Communicating with the Staff
  Step 5: Setting up Counseling and Debriefing Centers
  Step 6: Communicating with the Students
  Step 7: Informing Parents and the Community
  Step 8: Providing Funeral Information
  Step 9: Evaluating and Reviewing Team Performance
  Step 10: Initiating Remembance Activity

The following generic school critical incident protocol has been adapted from resources around the counties and from other states. This material is designed as a template for districts to use when developing school handbooks or as a resource to compare with existing critical incident response protocols when they are under review.

This protocol example features 10 steps. Because many school critical incidents involve the sudden death of people in the school community, the language in the steps is oriented toward responding to such events. The steps can be adapted for use with any type of traumatic event affecting a school.

Throughout the protocol steps, this template uses the word *principal* to refer to the principal or the designate.

Step 1—Gathering the Facts

1. The principal confirms the critical incident with appropriate sources of reliable information, as applicable:
   - Immediate family
   - Police
   - Coroner
   - School district personnel
   - Community resource personnel, such as a mental health worker
2. The principal collects information on the critical incident, by
   - Verifying of the details,
   - Identifying the individuals involved,
   - Evaluating the emotional status of the school and, if necessary, responding to the immediate safety needs of students and staff, or any combination of the previous actions
   - The principal consults with the families affected to determine their wishes concerning public announcements and information for school staff and students

Step 2—Contact with the District Team

1. The principal telephones the designated District Critical Incident Response Team leader. If the leader is unavailable, the principal contacts another member of the district team who in turn will call the other members of the district team.
2. The principal ensures that the predetermined media contact person for the district is informed. This person handles all media requests for information and arranges for the preparation of press releases, if necessary.

The decision of the family about privacy of information must be re-spected, and possible legal implications related to privacy issues must be considered.

3. The district team leader arranges for all involved schools and personnel to be informed by telephone. The timing of these calls should be sensi-tive to the needs of the school community that is most affected by the incident.

Step 3—Activate the School Team

1. The principal contacts the members of the school **Critical Incident Team** and calls them together for a meeting. The school team will implement an appropriate plan of action that takes into consideration both the wishes of the family or families and the needs of the school.

   In brief, at this initial meeting the team should
   - Distribute the Critical Incident Team Checklist.
   - Determine what needs to be done.
   - Clarify each person's tasks.
   - Ensure that confidentiality is maintained until information is shared with the whole staff, and clarify family privacy issues.

2. The school team notifies the rest of the staff, including secretarial, custo-dial, and other support staff, of a special staff meeting. If the critical incident occurred during an evening or a weekend, a scripted telephone tree message can be used to call staff members to a meeting before the next school day. The school team should not discuss the incident on the telephone unless it is already widely known in the community. Care should be taken about using the phone tree:
   - Ensure that each person understands the message about the staff meet-ing by asking him or her to repeat the message back to the caller,
   - Avoid leaving a message on an answering machine or voice mail or with a child, and
   - Reassign telephoning responsibilities of people who may be most af-fected by the incident.

3. Tasks for the school team to do before the start of the school day, if possible:
   - Determine further details of the event.
   - Ensure that the predetermined media contact person is provided with detailed information that is necessary to effectively carry out the role.
   - Determine the family's wishes regarding personal property if the inci-dent has been a sudden death or a suicide and ensure that personal

property is secure. For example, replace the lock on the individual's locker if the incident was a student death or an injury.

- Decide what course of action will be used to deal with potential memorial "shrines" created by classmates of the deceased after a student's death. It is important to establish a protocol on this matter. Allowing a memorial "shrine" in one instance, but not in the next, may raise questions of fairness and favoritism that can escalate emotions and introduce conflict unnecessarily.
- Assess whether teachers on call will be needed, and advise the appropriate person to contact them.
- Identify members of the school community who may be most affected by the incident, and plan support for these people.
- Assess the need for additional counseling support in the school, and ask the District Critical Incident Response Team to assist in making the necessary arrangements.
- Plan a meeting to inform the staff.
- Prepare a written statement for the staff meeting.
- Decide whether a letter will go home with students informing parents of the critical incident.

4. Tasks for the Critical Incident Response Team during the school day:
   - Supply a brief, written statement for office staff to use in referring incoming queries or media calls. A script helps to ensure that callers are redirected to the official media contact person.
   - Contact other nearby schools such as feeder schools that may be affected, and ensure that the district team has accurate information so that it can inform all schools in the district.
   - Activate plans for drop-in counseling centers, and assign counselors and other staff as appropriate.
   - Contact required outside resource people as appropriate—for example, mental health services, the police liaison officer, and the Health Department.
   - Bring in additional support staff, if needed, with the help of the district team.
   - Lower the flag when appropriate. This is a potentially contentious issue, particularly in the case of a suicide, which needs to be discussed by the staff as part of the advance planning for a critical incident.
   - Prepare the letter to the parents if one is needed.
   - Implement the planning for a Critical Incident Stress Debriefing for the staff for the end of the school day, if possible.

Step 4—Communicate With All school Faculty Staff Members

1. Inform all staff members of the critical incident at an emergency staff meeting prior to the start of school, if possible. In addition to teachers, be sure to inform secretaries, custodians, teacher assistants, and itinerant staff such as therapists, cafeteria workers, bus drivers, the public health nurse, and playground supervisors, of the meeting. After the meeting, inform all staff members who were unable to attend the meeting.

2. Carefully orchestrate the staff meeting in order to assure the staff that the team's plans are in place. All members of the Critical Incident Response Team should attend. Include the following in the meeting:
   - Advise the staff members to deal with students at a level of their comfort.
   - Reassure staff members that they will be supported in their efforts to give comfort to students and that additional help is available to anyone who needs it, staff or students.
   - Remind staff members of items in their critical incident handbook that may be useful over the next few days, and provide them with written directions for the day as soon as possible, during or after the meeting.
   - Introduce any people from the district team or the community support staff who are in attendance at the meeting and who may be present in the school to provide support to staff or students.

3. Develop a plan for the day with the staff:
   - Maintain a regular school schedule, if possible.
   - Cancel special activities, if necessary.
   - Carefully state the information that should be given to students during class discussion, and provide all staff members with additional copies of agendas to use for class discussions with students.
   - Inform the staff of the counseling services that are available to staff, students, and parents. In the case of a sudden death or a suicide, consider assigning a counselor to visit the scheduled classes of the deceased.
   - Identify students who are the closest friends or relatives of the deceased or injured, and make plans to inform them, using with additional sensitivity and support.
   - Identify students at risk, those who are vulnerable to stress or changes in routines, and make specific plans for each student. This task can be assigned to a key staff member, such as a counselor, a special education teacher, or a child-care worker.
   - Ensure that staff members who are absent get information. Make plans to assist on-call teachers with classroom discussions.
   - Plan to inform students who are absent. In the case of students who might be at risk, telephone their parents immediately.

4. Additional staff meetings may be needed:
   - Keep the staff informed throughout the day by calling short update meetings during breaks.
   - Gather information about student and staff needs throughout the day.
   - Provide all staff members with information about plans for the Critical Incident Stress Debriefing.

Step 5—Set Up Counseling Care Centers

As part of the protocol development, plans should be in place to designate counseling centers in case of a critical incident. When a traumatic event occurs, there is not sufficient time to carefully discuss how this service will be organized. Specific rooms or areas of the school can be designated for dealing with a potentially large number of people who are grieving or experiencing high levels of stress following a critical incident. Some ideas suggested by schools that have planned and used this type of service following a school critical incident include:

- Individual students can take a break during the day to visit the counseling center and get support in dealing with their emotional reactions to the death or the traumatic incident.
- It is important that support be available to students, at the moment they need it, in a private and supportive setting.
- Small group-counseling sessions may be helpful, if the personnel assigned to the centers have experience and training in counseling.
- Staff members in the centers should have written information to give to the students, such as a list of the normal stages of grief and guidelines on how to arrange for support from mental health workers.
- Large groups of students should not be allowed to congregate in the center.
- Schools should consider calling on elementary and secondary counselors from neighboring schools, when possible, to augment available counseling personnel.

Step 6—Talk with Students

1. Be sure there is a teacher in each classroom as the students come in for the day or the first class.
2. Give information on the critical incident in a low-key and factual manner, including
   - What happened,
   - When and where the events occurred,

- Who was there at the time of the incident,
- What happened after the event,
- Who might be seriously affected by the incident because of their relationship with people directly involved in the traumatic event, and
- What is going to happen next. In the case of a sudden death, try to have information available on the funeral arrangements.
3. Give the students an opportunity to react, discuss, and ask questions.
   - Allow time for the students to express their feelings. Keep in mind that reaction times may vary.
   - Give students permission to express what they uniquely feel. Listen and be empathetic.
   - Consider using activities to help students process their grief, such as art, poetry, or creative journal writing.
   - Once the talk seems to be over, begin the regular class routines in a flexible manner, allowing yourself time to respond to more questions throughout the day.

Teachers will need to be prepared to hear some unusual questions and to handle these questions in a matter-of-fact way. They will need to model, by their behavior, that the critical incident is serious, yet at the same time show warmth and understanding toward all students. Teachers should watch carefully for individual students who are having a hard time coping, to ensure that they get access to help in the counseling centers. It is better to over-refer than to under-refer. Teachers should not try to second-guess the level of grief of a student or a staff member, as people respond to trauma and grieve differently.

Following a critical incident, children may report other traumatic events in their lives, such as child abuse. All staff members should be clear on the protocol for reporting child abuse and neglect and be prepared to take action to get help for the students in areas that may seem unrelated to the current trauma situation.

Step 7—Inform Parents

Send a letter home with the students to inform their parents of the incident, if appropriate. Sample letter formats, provided at the end of this chapter and also at the end of chapter 3, can be adapted for use following a critical incident. In general, parents who are well informed are better equipped to support their children at home.

Information shared in such a letter should be carefully worded to ensure that personal and family privacy is respected.

Step 8—Share Funeral Information

In the case of a death, inform the staff and the students of plans for funeral arrangements. Many types of critical incidents involve sudden deaths: accidents, suicides, natural or physical disasters, or sudden acute health events. The school will need to provide information to the whole school community about formal occasion, such as funerals or memorial services.

- When appropriate, students and staff members should have the opportunity to attend the funeral. To do this, the school team should arrange permission from the district-level administration to dismiss the students.
- Decisions about allowing funeral attendance should be governed by the wishes of the family. Student and staff attendance at the funeral can provide support for the family, if that is the family's choice. Students should be informed of the family's wishes regarding attendance at the funeral service.
- The funeral service can help peers understand and accept the death of a friend or a colleague and can help to provide closure.
- Ensure that students who plan to attend the funeral are prepared by helping them anticipate what happens at funerals. Explain the purpose of various rituals, appropriate etiquette at the ceremony, and other topics as necessary, such as embalming, cremation, open caskets, burial, and specific cultural practices.

Step 9—Conduct a Critical Incident Team Debriefing

After each use critical incident, the critical incident response team should meet to review the events while they are still recent, preferably within two weeks to assess strengths and weaknesses. This will serve several purposes, it will improve the plans, raise staff skills about the use of the plan, and tie up loose ends and concerns following the critical incident. The meeting should include:

- A review of how well the plan guided the actions of the staff. Identify improvements that can be made in the school plan for future situations.
- A reevaluation of how well the actions taken as part of the plan were carried out. Appropriate changes can be made for next time, including additional training, if needed.
- Ensuring that counseling for school team members is available for staff members who feel that they still need to deal with their own feelings about their role in the critical incident.
- A plan to write letters of appreciation to all who helped.

Step 10—Remembrance Activity or Memorial Service

Family wishes should guide the planning of a remembrance activity after a critical incident that involved a student's or a staff member's death.

- Schools and districts are cautioned against holding a large assembly to honor the deceased because of the potential for group hysteria and for glorifying death in the case of a suicide. Large assemblies are not recommended for acute grief situations.
- Students or staff members may wish to express their grief and sympathy by contributing something in the name(s) of the deceased: a scholarship fund, school landscaping, a school plaque, books for the library, construction of a showcase, or some other appropriate means. Caution should be taken when establishing a permanent or highly visible memorial to remember a student who committed suicide.
- Staff members may need to provide leadership to students wishing to establish an appropriate remembrance, as the judgment of peers may be impaired following a traumatic event.

CRITICAL INCIDENT NO. 1:
PROCEDURES FOR THREATENED ACTS OF VIOLENCE

The following procedure is separated into several sections, in order to reflect those instances where a threatened act of violence may be received by specific individuals.

1. Any student, parent, teacher, or staff member, upon receiving information that a person is threatening to commit an act of violence, shall:
   - Assume the threat is serious.
   - Immediately report the threat to a parent, a guardian, the school staff, an administrator, or a law enforcement officer.
   - Be available and cooperative in providing a statement of information, with the understanding that the information source (a student) will remain anonymous, to the greatest extent possible.
2. Any school administrator, upon receiving information that a student is threatening to commit an act of violence, shall:
   - Assume the threat is serious.
   - If said student is on campus, immediately remove the individual from the classroom and segregate him or her into a secured area, pending further investigation.
   - Immediately notify the designated law enforcement officer assigned to the school, and provide the officer with complete information regarding the information received.

- Require the school staff member, if this is the source of the information, to provide immediate written statements regarding the information received.
- The designated law enforcement officer shall conduct an assessment interview of the subject making the threat. The assessment interview will include at least one administrator.
- NOTE: The primary purpose of the interview is to assess the available information, in an attempt to determine the authenticity of the threat and thus to decide what level of follow-up action is needed and appropriate.
- Once the assessment is complete, the law enforcement officer and the administrator shall convene privately to discuss the threat and consider options for follow-up action.
3. If it is agreed that the threat is credible,
   - The law enforcement officer shall immediately consult with the city or county commonwealth's attorney.
   - The school administrator shall take administrative action in accordance with school board policy.
   - The student's parents or guardian shall be notified in accordance with school board policy.
   - If it is agreed that the threat is not credible, the school administrator shall assume responsibility to institute any further action deemed necessary.
   - Once the situation has been assessed and action taken, the school principal assumes the responsibility for reporting to the superintendent.

RECOVERY TIME LINE

The successful management of critical incidents depends on the school taking appropriate action and providing support during and after the incident. The recovery time line following a critical incident will vary, depending on the circumstances. The following guideline is provided to outline necessary action in the event of a critical incident:

Tasks to Do Immediately

- Assess the situation.
- Ensure the safety and the welfare of the staff and students, and arrange first aid and emergency service, if needed.

Tasks to Complete During the First 24 Hours

- Notify the superintendent of schools and various emergency services.
- Where appropriate, ensure that the equipment and the area where the critical incident has taken place are not further disturbed.
- Organize a meeting with all relevant persons for the purpose of updating them on the critical incident and to discuss personal issues or concerns.
- Arrange counseling as needed.
- Work delicately with the media and refer them to the district information officer.
- Keep staff, students, and parents informed (e.g., set up a hotline number for them to call and place information on the school website. Information is power, and immediacy is critical.).
- Complete and forward a **Critical Incident Report** to the district superintendent.

Tasks to Complete Within 24–72 Hours

- Provide opportunities for the staff and students to talk about the critical incident with counselors.
- Provide support to the staff and helping professionals.
- Debrief all relevant persons.
- Ensure that relevant persons are kept up to date with information.
- Restore normal functioning and service delivery.
- Keep parents and the community informed.

Tasks to Complete Within the First Month

- Arrange a memorial service, if appropriate.
- When appropriate, encourage parents, clergy, and other support personnel in the community to participate in meetings to educate them and discuss students' welfare.
- Identify ongoing behavioral changes that may indicate the necessity for counseling or referral, and, when appropriate, refer students to outside sources for counseling.
- Continue to ascertain the progress of hospitalized staff members or students.
- Provide appropriate activities for classes to help students come to terms with or gain an understanding of the event.
- Be aware that the physical and mental health of helpers may be affected, and provide them with appropriate support. (See chapter 10 on "Compassion Fatigue" and therapeutic strategies for helping professionals.)

Tasks to Complete to Follow Through and Follow Up

- Identify ongoing behavior change that may indicate the necessity for further counseling and referral.
- Provide continued support, if needed.
- Consider planning grief and loss topics of study or discussion in appropriate courses or class sessions, to assess post-traumatic stress disorder or acute stress disorder.
- Plan for and be sensitive to the disturbing influences of anniversaries of the critical incident, requests from the media, and legal proceedings.

CRITICAL INCIDENT NO. 2: PROCEDURES FOR HANDLING FIGHTS IN SCHOOL SETTINGS

- Walk briskly—don't run.
- Get help along the way.
- Assess and evaluate
  1. The number of schools involved
  2. The size of the students involved
  3. Any weapons that are involved
  4. Proximity of individuals who can assist
  5. Whether there are several subtle things going on simultaneously that are being tangibly expressed in the conflict. Is there gang involvement? What other alliances might exist?
- Dismiss the gathered students to go back to their current classrooms (if before school, dismiss them to their homerooms).
- Identify yourself to the fighters.
- Call the students by name.
- Stay away from the middle of the conflict.
- Remove your glasses.
- Give specific commands in a firm, authoritative voice.
- Defer to rules, not personal authority.
- Separate the aggressor and the person who was victimized.
- Avoid physical force, if possible.
- Remove the participants to neutral locations.
- Obtain identification.
- Get medical attention, if necessary.
- Describe the incident in writing.
- Debrief the relevant teachers.
- Provide protection and support for the people who were victimized.
- Provide counseling—not simply the day after the event, but as long as necessary.

98 Crisis Intervention and Crisis Management

- Report the incident to law enforcement and other child-serving agencies that may be helping the child or the adolescent
- Manage the media
- Set up a recovery room, if necessary.
- Provide factual information to the staff, the students, and the school community, while maintaining the privacy of the students and staff members who were involved.
- Provide staff with information regarding workman's compensation, if applicable

CRITICAL INCIDENT NO. 3: LOCKDOWN PROCEDURES

In cases of an emergency requiring lockdown, staff and students will use the following procedure:

1. The principal or his designee will announce over the public address system that a lockdown is in effect.
2. One of the secretaries will be directed to call 911 and notify the police of the emergency and the need for immediate police assistance.
3. The following announcement will be made:
   A. Class in session (no lunches in progress)
      "Students and staff—It is necessary at this time to begin a schoolwide lockdown. All students are to remain in class. Students in the hall report immediately back to your room. Teachers lock your classroom door. No one is to leave the classroom until *an all-clear announcement* is made by an administrator. Ignore a fire alarm. If we need to evacuate the building, an announcement will be made."
   B. Class change in progress
      "Students and staff—It is necessary at this time to begin a schoolwide lockdown. All students and teachers report immediately to your next class. Teachers, be at your classroom door and lock it as soon as the students have arrived. Ignore a fire alarm. If we need to evacuate the building, an announcement will be made."
   C. During lunch bells
      "Students and staff— It is necessary at this time to begin a schoolwide lockdown. Students in the cafeteria are to report immediately to the (gym or auditorium—whichever is appropriate). Teachers lock your classroom doors. Students outside of their classroom at this time are to report back to your class immediately. No one is to leave his or her

classroom or designated area until an administrator makes an all-clear announcement. Ignore a fire alarm. If we need to evacuate the building, an announcement will be made."

   During the lockdown announcement, the administrator and the head custodian will lock the exit doors.
   D. Teachers are to do the following:
      i. Lock your door.
      ii. Tell the students that we have an emergency, and you don't know what it is.
      iii. Get the students to go to an area of the room that is away from the door and away from the windows.
      iv. Have the students stay there until an announcement is made. Members of the crisis team will come to your room and update you.
      v. Communications among administrators will be by walkie-talkie to assess situation and plan the next course of action.
      vi. The school nurse and the attendance clerk will report immediately to the main office during the lockdown announcement.

Security officers will report to the nearest classroom and will maintain radio contact with administrators.

CRITICAL INCIDENT NO. 4:
HOSTAGE SITUATIONS/BARRICADED CAPTOR

A hostage situation is any situation in which a person or persons are forced to stay in one location by one or more individuals. Weapons are usually in the possession of the hostage taker(s), and hostages are threatened with some degree of bodily harm should they not comply with the directives of the hostage taker(s). Certain demands are usually made of outside officials, in return for the release of the hostages.

- All hostage situations are dangerous events.
- A hostage taker might be a terrorist, a fleeing felon, a disgruntled employee (past or present), an employee's spouse, a drug or alcohol abuser, emotionally disturbed person, a trespasser, and, on occasion, a parent, a student, a or citizen who is usually angry about some situation and decides to resolve it by taking hostages and making demands to achieve some resolution.
- A hostage situation varies greatly, and no two incidents will be the same.

School Building Plan of Action

Upon notification of a hostage situation within any activity, event, school, or building under the control of the city/county public schools, the following procedures should be implemented:

- **Principal:** The principal/administrative head or a designated individual will assume command of the situation until the arrival of the police department at the scene. Security officers should work closely with the principal/administrative head/designee to ensure that this plan of action is safely achieved. School radios should be utilized when it is established that the hostage taker does not have one. If he does, radios should not be used.
- **Containment:** Appropriate actions should be taken to isolate the hostage taker and the victims under his control. It is important that no additional individuals be exposed to the hostage taker.
- **Evacuation:** Using a prearranged signal, immediately evacuate the building and ensure that egress of students and personnel is done in a manner that they do not go near the area controlled by the hostage taker. All individuals should proceed to a prearranged location out of sight of the building so that the possibility of injury from gunfire is minimized.
- **Reentry:** Ensure that no individuals enter or reenter the building until it is safe to do so.
- **Contact 911:** Immediately have a staff member contact 911 and give all available information to the dispatcher, who will relay the information to the city/county police department. Ensure that the caller remains on the line with the 911 dispatcher until police actually arrive at the scene. This will ensure that accurate, detailed information is relayed to responding officers, and school officials can respond to requests of the police department.
- **Contact the Office of the Superintendent of Operations:** Immediately have another staff member contact the Office of the Superintendent for Operations at _____ and give all available information to that office. Ensure that the caller remains on the line with the Office of the Superintendent until such time as directed to terminate the call by that office.
- **Deputy or assistant Superintendent of Operations:** The Office of the Superintendent for Operations will immediately contact the superintendent, the director of informational services, the coordinator of security, the director of transportation, and the director of school plant facilities.
- **City/County Police Department:** Upon response by the city/county police department, that department will assume control of the scene. The principal or the building administrator should maintain contact with the city/county police department and report to the Command Center when

Evacuation Procedures

The Critical Incidents Management Plan should contain procedures for the evacuation of the school during critical incidents. These procedures should include the following:

1. Ensure that an effective evacuation alarm system and procedure are in place.
2. Identify an evacuation assembly area that is a safe distance from the evacuated site, (e.g., football field, city park, church parking lot). A manageable assembly area should allow for crowd control, traffic control, and communications.
3. Establish priorities for evacuation (e.g., students with disabilities).
4. Ensure that exit routes are free of obstruction.
5. Record and display prominently all emergency and key local support personnel.
6. Define areas of responsibility and assign duties to appropriate staff members, including school administrative staff, counseling personnel, and support personnel such as secretaries, custodians, teaching assistants, and cafeteria workers.
7. Ensure that visitors are accounted for.
8. Identify an operational area for the administration to manage the evacuation.
9. Establish a recovery and communication room, if appropriate.
10. Provide after-hours contact numbers for local authorities, as well as hotline numbers and updated information on the local school website (e.g., provide locations of debriefing groups, contacts for clergy and spiritual leaders, as well as safe houses for students and families to congregate).

After the Evacuation

All faculty and staff members who manage evacuations should follow up with these procedures:

1. Ensure adequate supervision of all students (as well as that of a colleague should he or she become disabled).
2. Conduct a roll call, and account for all students assigned to each faculty member at that time period.
3. Report absentees and their last location to their team leaders.
4. Inform emergency authorities (e.g., police, medical technicians, HAZMAT teams, etc.) of missing students and their possible location.
5. Assist emergency authorities upon request.
6. Returning to the building is not permitted until the principal is assured that it safe to do so. This should be a collaborative decision between the principal, the central office personnel, and appropriate emergency services.
7. Students who have no transportation or no home to return to where there is adequate supervision because their parents cannot be located should be retained at the school and sheltered there until supervision can be secured.
8. The central office should be apprised of all transactions and actions that have occurred during and following the critical incident.

it is operational. *It is important that items such as building keys and detailed building plans be made available to the police department.* Important information such as camera and monitoring locations, hearing and broadcast devices, motion sensors, the location of radios, the availability of phones, and so on, must be conveyed to the police department. Anecdotal information regarding the cause of the incident, the identity of the hostages and hostage takers, and their location in the building is of great importance. The principal, the custodial staff, and plant personnel who are knowledgeable of the building design need to describe the premises using the detailed building plans.

- **Response by City/County Public Schools Officials:** The superintendent, the deputy superintendent for operations, the director of informational services, the director of transportation, the director of school plant Facilities, and the Coordinator of Security should respond to the Command Center.
- **Media:** The public information officer for the city/county police department will handle all press matters, as well as the dissemination of information to students and parents at the scene.
- **Director of Transportation:** The director of transportation will, at the direction of the superintendent or his designee, coordinate the utilization of school buses to evacuate students to another location or to their homes.
- **Director of School Plant Facilities:** The director of school plant facilities will interface with appropriate officials of the city/county police department to ensure that all their needs are met with regard to the facility under siege.
- **Negotiations:** It is important to remember that it is the philosophy of the city/county police department to end a hostage situation through negotiating tactics. Often this is a lengthy process. An assault is used only when all indications are that the hostage taker will harm the hostages and that lives will in fact be saved through such an assault.
- **Closure:** Upon the arrest of the hostage taker and the release of the hostages, the control of the school or the building will be returned to the school.

CRITICAL INCIDENT NO. 5: HOSTAGE SITUATION WITH A SCHOOL BUS

Consideration must be given to the possibility of a hostage situation occurring on a bus operated by city/county public schools. If such an incident occurs, the following procedures should be implemented.

- **Bus Driver:** The bus driver must assume a position of heightened responsibility for the welfare of the students on the bus, as well as for his or her own safety. Sound judgment, good decision making, knowledge of school and police procedures in handling such incidents, and training are the items that will be of greatest assistance to the driver should that individual become victimized. Students must be made aware of the behavior that will be required of them so that they will be safe and do not inflame an already volatile situation.

The bus driver should accomplish the following tasks if they can be done in a safe manner:

—Disable the bus or throw the keys away from the bus. This will eliminate the need to move the bus and will be helpful to the police department, which will respond to the scene as soon as the location has been established.

—Evacuate as many students as possible from the bus, and direct them to move to a position out of sight of the bus.

—Clear the area of as many students and others as is safely possible.

—Notify the transportation radio dispatcher of as much information as possible regarding your situation and location. If you are allowed to maintain radio contact, do so.

• **Transportation Department:** The dispatch office should call 911 and the deputy superintendent of operations, and all procedures set out in the Plan of Action for Buildings should be implemented.

CRITICAL INCIDENT NO. 6: EMPLOYEE HOSTAGE

A situation may arise in which a teacher, an administrator, or a school support staff member becomes a hostage. Other individuals, such as students, employees, and citizens, may become hostages at the same time. Remember that each incident involving hostages is different. Variables such as hostage takers, hostages, the motivation for the act, and the location of the incident make each occurrence unique. Sound judgment, good decision making, knowledge of school and police procedures in handling such incidents, and training are the items that will be of greatest assistance to you should you become a hostage.

Critical Responsibilities

• The main responsibility of individuals who have become hostages is to remain calm and act in a manner that will preserve their lives, as well as the lives of other hostages.

• If, in fact, the other hostages are students, city/county public school personnel have the additional duties of ensuring that these children are aware of the behavior that will be required of them so that they will be safe and do not inflame an already volatile situation.

- Initially, any school staff member may be the person who is thrust into the role of negotiating with the hostage taker(s). Always remain calm and request that the situation end by the release of the hostages or the escape of the hostage takers from the area. At all times, remain neutral regarding the reasons given by the hostage taker(s) for taking this action. The main focus is safety and the release of the hostages. Furthermore, responses of the hostage taker may be irrational or illogical, depending upon his or her mental condition and the stress of the situation.

The Role of the City/County Police Department

- Be prepared to wait, as the resolution of hostage situations routinely takes time. Be assured that the city/county public schools and the city/county police department are acting on your behalf, as quickly as possible.
- The city/county police department crisis negotiator will contact the hostage taker and begin the process of negotiating an end to the situation. If requested to talk to the negotiator, the city/county public schools' employee should do so. Answer all questions as fully as possible. At this point, the negotiator has the main responsibility to successfully end the situation.
- At the conclusion of the situation, the city/county police department will request that the staff member talk at some length with a police officer so that all pertinent information can be recorded.

CRITICAL INCIDENT NO.7: ALLERGIC REACTION

Possible symptoms include a general feeling of impending doom or fright, weakness, sweating, sneezing, shortness of breath, nasal itching, hives, vomiting, cough, restlessness, shock, hoarseness, swollen tongue, and severe swelling.

Checklist of What to Do

- ❑ Assess the situation, remain calm, and make the student or staff member comfortable.
- ❑ Move the person only for safety reasons.
- ❑ Send for immediate help and a medication kit (in cases of known allergies).
- ❑ Follow medical protocol for the student if on file

❑ Observe the student for respiratory difficulty and, if needed, call 911.
❑ Notify the parent or guardian.

CRITICAL INCIDENT NO. 8: ANGRY, HOSTILE PARENT

- Lower your voice and speak calmly.
- Be courteous and confident.
- Remain calm.
- Do not touch the person.
- Keep at a reasonable distance.
- Listen, Use "I" messages.
- Paraphrase what was said to confirm understanding.
- Allow the person an opportunity to vent.
- Meet in a neutral, protected location.
- Leave the door open or have another staff member join you.
- Avoid blame—focus on what can be done.
- Ask:
  —"How can I help you get the services you or your child needs?"
  —"How can we work together?"
  —"What kinds of support can we put in place to help your child succeed?"
  —"What can we do together to make this happen?"

CRITICAL INCIDENT NO. 9: ASSAULT BY INTRUDER

Checklist

- Assess the situation.
- If danger continues, institute a lockdown.
- Provide first aid.
- Question the injured person—make reasonable notes for a potential court case:
  1. Get a description of the assailant.
  2. Record all events.
  3. Contact the police (school resource officer, 911, or both)
  4. Notify the superintendent.
  5. Instruct the person answering the telephone to direct all requests to the Public Information Office.
  6. Complete the police information for charges.
  7. Prepare a written memo for the staff and the parents.
  8. Schedule follow-up programs for the staff and the students.
  9. Call an emergency staff meeting.

Essential Responsibilities

1. **Assess the Situation**
   - Request police assistance when the assailant or assailants are outsiders.
   - Determine the number of people injured.
   - Determine the amount of threat still pending—was this an isolated incident that is now over?
   - Is there continued danger to the individuals already involved or are any other people potentially being targeted?
   - Determine the need for first aid.
2. **Move Others to Safety**
   If the assailant has not been contained and continues to be a threat to others, institute a lockdown.
3. **Provide First Aid**
   Provide first aid for the injured via a nurse, a nurse's aide, a trained staff member, or 911. Have someone at the entrance to meet and direct the ambulance staff to the injured and designate a staff member to accompany the injured in ambulance.
4. **Question the Injured Individual(s)**
   Make notes that can be shared with the police upon their arrival. These notes may be helpful in a court case.
5. **Contact the Police**
   Contact 911 and your school resource officer.
6. **Notifications**
   - The Superintendent's Office should be contacted as soon as possible.
   - The Public Information Office will handle all media and community inquiries into the event(s).
   - The parents (or spouse) of the injured victim should be notified as soon as possible.
   - Inform the staff of the situation as soon as possible. A Crisis Team, identified for the school, can effectively deliver information to the other staff members so that your time can be used for other decisions or actions.
   - The Transportation Department can, in extreme emergencies, provide buses for early dismissal. The Transportation Department will notify the superintendent of the need for this dismissal.
   - The students will be able to deal with the situation by being informed of the facts as soon as possible, rather than receiving their "facts" through rumors.

- The other schools should be given the basic information as soon as possible by the Public Information Office, because siblings and neighbors will quickly learn of the disturbance.
- The Crisis Team may be needed to provide counseling support for students and staff in dealing with the trauma. This office may seek additional help from the county's Department of Human Resources.
- The parents of other students in the community will need to learn the real facts, just as their children have learned them, to reduce the rumor factor.
- After the crisis is over, the principal may wish to arrange a special press conference to give the media the same information that has been shared with the parents.

7. **Telephone Answerers**

   Prepare a statement for the individuals who answer the telephones to read. Instruct them that any further inquiries should be made to the Public Information Office. Give them the telephone number for the caller to use as a reference.

8. **Police Information for Charges**

   The police will need to be sure of details from you, as well as from the injured person(s). Assault/battery are chargeable offenses.

9. **Written Memo for Staff and Parents**

   As soon as the immediate crisis or danger is over, the staff and the parents will need to know, not only what occurred, but also why you took the action that you did. Individuals who know the correct facts can help to stop rumors and misperceptions.

10. **Follow-Up Programs**

    School counselors will arrange special counseling for students and staff through Pupil Personnel Services.

11. **Call an Emergency Staff Meeting**

CRITICAL INCIDENT NO. 10: BOMB THREAT

Bomb Threat/Telephone Threats

The principal must evaluate the seriousness of bomb threats or other disruptive types of demonstrations, using input from all sources; then act in such a manner as to reflect the best safety interests of those under his or her charge.

Bomb and other threats may originate in writing, in person, or over the telephone or be relayed through a second source.

Decision Making: Things to Think Through

All bomb threats must be taken seriously and be carefully analyzed. The bomb report should be treated as genuine until investigated and until a search of the school has been completed. Begin your decision-making process by gathering as much information about the bomb report as possible. Factors you will consider include:

1. Have there been national bomb incidents lately?
2. Have there been other hoaxes lately?
3. Has a hostile student been suspended recently?
4. Are exams scheduled for today?
5. Is it senior skip day?
6. Is there any unexplained student unrest?
7. Are any rumors circulating about a student threatening to harm others?
8. How much information did the caller provide? (You can generally get more information out of a caller when it is not a hoax.)
9. How serious was the voice of the caller?
10. Were any specific details given?
11. Are any chemicals missing from school supplies?
12. Did the caller have knowledge of the design of the school?
13. Have there been any recent break-ins? (Look for evidence of illegal entry.)
14. Did the caller give repeated warnings? This seriously escalates the degree of danger.

Check your surveillance tapes. Large-scale bomb incidents, such as the Oklahoma City bombing and that of the World Trade Center, received no warnings.

The Building Administrator or Designee Shall

- Notify the authorities.
- Consider the safety of the students and the staff as the prime factor. If advised, direct the students and the staff to safe areas of the campus. Nothing is to be touched or altered; do not open desks or lockers.

Basic Documentation for a Bomb Threat

- Keep the caller on the line as long as possible.
- Notify the principal/building director.
- Write down all the information obtained in the exact words. Use the record sheet immediately following these instruction pages; place copies of the bomb threat sheet at the switchboard and other appropriate phone locations.
- Find out what time the bomb is due to go off
- Document in writing, as soon as possible, other types of threat contacts, including:

    — Specific **time** the message is received.
    — **Date** and **day** of the week.
    — Exact wording of the threat.

    _____

    _____

    _____

    — Estimation of sex, age, and cultural background of person making call.
    — Make note of background noises, the tone of voice.

Questions to ask the caller:

Where is it? _____

What time will it explode? _____

What type of device is it? _____

Why are you doing this? _____

What is your name? _____

FIGURE 4.1

Do Not Reenter the Building Until Authorized

- Alert the staff of the situation and implement a building search procedure (see below):
- School activities should be continued as normally as possible in designated safe areas.
- The recommendation to close the school will be made only after consultation between the Central Office, security, and the building administrator.
- Submit written reports as appropriate to the director, Department of Facilities, following the incident.

Confidential Building Search Procedures for Use by Staff Only

The principal or the assistant principal will

1. Call the police department.
2. Call the superintendent's office.
3. Call maintenance department.
4. Notify the school staff by prearranged signal.

The Signal

Use a prearranged intruder or lockdown announcement over the public address system, such as the following:

"PLEASE BE CERTAIN TO SEND LUNCH MONEY TO THE OFFICE TODAY."

A fire drill will be called about 15 minutes before the threatened time, if known.

- Following the signal, the staff will conduct a thorough search of assigned areas, as outlined further on. If anything is found, it should not be touched in any way. Get an adult to "watch it," while you report it personally to the principal. Following the search, each staff member responsible for searching areas (all teachers and others) must send a note to the office reading, for example, "Brown—Clear."
- Responsibilities for the search effort: All search efforts should be conducted quietly and quickly without alarming or informing the students. Each teacher will search his or her own area, in addition to the following search responsibilities:

Custodial closets	Lead custodian I
Girl's bathroom	Principal, assistant, or designee
Boy's bathroom	Principal, assistant, or designee
Mechanical room	Lead custodian I/HAZMAT team
Media center	Librarian
Food service area, dining room	Cafeteria manager
Principal's office and other areas	Office personnel
Outdoor storage	Lead custodian I
Other areas throughout building	Youth service officer

Checklist

❏ Listen carefully to the caller to gain as much information as possible. Notify the building school resource officer if the caller is in the building.

❏ If the threat appears to be a crank call, ask teachers to survey their instructional areas and nearby restrooms.

❏ If the call could be real and the school resource officer is not in the building, call 911 immediately.

❏ Evacuate the building. NOTE: *DO NOT USE THE P.A. SYSTEM, TURN LIGHTS ON OR OFF, OR USE WALKIE-TALKIES BECAUSE THEY COULD SET THE BOMB OFF.*

❏ Notify the Superintendent's Office

❏ Follow the established Policy regarding return to the building.

❏ If necessary, contact transportation to arrange for early dismissal.

❏ Perform follow-up activities.

Response to a Suspected Device

1. This may take the form of a suspected article being found either in the building or on the grounds or the delivery of such an article by messenger or mail.

2. The principal must evaluate the threat and make a decision to evacuate. Staff and students should evacuate the area or the building to a safe location.

3. The designated evacuation area should afford safety in respect to the detonation of the device.

4. The principal or a designated person should contact the police at the first available opportunity and be in a position to inform them of the following:
   • Exact location of the device;
   • Description of the device; and
   • Exact location of the principal or a person who can assist the investigating police officers upon their arrival.

5. The principal, if time allows, must ensure that classified documents or valuables are secured immediately after the evacuation of all personnel.

Doors and windows should be opened to vent fumes from possible explosion. Gas and electricity should, if possible, be disabled.

6. Ensure that all personnel reach the designated "safe area" and remain there.
7. Place responsible people at all entry points to prevent visitors and voyeurs from approaching the suspected danger area until the arrival of the police and emergency medical personnel.
8. When required, the principal should accompany the police to ensure that the police quickly find the exact location of the device, so that the safety measures already implemented can be assessed.
9. The principal should be prepared to assist the police, if required, in making a full search of the building to locate further devices.

CRITICAL INCIDENT NO. 11: BUS ACCIDENT

Goals
- Safety
- Containment
- Effective communication
- Mobilization
- Assessment and follow-up

Prevention

Have a clear operation plan and be familiar with that plan. Maintain a bus accident folder, including a list of each bus number, with names and emergency telephone numbers of all occupants.

Intervention

In the event that a bus accident occurs and the school has been contacted for assistance, the principal or the designee determines and coordinates the appropriate responses. Interventions may include

At the Scene

- Provide emotional support.
- Be available and attend to the injured, as directed by emergency medical personnel.
- Be available, attend to the uninjured, and account for everyone involved.

At the School

- Provide coordination.
- Provide emotional support and attend to the affected students.
- Provide information to the faculty and staff.
- Call mental health professionals for assistance, as needed.
- Contact the parents of the students who were involved.

At the Hospital

- Provide emotional support for the injured and their families.

Follow-up

- Send a letter to the parents.
- Assess the response procedures, debrief the Critical Incident Team, and follow up with the faculty and the staff, students and families, as well as with school and community agencies.

CRITICAL INCIDENT NO. 12:
BUS/AUTO ACCIDENT ON TRIPS AWAY
FROM THE SCHOOL DISTRICT

Precautionary Measures Before Leaving the District

- School buses, by law, are required to carry first aid kits. Check to see if one is in place.
- In all automobiles take along a first aid kit on every field trip.
- Take a list of students in attendance. Include for each person a home telephone number, names of parents, parents' work telephone numbers, home addresses, and any pertinent health or medical information.
- Take a list of emergency phone numbers (listed further on).
- Take a list of chaperones and teachers who are in attendance on the trip, their home addresses and home phone numbers, the names and work telephone numbers of spouses or nearest relatives, and medical and health information for each person.
- Follow school board policy and administrative regulations on field trips.

In the Event of an Accident

- Remain calm.
- If a threat of fire exists, move the children to safe place.
- Call emergency vehicles/services: police, fire, ambulance, and local highway patrol; begin the administration of first aid.

Have the Following Phone Numbers Available for the Trip

- The superintendent and his or her immediate staff.
- The director of pupil transportation.
- The public information officer (who will notify the superintendent).
- The principal.
- The assistant principal.

Do not issue statements to the press. Refer the press to the public information officer.

CRITICAL INCIDENT NO. 13: CHILD ABDUCTION OR LOST CHILD

Checklist

1. Telephone the police.
2. Call the superintendent's office to report the incident.
3. Notify the parents of the child. Establish a communication plan with them, if necessary.
4. Identify a team to work on the crisis while the rest of the school maintains the normal routine. Designate personnel to deal with phone communications and so on and other administrative staff members to assist as appropriate.
5. Obtain a full description of the child and pull out his or her school picture to assist police.
6. Search the school building and grounds.
7. If an abduction, try to obtain a description of the suspect from witnesses.
8. When the child is found, contact the superintendent, contact the parents, notify the child's teacher, and fill out a Crisis Incident Report.

9. Prepare a memo to inform the staff and the parents of the incident and the actions taken. Give factual information to respond to questions knowledgeably.
10. Arrange for counseling for the staff and students, if necessary.
11. Call an emergency staff meeting.

Preventative Activities That May Help Prevent Childnapping Situations

- The school secretary should have at her desk a list of students who are not to be released to anyone except a particular parent or guardian.
- Emergency cards of such students should be tagged.
- Before releasing a child to anyone except a parent or a guardian on the list, the school secretary should check with the custodial parent or guardian for approval; a record of the time and date of the phone approval should be kept.
- When a parent telephones a request that a child be released from school, the identity of the caller should be confirmed (by a separate call to the parent or guardian, if needed) before the child is permitted to leave. In the event of any doubt, the message and the phone number should be written down; a return call should be made after cross-checking the phone number with those on file in the child's folder or on the emergency card.

CRITICAL INCIDENT NO. 14: ARMED AND DANGEROUS INTRUDER

Checklist

1. Contact the police (911).
2. Instigate lockdown procedures; after the police arrive, if the danger is confined, begin orderly evacuation away from the danger.
3. Notify the superintendent.
4. When the police arrive, in accordance with preplanning, they assume control of the incident and negotiations.
5. No school personnel should circulate through the building; after evacuation, no individuals should enter or reenter the building.
6. Instruct the person answering the phone to direct all requests to the Public Information Office.
7. Keep the telephone lines open for police use (pay telephones as well).
8. Provide information to the police about the building layout and what is known about the background of the hostage taking.

Essential Responsibilities

1. Contact the police. Hostage taking or endangering the safety of others is a criminal offense.
2. Secure all classrooms (lockdown). The more closely contained the intruder can be kept, the less danger there is to others and the easier it is for the police to apprehend the individual.
3. Notification
   - The Superintendent's Office should be contacted as soon as possible.
   - The Public Information Office will handle all media and community inquiries.
   - After the crisis is over, the Public Information Office may wish to arrange a special press conference to give the media the same information that has been shared with the parents.
4. Staff members must keep the students restricted to their current location; students should not be released for any reason until permitted by the police.
5. No personnel should be circulating. For the same reason as number 4, all staff members should be protected from involvement in the crisis whenever possible.
6. Telephone answerer: Prepare a statement to be read by the individuals who answer the telephones. Instruct them that any further inquiries should be made to the Public Information Office. Tell them the telephone number to give to callers.
7. Keep the phone lines open. The police and other public safety personnel have the highest priority for use of the phones. Even the pay phones should be available to the police.
8. Provide the police with maps of the buildings and grounds. Involve people with the greatest knowledge of the facilities, such as the head custodian. Also, provide any anecdotal information about possible reasons for the hostage taking, precipitating events, and so on.
9. Identify people who are familiar with the facility. People who are familiar with the entire building should be available to discuss the interior room arrangements, and so on. These individuals should remain at a chosen location away from the scene.

CRITICAL INCIDENT NO. 15: INTRUDER OR TRESPASSER

Checklist

1. Determine the whereabouts of the intruder/trespasser.
2. Isolate the individual.

3. Determine the extent of the crisis.
4. Make reasonable notes for a potential court case.
5. Contact the police—911.
6. Move other students and staff members from the area.
7. Notify the superintendent.
8. Instruct the person answering the telephone to direct all requests to the Public Information Office.
9. Complete and submit information for charges to the police.
10. Prepare a written memo for the staff and the parents.
11. Complete a Crisis Team Report.
12. Call an emergency staff meeting.
13. Schedule follow-up activities for the staff and the students, including a security plan review.

Essential Responsibilities

1. Determine the whereabouts of the intruder. Use school maps to assist the police and staff members in locating the intruder.
2. Isolate the intruder from rest of building and from the students.
3. Determine the extent of the crisis.
   Trespassing with no safety hazard may be dealt with by informing the intruder of the offense being committed. If the trespasser refuses to leave, wait for the police to arrest him or her.
   If the trespasser has previously been warned (placed on notice), trespass charges may be filed without the arrest of the offender.
   Trespassing with a threat to others' safety will require assistance from the police. Trespass charges should be filed.
4. Make notes. Recording what has occurred can provide important information to the police and in subsequent court cases.
5. Move other students or staff or members.
   Staff members may be asked to keep their students in certain areas or to keep them out of certain areas. The staff should move students as quietly and quickly as possible when directed to do so.
6. Contact the police.
   Trespassing is a misdemeanor or a felony, depending upon the location of the intrusion.
7. Notification
   • The Superintendent's Office should be contacted as soon as possible.
   • The Public Information Office will handle media and community inquiries.

- Keep the staff informed of actions. A Crisis Team, identified for the school, can effectively deliver information to other staff members so that the administrator's time can be used for other decisions or actions.
- The Transportation Department can, in extreme emergencies, provide buses for early dismissal.
- The students will be able to deal with the situation by being informed of the facts, as soon as possible, rather than receiving their "facts" through rumor.
- Other schools should be given the basic information as soon as possible by the Public Information Office, because siblings or neighbors will quickly learn of the situation.
- The parents of the students in the community will need to learn the real facts, just as their children have learned them, to reduce the rumor factor.
- After the crisis is over, the Public Information Officer may wish to arrange a special press conference to give the media the same information that has been shared with the parents.

8. Telephone Answerer
   Prepare a statement for the individuals who answer the telephones to read. Instruct them that any further inquiries should be made to the Public Information Office. Tell them the phone number to give to callers.
9. Police information for charges
   The police will need to be sure of details from you, as well as from others interviewed. Trespassing is a misdemeanor or a felony, depending upon the location of the intrusion.
10. Written memo for the staff and parents
    As soon as the immediate crisis or danger is over, the staff and the parents will need to know, not only what occurred, but also why you took the action that you did.
11. Crisis Team Report
    Submit it within 24 hours.
12. Follow-Up Activities
    Provide counseling for students and staff. The building security plan should also be reviewed.
13. Call an emergency staff meeting.

CRITICAL INCIDENT NO. 16: RAPE

When a school is notified that a rape has occurred to a student or a staff member, the Crisis Response Team and the school must protect the identity and right to privacy of the rape survivor and the alleged perpetrator. News of the incident should be contained as much as possible. Appropriate response by the school staff will be directed toward minimizing the fear of fellow students and quelling the spread of rumors. As opposed to convening a Crisis Response Team meeting and alerting the student body, services provided to the survivor and her or his family should be kept confidential and should be coordinated with outside providers, such as a rape crisis team or the hospital emergency room.

Rape Becomes A Crisis to Be Managed by the School Staff Only When One or More of the Following Conditions Exist

- A rape occurs on campus.
- A member of the rape survivor's family requests school intervention.
- The rape survivor's friends request intervention.
- Rumors and myths are widespread and damaging.
- Students witness police action or the emergency services response.

When one or more of the previous conditions exists, the following should be implemented:

- Direct the person providing the information not to repeat it elsewhere in the school.
- If the rape occurred on campus, notify the appropriate law enforcement office, local rape crisis team, or both.
- If office staff members heard the report, tell them not to repeat or give out any information within or outside school unless they are specifically told to do so.
- Designate the Crisis Response Team member closest to the rape survivor to talk to her or him about the types of support the survivor and the closest friends need and the person(s) the rape survivor would like to provide that support.
- Provide space in the school for the rape survivor and identified peers to receive support services. Provide necessary passes to release these students from class to receive services.

Rape is a crime of violence. For the rape survivor, it is often an experience of fear, loss of control, and humiliation, as well as violence. Rape survivors may experience a full range of emotional reactions. It is extremely beneficial for rape survivors to seek emotional support regarding the assault.

Monitor any school intervention in a rape incident with the following checklist:

Rape Response Checklist

The school is involved in the incident because:

❑ The rape occurred on campus.
❑ The survivor's family requests school intervention.
❑ The survivor's friends request intervention.
❑ Rumors and myths are widespread and damaging.
❑ Students witness police or emergency services response.

Collectively, the school division and the school must ensure that:

❑ Information providers or recipients, or both are enjoined not to repeat the information elsewhere.
❑ Steps are taken to protect the survivor's identity and right to privacy.
❑ Law enforcement and a rape crisis agency notified, if appropriate.
❑ A Crisis Team member who is closest to the rape survivor is designated to talk with the survivor and to determine the type of support and the support provider that is desired.
❑ The rape survivor is encouraged to seek additional support from a community rape crisis agency.
❑ Space is provided on site for the rape survivor and identified peers to receive support services.
❑ School services are coordinated, as is appropriate and legal, with outside service providers.
❑ Action is taken to quell rumors.
❑ All records related to the rape incident and services provided are stored in a confidential file.

CRITICAL INCIDENT NO. 17: SHOOTINGS, STABBINGS, ASSAULTS

Checklist

☑
❑ Assess the situation.
❑ Call 911.
❑ Notify the police/school resource officer.
❑ Call for an ambulance.
❑ Use the emergency signal—all students and staff are to stay in their classrooms, secure the door, and stay on the floor.
❑ Establish a command post with several telephones available.

❑ Implement first aid procedures until the rescue service arrives.
❑ Notify the Superintendent's Office.
❑ Keep a written log of events.
❑ Prepare a written memo for the staff and the parents.
❑ Implement all necessary follow-up activities.
❑ Call an emergency staff meeting.

Essential Responsibilities

1. Notify the police and other necessary emergency staff.
2. Determine whether the perpetrator is still on the premises—determine the number of injured or dead and identify the witnesses.
3. The emergency signal to the staff and the students should convey the seriousness of the situation. Follow-up announcements will be necessary to keep everyone informed. Prepare a general statement of the facts.
4. Establish a command post to handle the load of the Crisis Team and to direct the press and concerned members of the community to the Public Information Office.
5. Implement necessary first aid procedures through trained staff members, the school nurse, a nurse's aide, the physical education department, the athletic trainer, or any combination of these. Direct rescue personnel to the injured and give any required assistance. Designate a staff member to accompany the injured in the ambulance.
6. Contact the Superintendent's Office.
7. Identify a place where a log of events will be kept. Document all information about the individuals involved, the events, and the actions taken.
8. Keep the staff informed through a memo or an emergency staff meeting. Parents may be informed through a letter sent home with the students.
9. Follow-up management should be well delegated. Crisis counseling for students and staff may be needed, and security concerns should be considered. All staff members will assist in restoring the building to a normal state. Reopen the school as soon as possible.
10. Call an emergency staff meeting.

Handling a Weapon-Wielding Student

• Evacuate the area.
• Evaluate the perpetrator.

- Isolate him or her.
- Negotiate.
- Remain calm.
- Get help.
- Avoid heroics.
- Don't threaten.
- Keep a safe, nonintimidating distance.
- Avoid abrupt, impulsive movements.
- Look for a place to dive or jump.
- Report the incident to law enforcement.

CRITICAL INCIDENT NO. 18: TERRORIST ACTIVITY

Prevention strategies against terrorist activities should include implementing plans to consider both safety and security, such as

- Assessing the access to, and the security of, the school, including where cars are parked
- Identifying the means of communication from all areas in the school (including portable classrooms) in an emergency situation
- Regulating and restricting access by visitors (such as using only one entrance into the building and locking all other entrance areas; providing visitor badges and enforcing sign-in procedures)

Terrorist intruders may threaten to use violence or use themselves as human bombs. The Critical Incident Team should have preidentified procedures for evacuation to another floor, safe areas, or multiple safe areas, rather than to an external location within the school. Plans should be in place to use neighboring schools as possible evacuation locations. Such procedures may include special alarm signals for such types of evacuations and locking off sections or entire rooms of the building to protect the staff and students from terrorists.

Checklist

If terrorist activity does occur:

☑
❑ The staff and the students who are not involved should be evacuated to a safe area.

❑ The principal should contact the police and the superintendent at the first available opportunity and be in a position to inform them of the following:
   1. The name and address of the school, including the nearest cross street and available vehicle access
   2. The exact location and number of terrorists known
   3. The threats or demands made by the terrorists
   4. The number of hostages
   5. The types and number of weapons, for example, firearms, chemicals, suicide bombers
   6. The exact location of the principal or a person who can assist investigating police on their arrival
❑ Instruct the teachers, the students, and the staff to remain calm and obey the demands of the terrorist.
❑ Avoid any action that might provoke an incident resulting in death or injury to the staff and students.
❑ Conduct a roll call in a safe area.
❑ Decide when to reopen the school, in consultation with emergency services.
❑ Arrange for appropriate counseling support.
❑ Implement procedures to resume normal school activities.

Types of Terrorist Attacks

According to the Federal Emergency Management Administration (FEMA), the weapons of mass destruction (WMD) likely to be used by terrorists fall into four categories: (1) conventional, (2) chemical, (3) biological, and (4) nuclear. Specific guidelines for schools have not yet been developed; however, some preliminary considerations are set forth in the following sections.

Conventional Weapons

Conventional weapons include bombs and other explosive devices. The goal is to place students and staff in a protective space, to increase the distance from the blast area, or both.
Possible actions include:

❑ Moving everyone to basement rooms, if practical;
❑ Moving people to interior hallways, away from windows; closing doors to exterior rooms;

❑ Having the students and the staff assume "duck and cover" positions;
❑ Shutting off gas and utilities;
❑ If the school buildings themselves are targeted, consider evacuation to other schools or community spaces, such as community centers or churches; and
❑ Releasing students to their parents or other authorized persons, in accordance with emergency release procedures.

Chemical Weapons

The goal is to limit people's exposure to contaminated air.

❑ In the absence of gas masks, which are not available in sufficient quantity and which present other practical problems, get all the students into the buildings, close all the windows and doors, and shut off the heat, ventilation, and air conditioning (HVAC) systems.
❑ Ground-level spaces are preferable to basement areas because vapors may settle and become trapped in basements.
❑ Decisions to evacuate should be based on reliable information from public safety officials about the location of the chemical release and the direction and the speed of winds carrying the agent toward or away from the school.
❑ If students are released to parents, procedures to minimize the penetration of airborne substances must be employed.

Biological Weapons

Biological weapons present a unique challenge because symptoms may not be present for days or weeks following exposure. Schools must rely on medical expertise in developing procedures for responding to a biological attack. Consider the following:

❑ If an attack is identified while it is occurring, schools should get students into the buildings, close all the doors and windows, and shut down the HVAC systems. Just as with chemical weapons, the goal is to prevent or reduce people's exposure to the substance.
❑ Release students to their parents or other authorized persons, in accordance with emergency release procedures.
❑ Because many biological weapons are contagious, the school will likely be closed after an attack, pending clearance by medical authorities,

Nuclear Weapons

Just as with conventional weapons, the goal is to place the students and the staff in a protected space, to increase the distance from the blast area, or both. Such weapons present a threat not only from the effects of the blast but also exposure to radiation. Possible actions include:

❑ Moving to basement rooms, if practical;
❑ Moving to interior hallways, away from windows; closing the doors to exterior rooms;
❑ Having the students/staff assume a "duck and cover" position;
❑ Shutting off gas and utilities; and
❑ Releasing students to their parents or other authorized persons, in accordance with emergency release procedures.

Critical Incident Faculty Skills Inventory
(To be conducted annually)

Name _____ Room # _____

Please check any of the following in which you have expertise or training:
Emergency response:

_____ First aid

_____ CPR

_____ EMT

_____ Firefighting

_____ Search and rescue

_____ Law enforcement source

_____ CB radio

_____ Ham radio

_____ Emergency management

_____ CISD (Critical Incident Stress Debriefing)

_____ Other (specify)

_____ Mobile or cellular phone that could be used in an emergency

Phone numbers: (Home) _____

(Cell) _____   (Pager) _____

FIGURE 4.2

Authorization to Release Children in an Emergency

Our school has developed an emergency plan in case of any disaster that might occur. This is done in compliance with the division policy. The emergency plan is devoted to the welfare and safety of your child during school hours. The plan is available for inspection in the school office.

We are requesting your assistance at this time:
Should there be an emergency, such as a major fire, tornado, explosion, and so on, your child may be required to remain in the care of the school until it is deemed safe by an Emergency Services authority that the child can be released. At that point, children may be released only to properly authorized parents or designees. Therefore, please list as many names (with local telephone numbers and addresses) as possible, of those persons to whom you would allow your child's release in the event of an emergency. Be sure to notify those persons listed that you have authorized their supervision in case of emergency.

In the event that you are unable to come to school, it is essential that others be designated to care for your child. No child will be released to the care of unauthorized persons.

We appreciate your cooperation in this important matter.

Child: _____ **Teacher:** _____ **School Year:** ____

Please release my child to any of the persons listed below:

Name	Phone	Address	Relationship
_____	_____	_____	_____
_____	_____	_____	_____
_____	_____	_____	_____
_____	_____	_____	_____

Parent/Guardian:_____ **Date:** _____
                                          Signature

Home Phone: _____ **Work Phone:** _____

FIGURE 4.3

SCHOOL LETTERHEAD

Dear Faculty and Staff Members:

We would like to thank you for your support during the recent crisis at our school. Your professionalism and dedication were evident as we all worked to quiet and soothe frightened students and allay their fears while still tending to instructional responsibilities.

We know that this has been an extremely difficult time for you, as well as for the students. Without your courage and concern, our school could not possibly have come through this crisis as well as we did.

Thank you once again. Your expertise and commitment have enabled all of us to work together as a team to overcome this tragic situation.

Sincerely,

Principal

School Guidance and Counseling Director

FIGURE 4.4
Sample Thank-You Letter to the Faculty and Staff Members

(To be mailed to parents at the beginning of each school year)

SUGGESTED LETTER FORMAT:

In a letter to parents, mailed in September of each year, the school will inform parents as to the proper procedures to follow in picking up a child/ children in a crisis situation, such as a tornado, a chemical spill, or other crises.

Among the types of information that will be contained in the letter are:

Specifications indicating that school is one of the safest places for students to be during most crises or natural disasters.

Instructions showing that students will be kept at school until the crisis is determined to be over.

Instructions emphasizing that students will be released to parents who come to get them.

Instructions NOT to phone the school and tie up the few telephone lines, which will be needed for emergency use.

Instructions emphasizing that when a person other than the parent comes to get a student, the building administrator will first check with the student and that a record is kept as to the person picking up the student; if there is any doubt that a parent does not want the student released, then the student will be kept at school.

Principal of School

FIGURE 4.5
Letter to Parent Regarding Procedures for Picking Up Children
in the Event of a Critical Incident

Chapter 5

Disasters and First-Response Procedures

The short-term emotional effects of a disaster—fear, acute anxiety, feelings of emotional numbness, and grief—may be obvious. For some survivors, these feelings fade with time. But for many others, there may be long-term emotional effects that are both obvious and subtle. Some of the emotional effects are direct responses to the trauma of disaster. Others are longer-term responses to the interpersonal, societal, and economic effects of the disaster. In any case, in the absence of well-designed interventions, up to 50% or more of the survivors of a disaster may develop lasting depression, pervasive anxiety, post-traumatic stress disorder, and other emotional disturbances. *Even more than the physical effects of disasters, the emotional effects cause long-lasting suffering, disability, and loss of income.*

DELAYED EFFECTS OF DISASTER

Certain emotional effects of a disaster may not appear until after a considerable delay. For some survivors, initial relief at having been rescued and initial optimism about the prospects of recovery may produce a "honeymoon stage." Over a period of months or even years, this may give way to a realization that personal and material losses are irreversible. Loved ones who died will not return. Disruptions in the family are permanent. Old jobs will not reappear. A long-term reduction in one's standard of living has occurred. Depression and anxiety are often recurrent feeling states. *Although most survivors of disasters are usually relatively free of distress a year or two after the event, a quarter or more of the survivors may still show significant symptoms, whereas others, who previously were free of symptoms, may first show distress a year or two after the disaster.*

CHILDREN

Two myths are potential barriers to recognizing children's responses to disaster, and they must be rejected:

1. that children are innately resilient and will recover rapidly, even from severe trauma; and
2. that children, especially young children, are not affected by disaster unless they are disturbed by their parents' responses.

Both of these beliefs are false. A wealth of evidence indicates that children experience the effects of disaster more than adults realize. Even very young children are directly affected by experiences of death, destruction, terror, and personal physical assault and by experiencing the absence or the powerlessness of their parents. They are also indirectly affected by identifying with the effects of the disaster on their parents and other trusted adults (such as teachers) and by their parents' reactions to the disaster.

Symptoms Shown by School-Aged Children After A Disaster

Children manifest a vast array of symptoms following a disaster. Often they are unable to put feelings into words, so their grief and loss are revealed in their behavior. The following are some of the symptoms that school-aged children show after a disaster:

- Depression
- Withdrawal
- Generalized fear, including nightmares; highly specific phobias of stimuli associated with the disaster
- Defiance
- Aggressiveness, "acting out"
- Resentfulness, suspiciousness, irritability
- Disorganized, "agitated" behavior
- Somatic complaints: headaches, gastrointestinal disturbances, general aches and pains. These may be revealed by a pattern of repeated school absences.
- Difficulties with concentration
- Intrusive memories, thoughts, and sensations, which may be especially likely to appear when the child is bored, at rest, or when falling asleep
- Repetitive dreams
- Loss of a sense of control and of responsibility
- Loss of a sense of a future

- Loss of a sense of individuality and identity
- Loss of a sense of reasonable expectations with respect to interpersonal interactions
- Loss of a realistic sense of when he or she is vulnerable or in danger
- Feelings of shame
- Kinesthetic (bodily) reenactments of aspects of the disaster; repetitive gestures or responses to stress reenacting those of the disaster
- *"Omen formation":* The child comes to believe that certain "signs" preceding the disaster were warnings and that he or she should be alert for future signs of a disaster
- Regression: Bed-wetting, soiling, clinging, heightened separation anxiety
- Post-traumatic stress disorder syndromes much like those of adults
- Reenactments of aspects of the disaster in play, drawing, or storytelling. In part, this can be understood as an attempt at mastery. Drawings may reflect images of trauma.

TASKS AT DIFFERENT STAGES FOLLOWING A DISASTER

I. The Rescue Stage (Immediate Post-Impact)

1. Provide "defusing" and crisis intervention services for relief workers. (This is important and often overlooked.)
2. Ensure the safety of survivors and see that physical needs are met (e.g., housing, food, clean water, etc.).
3. Seek to reunite families and communities.
4. Provide information, comfort, practical assistance, and emotional "first aid."

II. The Early Inventory Stage: First Month

1. Continue the tasks of the Rescue Stage.
2. Educate local professionals, volunteers, and the community with respect to the normal reactions of trauma.
3. Train additional disaster counselors, if necessary.
4. Provide short-term practical help and support to survivors.
5. Identify those most at risk and begin crisis intervention, "debriefing," and similar efforts.
6. Begin reestablishing community infrastructure: jobs, housing, safety, and security.

III. The Late Inventory Stage: Months 2 and Beyond

1. Continue the tasks of the Rescue and Early Inventory Stages.
2. Provide community education.
3. Develop outreach services to identify those in need.
4. Provide "debriefing" and other services for disaster survivors in need.
5. Develop school-based services and other community institution-based services.

IV. The Reconstruction Phase

1. Continue to provide defusing and debriefing services for relief workers and disaster survivors.
2. Maintain a hotline or other means by which survivors can contact counselors.
3. Follow up with those survivors treated earlier.

CHILDREN HAVE SPECIAL NEEDS AFTER A DISASTER

For the most part, the same principles that apply to adults apply to children, with appropriate adaptations for their age (i.e., use language appropriate to the child's age; be concrete). The various child-specific reactions to disaster discussed earlier suggest several additional principles for work with children:

- Children are affected both directly by the disaster and indirectly, by observing and being affected by their parents' reactions. Unless there are strong reasons to the contrary, such as an abusive parent–child relationship or the physical or psychological unavailability of the parents, involving children together with their parents should be a major part of treatment. It is helpful to encourage parents to discuss what happened in the disaster with their child; to recognize, accept, and understand their child's reactions; and to communicate openly about their own reactions.
- A barrier to identifying children in need of services may be the parents' ignoring or denying signs of distress in their children or attributing regressive behaviors such as bed-wetting or acting out as attention-seeking behaviors. Parents should be educated about these issues so that they can meet their children's needs and future adjustment.

Parents may benefit from education with regard to appropriate responses to particular behaviors and to the helpfulness of specific treatments, as well. For example,

1. Regressive behaviors, such as bed-wetting, should be accepted initially. The child should be comforted without parents making demands. He or she should not be shamed, criticized, or punished. Later, normal expectations can gradually be resumed.
2. Behavioral interventions (systems of rewarding desired behaviors and setting limits on undesirable behaviors) are the most useful responses to inappropriate behaviors.
3. Physical comforting may be useful in reducing anxiety levels among children. One study has shown that regular back and neck massages may be helpful.
4. Children need reassurance and permission to express their own feelings without fear of being judged.
   - Children may have special concrete needs—toys, bedding, special foods, the availability of age-appropriate activities (play groups, school, chores, and routines). Parents also benefit when these are provided, because they help the parents cope with the demands their children place on them. Ongoing child-care services, to enable parents to return to work or to deal with the practicalities of resuming to normal functioning, are also needed.
   - Separation of children from their parents should be avoided, if at all possible. When it is absolutely necessary (for the child's safety or because of the inability of the parents to care for the child), efforts should be made to ensure that the child is accompanied by other familiar and important figures in his or her life, such as a grandparent, an older sibling, or a teacher.
   - Children are especially prone to drawing inaccurate conclusions about the cause of the disaster, about their own actions, and about the normality of their current feelings. For example, they may believe that they are somehow to blame for what happened. Exploration and correction of these ideas are part of treatment.
   - Younger children (up to 10 or 11, at least) may not be able to use language effectively to describe their feelings or to work through their reactions. Drawing, play with puppets, role-playing, or writing that is not specifically focused on the disaster (e.g., poetry, stories) may be useful ways to enable a fuller exploration of responses.
   - Children should be given time to experience and express their feelings, but as soon as possible, a return to the structure of household routines should be pursued.
   - Schools play a key role. They provide a safe haven for children during the day and serve as a structured environment that helps the child regulate his or her reactions. A rapid return of children to school and the monitoring of attendance and of unusual symptoms are helpful. (It is not unusual for children to want to be with their parents following

immediately a disaster. Child-care services may be needed. When children return to school after a disaster, they should not immediately be rushed into ordinary school routines. Instead, they should be given time to talk about the event and to express their feelings about it (without forcing those who do not wish to talk to do so). In-school sessions with entire classes or groups of students may be helpful. The school can also hold meetings with parents to discuss children's responses and provide education for parents in how to respond to children after a disaster.

- Children, like adults, benefit from feeling a sense of control over frightening situations. Involving children in age-appropriate and situation-appropriate tasks that are relevant to relief efforts (e.g., collecting supplies for disaster survivors or taking on responsibilities such as caring for younger children in a shelter) is helpful both to the child and to other survivors of the disaster.
- The repetitive graphic images of the disaster shown on television can generate anxiety. Exposure to television accounts of the disaster should be limited. An adult should be present to monitor and protect the child from overwhelming graphic images and to talk about what the child is watching.

DISASTER INCIDENT NO. 1: TORNADO/SEVERE WEATHER

Each school should develop a tornado drill annually. Procedures for both Tornado *Watch* and Tornado *Warning* should be practiced. Each school should create a map to determine *areas of shelter* to be used during a tornado emergency. Areas under large roofs (gyms and cafeterias) and areas with considerable expanses of glass should not be used as shelters. The safest shelter areas are interior windowless rooms and hallways that have load-bearing walls and are on the lowest possible level. Upon request, risk management and security staff members will assist the school staff in conducting a building assessment.

TORNADO WATCH—**No funnel clouds have been sighted, but weather conditions exist that are conducive to their formation.**

Principal's Responsibilities

1. Advise teachers and staff via the public address system that a tornado *watch* is in effect.
2. Advise teachers to review the "drop and tuck" command and the designated *areas of shelter* with students.

3. Designate staff members to monitor National Oceanic & Atmospheric Administration (NOAA) and television broadcasts for additional information.
4. Bring students located outside of the building or in portable classrooms into the main building.
5. Advise the custodian to be prepared to shut off the main gas supply valve in the event of a tornado *warning*.
6. Ensure that a plan is in place to assist special needs students and staff.
7. Have an alternate plan of communication ready should there be a loss of power (e.g., bull horn, phone tree, runners, cellular phones, walkie-talkies).

Teachers' Responsibilities

1. Review the "drop and tuck" command and the designated *areas of shelter* with students.
2. Close the windows and blinds.
3. Be prepared to "drop and tuck" under desks if the immediate command is given over the public address system or if there is an immediate need to do so.

TORNADO WARNING—**A funnel cloud(s) has been sighted or indicated on radar. The approximate location and the direction are usually broadcast during the warning.**

Principal's Responsibilities

1. Advise teachers and staff of the tornado *warning*.
2. Advise all teachers to escort classes to their predesignated *areas of shelter*.
3. Notify predesignated staff members to keep a look out in order to spot tornado funnels. Depending on their position, these staff members may need a means to make immediate contact with the principal if a funnel cloud is sighted.
4. Be prepared to give the "drop and tuck" command via the P.A. system if danger is imminent. Occupants may need to "drop and tuck" under desks if they have not yet been moved to *areas of shelter* in the school.
5. Delay all bus departures.
6. Parents picking up students should be advised of the tornado *warning* and be persuaded to stay with their child.
7. Have immediate access to the contents of the "Emergency Management Kit," and distribute flashlights as necessary.

Teachers' Responsibilities

1. Escort students to the predesignated *areas of shelter.*
2. Take a class roster and an account for all students.
3. Ensure that students sit quietly against a wall on the floor and that they understand the "drop and tuck" command.
4. Close all fire doors and gates along the corridor to minimize injury from flying debris.

Custodial Staff's Responsibilities

1. Shut off the main gas supply valve.
2. Be prepared to shut off all other utilities, if necessary.

Bus Drivers' Responsibilities

1. Drive at a 90° angle from the funnel cloud, and seek shelter in the closest building if there is time.
2. If no building is available, highway underpasses can provide protection. Park the bus downwind so that it will not be blown back to your position. Escort the students to shelter up under the underpass.
3. If caught out in the open, escort the students to a low area, such as a ditch, a ravine, or a culvert.
4. Have the students lie face down, with their hands covering their heads.
5. Report in as soon as danger has passed.

DISASTER INCIDENT NO. 2: BUILDING IS STRUCK BY A TORNADO

Principal's Responsibilities

1. Ensure that utilities are shut off.
2. Call 911 and give a situation report.
3. Determine who was injured and administer first aid.
4. Carefully evacuate damaged areas.
5. Notify:
   - The superintendent
   - Risk management and security
6. Take roll call and conduct a search for missing students and staff members, if it is safe to do so.
7. Account for and release students to parents only after a complete roll call has been reported.

TABLE 5.1
The Fujita Scale

F-Scale Number	Intensity Phrase	Wind Speed	Type of Damage Done
F0	Gale tornado	40–72 mph	Some damage to chimneys; breaks branches off trees; pushes over shallow-rooted trees; damages sign boards.
F1	Moderate tornado	73–112 mph	The lower limit is the beginning of hurricane wind speed; peels surface off roofs; mobile homes pushed off foundations or overturned; moving autos pushed off the roads; attached garages may be destroyed.
F2	Significant tornado	113–157 mph	Considerable damage. Roofs torn off frame houses; mobile homes demolished; boxcars pushed over; large trees snapped or uprooted; light object missiles generated.
F3	Severe tornado	158–206 mph	Roof and some walls torn off well-constructed houses; trains overturned; most trees in forest uprooted
F4	Devasta-ting tornado	207–260 mph	Well-constructed houses leveled; structures with weak foundations blown off some distance; cars thrown and large missiles generated.
F5	Incredible tornado	261–318 mph	Strong frame houses lifted off foundations and carried considerable distances to disintegrate; automobile sized missiles fly through the air in excess of 100 meters; trees debarked; steel re-inforced concrete structures badly damaged.
F6	Incon-ceivable tornado	319–379 mph	These winds are very unlikely. The small area of damage they might produce would probably not be recognizable along with the mess produced by F4 and F5 wind that would sur-round the F6 winds. Missiles, such as cars and refrigerators would do serious secondary damage that could not be directly identified as F6 damage. If this level is ever achieved, evidence for it might only be found in some manner of ground swirl pattern, for it may never be identifiable through engineering studies

A key point to remember is this: the size of a tornado is not necessarily an indication of its intensity. Large tornadoes can be weak, and small tornadoes can be violent. The Tornado Project, P.O. Box 302, St. Johnsbury, Vermont 05819, Reprinted with permission.
Source: The Tornado Project, P.O. Box 302, St. Johnsbury, Vermont 05819.
Reprinted with permission.

Drop and Tuck
– Protect Yourself –
– Lie Face Down –
– Draw Your Knees Up Under You –
– Cover the Back of Your Head With Your Hands –

FIGURE 5.1
Information obtained at: www.doe.state.in.us/safety/level3/tornado.htm
and www.fema.gov/library/tornado.htm Reprinted with permission.

8. Maintain a list of all injured students and staff members. Keep an accurate record of the hospitals to which any were sent.
9. Establish a means to disseminate information to parents and the media.

Tornado Danger Signs

Severe Thunderstorms—Thunder, lightning, heavy rains, and strong winds
Hail—Pellets of ice from dark-clouded skies
Roaring Noise—Like a hundred railroad locomotives; a crashing, thunderous sound
Funnel—A dark, spinning "rope" or column from the sky to the ground

DISASTER INCIDENT NO. 3: WINDSTORM

Warnings of an impending windstorm may be received in time to allow students and staff to go home before the emergency. However, if the warning time is insufficient to allow this, or if high winds develop during school hours without warning, the following emergency actions should be implemented.

1. Direct the students and staff to assemble inside buildings:
   • Stand against interior walls or hallways on lowest floor possible (tops of buildings are often torn off).
   • Stand away from windows.
   • Avoid auditoriums, gymnasiums, and other enclosures that have long roof spans.
   • Avoid classrooms that will bear the full force of the wind.

- Bring students inside who are in portable classrooms.
- Close the windows and blinds on the side of the building that will receive the full force of the wind.

2. Secure loose objects that are in open areas—for example, garbage bins.
3. Close down any school utilities that may cause additional hazards (e.g., gas and electricity).
4. Ensure that all personnel have taken shelter.
5. Notify the Central Office of the circumstances and take action.
6. Notify utility companies of any break or suspected breaks in the lines.
7. Keep the students and the staff at school until it is safe to return to normal activities or to go home.
8. Check class attendance to account for all students and support staff members.

DISASTER INCIDENT NO. 4: EARTHQUAKES

The effects of an earthquake vary, depending upon geographic location, ground type, intensity of the earthquake, and the construction of the building. In the event of an earthquake, implement the following procedures:

Indoor Procedures

- Take cover under a door frame, a bench, a desk or a table.
- Keep away from the windows.
- Crouch under a desk or a table.

TABLE 5.2
Earthquake Magnitude and Effects

Magnitudes	Earthquake Effects Estimated	Number Per Year Worldwide
1.0–3.0	Generally not felt but recorded.	3,000,000
3.1–4.0	Often felt, but only minor damage.	50,000
4.1–6.0	Slight damage to buildings.	15,000
6.1–6.9	Can be destructive in areas where people live.	120
7.0–7.9	Major earthquake. Causes serious damage.	20
8.0	or greater = Great earthquake. Total destruction to nearby communities.	1

Source: FEMA.gov.U.S. Office of Homeland Security. Public domain.

> **Safety Chant**
> If inside, drop and cover.
> That's where you'll be safe.
> If outside, stay outside.
> Find an open space.

FIGURE 5.2

- Face away from the windows.
- Bend your head close to your knees.
- Use one hand to hold onto the table leg (approximately 6" from the floor to avoid pinching your fingers) and protect your eyes with the other hand.

If No Desk or Table Is Nearby

- Kneel against an interior wall.
- Face away from windows.
- Bend your head close to your knees.
- Clasp your hands on the back of your neck.

Outdoor Procedures

- If outdoors, stay away from buildings, high walls, electrical power lines, and trees.
- If beside a big building, seek refuge under archways and doorways to protect yourself from falling debris.
- Stay outside.
- Go to an open area away from hazards.

WHEN THE EARTHQUAKE STOPS

1. Immediately evacuate the building, if possible, in case of its collapse.
2. Assemble the students and the staff away from the building but not under trees.
3. Take attendance using class rolls.
4. Contact emergency services
   - If time permits, turn off all computers and other appliances prior to evacuation.

- If damage has occurred, turn off electricity, gas, and water.
- Do not use telephones, other than for emergency purposes, because lines will become overloaded.

DISASTER INCIDENT NO. 5: EXTREMES OF TEMPERATURE

Heat

Heat waves occur during the summer months. Schools should continue to operate as usual without a disruption of normal routines. Staff members working outdoors and students and teachers involved in outdoor activities are the most vulnerable and will be the most likely to experience problems that are associated with the sun and intense heat. Heat stroke can occur in extreme situations and includes tiredness, weakness, blurred vision, headaches, nausea, breathlessness, and heart palpitations. Recovery from heat stroke will be expedited when the individual is removed from the heat, rests in the shade, and is given a cool drink.

Essential Precautions

The following precautions should be utilized to assist all students and staff members in adjusting to transient heat wave conditions and to prevent problems from occurring:

1. Encourage students and staff to drink at least two liters (six to eight 8 oz. bottles) of water a day to avoid dehydration.
2. Encourage the wearing of hats and light protective clothing.
3. Reschedule outdoor activities to a cooler period of the day (e.g., physical education class in the early morning, rather than in the heat of the day).
4. Encourage students to remain in shaded areas during recess and lunch periods.
5. If students are removed from classrooms, ensure that they are taken to the coolest location possible.
6. Ensure that blinds, fans, and cooling units are working efficiently.

DISASTER INCIDENT NO. 6: FIRE PROCEDURES

Approximately 80% of fire fatalities are caused by smoke inhalation or breathing of super-heated air and gases; therefore, it is critical to evacuate without delay. In the event that a fire is detected within a school building, proceed according to the following plan:

1. Sound the **Fire Alarm** by pulling the alarm system located in the halls or in specific rooms. Call the fire department about the location and the nature of the fire within the school.
2. Close all doors and windows, including any doors separating sections of the building and at the stairwells, to confine the fire.
3. Evacuate the building immediately to at least 300 feet from the structure and out of the fire department's operational area.
4. Make special provisions for handicapped students.
   • Specific people, plus alternates, should be assigned to assist specific handicapped individuals.
   • Evacuation plans for the handicapped should be reviewed, practiced and, periodically updated.
5. Initiate a roll call. Each teacher should leave the room with the roll book to check student names. In order to avoid confusion, all student absences should be recorded.
6. Render first aid as necessary.
7. Notify utility companies of a break or a suspected break in lines that might present an additional hazard.
8. Keep access roads open for emergency vehicles.
9. Have fire department officials declare the area safe before allowing students and staff to return to school.
10. If the school needs to be closed and students transported to another location or home, contact the director of transportation at_____.

   Any time elementary students are sent home during the regular school day, it is important to send teachers on the buses for the purpose of bringing back those students who cannot be placed in the hands of competent persons. In some cases they may be housed at another school until dismissal time.

NOTE: The custodial staff, administrators, and other appropriate personnel should be trained to use fire extinguishers to fight small fires. However, they should not endanger their lives in doing so.

Arson Cases and Fires

• School administrators have only an administrative investigative responsibility. Fire investigators, police, or both will investigate all fires.
• In support of the investigative efforts by outside agencies, develop a list of events that have recently occurred in the school: disgruntled students or employees, prior fires, rivalry among students or between schools, or gang activity.

False Fire Alarms

- All false alarms should be reported to the alarm-monitoring facility, which will notify the fire department.
- Using a floor plan of the school, locate each fire alarm station on this plan. Every time an alarm is sounded, record the exact location, date, and time of the alarm. The purpose is to develop a pattern to the alarms. By establishing a time pattern, one can assign staff members to provide a greater adult presence in halls and stairwells.
- If false fire alarms are a persistent problem, consider initiating a sign-in/sign-out log in each classroom. Have each teacher record the name, the time, and the destination of each student leaving the classroom and the time each student returns. These lists will be a valuable asset in attempting to develop a list of suspects.
- Consideration should be given to installing special covers over the pull stations that will sound a local alarm prior to sending a general alarm. Schools using this type of device have found a marked decline in alarms. Before any such device is installed, check with the fire department to get its approval.
- *Other considerations:* A very effective tool in reducing false fire alarms is to involve the student body in a program that gives students some responsibility for "guarding" fire pull stations. Generally, this requires little time and causes very little disruption to the school program. Stationing students at key locations 3 to 5 minutes before and after classes change often eliminates false fire alarms.

DISASTER INCIDENT NO. 7: MANAGING EMERGENCY SHELTERS

Selected school buildings have been designated as emergency shelters and may be opened during hurricanes and other emergencies. Decisions as to which schools will be opened depend on specific conditions and the type of emergency. The decision to open a school is made by the county's/city's coordinator of emergency services, in conjunction with the superintendent's staff.

A. The Following School Buildings Have Been Designated as Emergency Shelters

Hickory High School
Deep Creek High School
Hugo Owens Middle School

Indian River Middle School
Deep Creek Central Elementary Middle School
Chittum Elementary School
Cedar Road Elementary School

NOTE: In extreme emergencies, schools other than those listed here may be opened as shelters.

B. *Shelter Operation*

1. School personnel. A minimum of three school employees are to be on duty at each shelter. They are
   - *Building administrator*—Either the principal or the assistant principal. Duties include coordinating building use with the appropriate county employees and safeguarding school property. The principal may ask teachers to volunteer to assist at the shelter.
   - *School custodian*—Duties include maintaining the facility, cleaning appropriate areas, supplying necessary restroom supplies, and cooperating with county employees. The custodian should secure areas not to be used by evacuees.
   - *Child nutrition service employees*—Either the cafeteria manager or another person designated by the child nutrition services department. Duties include supervising safe operation of the kitchen and safeguarding school property. Supplies of food will be delivered to the shelter by the child nutrition services department.
2. County employees. In addition to school personnel, each shelter will be staffed with the following county employees: a shelter manager, a nurse, a social worker, a police officer, and additional county employees.
   The shelter manager shall be responsible for
   - Providing adequate facilities;
   - Preparing the building to receive evacuees (including removal of furniture, allocation of sleeping space, placement of cots, distribution of supplies, etc.);
   - Identifying the of evacuees;
   - Maintaining communications, both with the facility and with the Emergency Operations Center;
   - Transferring of sick or injured people to casualty treatment centers. Requisition and dispersal of food supplies, soap, towels, and first aid supplies;
   - Enforcing safety measures;
   - Arranging for transportation; and
   - Scheduling use of sanitary facilities and enforcing standards of cleanliness.

NOTE: Additional personnel may be added, depending on the number of persons occupying the facility.

3. Additional Suggestions
   - Electrical service may be disrupted during the emergency, and alternate sources of light may be in short supply. Try to secure several flashlights prior to opening the shelter.
   - Assist the shelter manager in posting notices of shelter rules. These may vary, depending on circumstances, but should probably include
     ❑ Evacuees must register.
     ❑ No pets are allowed.
     ❑ No alcohol is allowed.
     ❑ Be considerate of others.
     ❑ Avoid activities that will disturb others (loud radios, etc.).
   - Do not admit people until the shelter has been officially opened.
   - Have a supply of board and card games, if possible.
   - Keep evacuees informed of the situation via TV or radio. Set up a separate room, if possible.
   - List emergency telephone numbers.
     ❑ City emergency services
     ❑ Fire, police, rescue

DISASTER INCIDENT NO. 8: AIRCRAFT DISASTER CRASHING INTO OR NEAR SCHOOL BUILDING

Checklist of What to Do

❑ Call police, fire, and rescue departments.
❑ Call the Superintendent's Office.
❑ Call the school district's information officer.
❑ Utilize the emergency exit plan modified to maximize the safety of students and staff.
❑ Assemble the students and the staff in an area as far from the scene as possible, uphill and upwind of the crash site.
❑ Account for all building occupants and determine the extent of their injuries.

DISASTER INCIDENT NO. 9: CHEMICAL SPILL

If the Chemical Spill is Inside the Building

- Evacuate the area immediately.
- Check the Material Safety Data Sheet (MSDS)* to determine the urgency of the situation.

- Notify the building principal/supervisor/director as soon as possible.
- The building principal/supervisor/director will call the fire department, if deemed necessary, for consultation.
- Notify the superintendent of operations

*In the lab file, the principal's office, or the custodian's office

If the Chemical Spill Is Outside the Building

- Ensure that all students are in the building and that they remain there.
- Shut off all outside air ventilators.
- If you are not alerted to the situation by division personnel, phone
  Environmental Health & Safety
  Director of Facilities of Services
- Keep telephone lines clear for emergency calls only.
- Release students to parents or a designee only.

THE ROLE OF THE SCHOOL IN HOMELAND SECURITY

Many of the strategies that would be used in a natural disaster, such as an earthquake or a tornado, have significant application for managing the effects of a terrorist attack involving explosions or chemical, biological, or radiological warfare. Although many people find it more unsettling to deal with a human-caused terrorist attack than to deal with a natural disaster, the key for both is to be prepared. In the event of a major terrorist attack in any given area, school officials and staff members could be called upon to assume more responsibility than they ever imagined. Depending on the severity of the attack, communications systems could be disabled. Accurate information or directions from authorities could be delayed. Emergency response services could be critically overburdened and not readily available. Working without assistance, schools could be called upon to provide shelter, food, medical attention, and guidance to students for extended periods of time beyond typical school hours. The physical and emotional endurance of staff members would be sorely tested as they assume parenting roles, providing physical, emotional, and spiritual support to their charges.

The general measures that follow are divided into two classifications: (1) establishing and maintaining a safe school and (2) implementing recommendations for maintaining the safety of a school under the threat of war and terrorism. These measures can be tailored to local schools and communities to help develop a safe schools plan and to prepare school officials and community leaders to respond to a crisis of significant magnitude.

The National School Safety Center (2003) offers the following guidelines for "Homeland Security in a Post 9/11 Environment":

1. **Identify a specific procedure for evaluating and responding to threats.** Every campus should have a series of threat assessment protocols so that school officials can effectively work with mental health and law enforcement professionals in handling circumstances that could result in potential violence or harm. Also, make certain that students are on your team. For the most part, students are the best information resources for inside threats. Recent studies by the U.S. Secret Service revealed that, in the vast majority of student shootings, other students on the campus were aware of the event before it occurred. Having a tip line or a safe reporting mechanism in place for students is critical.

2. **Identify the potential disasters that could occur, based on the school's setting and climate.** Such disasters may include:
   — Civil unrest/demonstrations/rioting
   — Bomb threats/explosions
   — Intruders/unauthorized visitors
   — Hostage taking
   — Sniper attacks
   — Extortion
   — Assault/battery/rape
   — Weapons possession
   — Drug abuse/trafficking
   — Gang-related violence/drive-by shootings
   — Kidnappings/abductions
   — Child abuse/neglect/molestation
   — Life-threatening illness
   — Accidental injury or death
   — Intentional injury or death
   — Utility failures
   — Chemical spills
   — Automobile accidents
   — Natural disasters: earthquake, flood, tornado, fire, hurricane, tsunami
   — Mass transit disasters: falling aircraft/train derailment/bus accidents

3. **Control campus access.** Minimize the number of campus entrance and exit points used daily. Access points to school grounds should be limited and supervised on a regular basis by individuals who are familiar with the student body. Campus traffic, both pedestrian and vehicular, should flow through areas that can be easily and naturally supervised. Delivery entrances used by vendors should also be checked regularly. Parking lots often have multiple entrances and exits, which contribute to the vandalism and defacement of vehicles and school property. Vehicular and pedestrian access should be carefully controlled. Perimeter fencing should be considered. Bus lots should be secured and monitored. Infrequently used rooms and closets should be locked. Access to utilities, roofs, and cleaning closets should be secured.

4. **Identify specifically assigned roles and responsibilities.** Specific policies and procedures that detail staff members' responsibilities for security should be developed. These responsibilities may include monitoring hallways and restrooms, patrolling parking lots, and providing supervision at before-school and after-school activities. Specific roles and responsibilities should also be assigned for times of crisis, including the appointment of a Crisis Team.

5. **Identify whom to call in a crisis.** Maintain an updated list of whom to call in case of various kinds of crises. Develop a close working partnership with these emergency responders. When a crisis occurs, school officials do not have the time or the luxury to find out who handles chemical or biological disasters or who handles bomb threats. Know the extent of the services offered by these agencies. Find out what to do when an emergency responder is not immediately available. Develop a close working partnership with law enforcement officials. Get to know your school police before there is a crisis. Develop a memorandum of understanding as to the role of a police officer on campus. Determine in advance who will lead, who will follow, and how searches, interrogations, and other issues will be handled. Create a close working partnership with mental health professionals who can assist school officials in evaluating and assessing potentially dangerous students who may threaten or intimidate others. The counselor or the psychologist can also be an important partner in the aftermath of a crisis.

6. **Provide training for all members of the school community regarding cultural awareness and sensitivity.** It is important to consider the impact of cultural influences on a school community's ability to create and maintain safe, secure, and peaceful schools. Cultural influences will directly affect the information, strategies, and resources that will be used in safe school planning. The sensitivity to cultural influences also applies to creating a plan to manage and respond to a crisis.

7. **Establish an Emergency Operation Communication System.** In addition to campus intercoms and two-way radios, it is important for school officials to be able to communicate with law enforcement officers and outside telephone providers. This includes the use of cell phones.

8. **Implement a uniform school crime reporting and record-keeping system.** When school administrators know what crimes are being committed on their campus, when and where they are committed, and who is involved, it speaks volumes about the types of strategies and supervision that should be implemented. In addition, it is important to conduct some level of crime analysis to determine what, if any, linkages exist among various aspects of criminal activity on the campus.

9. **Identify potential and reliable sources of information to be accessed once a crisis situation develops.** Prepare a plan that identifies the first and subsequent contacts you will make to access credible information and appropriate directions for action.

10. **Perform an assessment of your school's risk during a national crisis.** This includes:

    a. Evaluating health and medical on-site preparedness;

    b. Checking the availability and the accessibility of local emergency services, including HAZMAT (hazardous materials), fire, emergency medical, law enforcement, and local and federal emergency-management agencies;

    c. Identifying potential terrorist targets in your local community;

    d. Identifying and taking inventory of potential informal contacts in the community who could provide food, water, shelter, medical aid, power sources, and other forms of emergency support; and

    e. Reviewing viable communications plans, such as phone chains and parent contact information.

    f. **Be observant of the things transpiring on campus.** During periods of high alert, an additional level of vigilance must be in place. Everyone who comes onto the campus must have a legitimate purpose. It is important to have a uniform screening policy for all visitors, including vendors and delivery or service personnel. All visitors should be required to sign in at the school office, state their specific business, and wear or visibly display a visitor's badge. All school employees should be advised to greet visitors or any unidentified people and direct them to the main office, to ensure that these visitors have legitimate business at the school. Teachers and staff should be trained to courteously challenge all visitors. "May I help you?" is a kind, nonthreatening way to begin.

       Confirm the identity of service personnel and anyone seeking access to operational systems, such as heating/air conditioning units, gas or electric utilities, telephone systems, security systems, maintenance areas, and other related locations. Maintain accurate records of service and delivery personnel, including a log of dates and times of service delivery, types of services, full names of service personnel, company represented, and vehicle information.

       Develop procedures for identifying and keeping track of volunteer workers on campus. Enforce sign-in/sign-out procedures for volunteers.

       During periods of high alert, be on the watch for suspicious people, packages, and activities on or near your campus. Notify authorities of these observations. Things to watch for include someone photographing or videotaping on or near your campus, unidentified or unfamiliar vehicles parked on or near campus for extended periods of time, unclaimed packages or backpacks left unattended, or unfamiliar people seeking information that is out of the ordinary.

g. **In view of Homeland Security recommendations, it is especially important to pay added attention to the possibility of the following kinds of disasters. Review and revise your crisis plans accordingly.**
   Bomb threats/explosions
   Suicide bombings
   Intruders/unauthorized visitors
   Biological/radiological attacks
   Utility failures
   Mass transit disasters: Falling aircraft/train derailment/bus accidents

h. **Assemble your Crisis Response Teams** to reacquaint members with each other and with crisis plans and procedures. Enlist new team members as needed.

i. **Provide training to all school staff members regarding crisis preparation.** Detail each person's responsibilities during a crisis. Train everyone to be observant and watchful of suspicious or out-of-the-ordinary activity; show people how to identify and what to do with suspicious packages, how to turn off utilities and heating or air systems and who will be responsible for doing so, and how to administer basic first aid.

j. **Conduct an inventory of campus provisions**, including food, water, alternative power sources, materials for sealing doors and windows, and medical and first aid supplies that will be available during an emergency. Consider assembling emergency kits and food and water supplies for every classroom. In some cases, this may be as simple as expanding already existing student disaster-preparedness kits. Enlist parent and community groups to help pull together the supplies for these kits. Maintain an updated record of any hazardous chemicals and cleaning agents that may be stored on campus. Be sure that such materials are securely stored, according to local and federal regulations.

k. **Review and, if needed, revise existing plans for evacuation, alternative shelter, temporary lockdown, and shelter-in-place.** Be prepared to put any combination of these into effect. It is possible that a situation will call for a simultaneous lockdown of one section of the building while evacuating other parts of the school.

l. **Keep parents informed of your crisis plans, procedures and protective policies**, particularly with regard to reuniting parents and children after a crisis event.

m. **As is appropriate to your community and degree of risk, conduct emergency drills** for evacuation, lockdown, or shelter-in-place procedures so that staff and students are familiar with the appropriate response in an actual emergency.

Creating safe schools is a joint responsibility involving students, parents, teachers, school officials, local law enforcement, judges, emergency personnel, social service, and a variety of other youth-serving professionals. The bottom line is that if we are going to require young people to attend school, then it is our responsibility to provide them with a safe, secure, and welcoming environment. In this time of heightened potential for terror, including the use of chemical, biological, and radiological weapons in our communities, it is more important than ever for our schools to be prepared to respond in appropriate ways (National School Safety Center, 2003).

CONCLUSION

A disaster or a critical incident is frightening to everyone, especially children and adolescents who are contained in a building, having no contact to their families. Eighteen possible critical incidents were cataloged in chapter 4 and eight disaster incidents in this chapter, to provide adults with the necessary directions and skills to resolve such traumatic events when they occur. Today, schools and communities are confronted with both domestic and international threats of violence on a daily basis. Perceived as a safe haven, schools continue to be held responsible not only for educating youths, but also for providing for their safety and security. Parents and concerned communities look for the school's inherent leadership in providing safety and security in uncertain times.

Schools are increasingly looked upon as the central hub of stability within a community. Essentially, knowledge is power, and, collectively, schools have access and have forged important relationships to valuable human resources within the communities they serve. These resources are invaluable and include everyone from custodian to counselor; principal to school psychologist; teacher to special needs educator; nurse to social worker; resource officer to police representative; and cafeteria worker to probation officer. All of these relationships work independently and cooperatively on a daily basis. The people in these collective relationships can also mobilize to serve the community at a moment's notice.

Helping Your Child After a Disaster

Children may be especially upset and may express feelings about the disaster. These reactions are normal and usually will not last long. Listed below are some problems you may see in your child:

- Excessive fear of darkness, separation, or being alone
- Clinging to parents, fear of strangers
- Worry
- Increase in immature behaviors
- Not wanting to go to school
- Changes in eating/sleeping behaviors
- Increase in either aggressive behavior or shyness
- Bed-wetting or thumb sucking
- Persistent nightmares
- Headaches or other physical complaints

The following will help your child:

- Talk with your child about his or her feelings about the disaster. Share your feelings, too.
- Talk about what happened. Give your child information he or she can understand.
- Reassure your child that you are safe and together. You may need to repeat this reassurance often.
- Hold and touch your child often.
- Spend extra time with your child at bedtime.
- Allow your child to mourn or grieve over a lost toy, a lost blanket, a lost home.
- If you feel that your child is having problems at school, talk to his or her teacher so that you can work together to help your child.

Please reread this sheet from time to time in the coming months. Usually, a child's emotional response to a disaster will not last long, but some problems may be present or may recur for many months afterward. Community mental health centers are usually staffed by professionals skilled in talking with people who had experienced disaster-related problems.

FIGURE 5.3
Sample Information Sheet to Share with Parents

Chapter 6

Strategies for the Resolution of Grief and Loss

Grief is a tidal wave that overtakes you,
smashes down upon you with unimaginable force,
sweeps you up into its darkness,
where you tumble and crash against unidentifiable surfaces,
only to be thrown out on an unknown beach, bruised, reshaped . . .
Grief will make a new person out of you,
if it doesn't kill you in the making.

Stephanie Ericcson

MEETING THE EMOTIONAL NEEDS OF STUDENTS AND SURVIVORS

Balk (1983) identified acute emotional responses of students after the death of a peer. He revealed that although peer support and chances to talk with friends about the death at such a time of loss were important aids in coping with death, many peers feel uncomfortable talking about death. They frequently avoid the survivors, to decrease their own discomfort of not knowing what to say or how to say it. Young people sometimes hide their feelings of grief because such feelings often are not considered acceptable in public. As a result, youths are often confused about the source of their recurring grief reactions.

Furthermore, young people often take cues about how to react from the adults around them, more than from the event itself. It is crucial that counselors, teachers, administrators, and support personnel process the emotional needs of survivors. Structured opportunities to talk about the loss enhance coping skills. Validation of feelings as a perceptual check is particularly important to children and adolescents. Talking about the death and

related anxieties in a secure environment that fosters trust provides a means
to "work through" the loss experience. It also serves to prevent *destructive
fantasy building*, which often occurs when young people cannot test their
perceptions and feelings against reality.

Hawton (1986) and Perrone (1987) found that peers of adolescents
who attempted suicide are vulnerable because the rate of suicide is higher

- Among people with unstable social relationships;
- When a population is self-contained;
- When imitative behavior is common;
- When the element of bravado exists; and
- When the act is sure to be noticed.

Teachers and staff also need help in understanding and handling young
people's normal, yet often inappropriate, reactions to death. A paramount
need is for counselors, teachers, and other support personnel to process the
emotional needs of survivors.

With adequate preparation, counselors, teachers, administrators, and
other helping professionals can provide the curative environment that fosters a responsive and healing process. Collective efforts to provide structured programs and secure environments to work through significant losses
are critical. Furthermore, all schools should have a detailed **Crisis Communication Contingency Plan.** Fundamentally, schools need plans that include steps take to prevent further harm and a referral network for students
and their families who are in need of long-term mental health counseling
(Sheeley & Herily, 1989).

Students often key into the behavioral clues provided by adults who
are around them and allow these clues to give direction to their own reactions. Without an available plan of action, normal coping mechanisms for
many students (and staff members) will break down, and disorganization
will occur. Furthermore, if students are not led to discover a balanced resolution to the traumatic event, disorganization will leave survivors vulnerable
to developmental crises over identification with the deceased. Therefore, it
is paramount to process the emotional needs of survivors.

BEHAVIOR MANIFESTATIONS OF LOSS

The reactions of survivors who have experienced a suicide or a sudden loss
are likely to be complex, but typically include some of the following characteristics:

❑ *Denial and numbness* dominate during the first 24 hours and includes a refusal to accept the fact of loss or a selective denial of painful memories.

❑ *Anger* is often directed toward the deceased, as well as toward medical or emergency services, family, friends, teachers, administrators, and others in positions of authority.

❑ *Blaming others/blaming self* occurs, especially with a "suicide note." For example, the family may blame teachers, counselors, administrators, or teachers for not intervening or recognizing a problem and communicating their concerns. Conversely, administrators, counselors, and teachers may blame parents, stepparents, or estranged caregivers if the family has a history of domestic problems.

❑ *Shame and regret.* Shame occurs because of the stigma associated with the death, or regret for not recognizing warning signs and self-destructive or violent patterns of behavior.

❑ *Guilt* revolves around what survivors might or should have done to prevent the suicide or sudden death, as well as ideation about feeling responsible for the death; regretting other relationship issues or disappointment in the past, such as not making the athletic or scholastic team; being part of a romantic breakup; or not intervening when a peer was harassed or bullied. A suicide note also eliminates the opportunity for survivors to say good-bye or communicate unresolved conflicts with the deceased. Those left behind are faced with a triple loss: from death, from rejection, and from disillusionment. Suicide takes away self-worth. All these factors operate to increase the potential of hostility in the mourner and the danger of the mourner turning it upon himself or herself as the "only available or most appropriate target."

❑ *Fear* manifests in relation to one's own destructive impulses: fear of being alone; fear of revealing repressed secrets, such as abuse; or fear of loss of control.

❑ *Intellectualization* often dominates the dialogue of well-meaning adults in their effort to search for meaning; to seek justification; and as a defense mechanism to obsess over the event, rather than to confront painful feelings.

❑ *Hostility* is often directed toward the people who must confront the loss (e.g., the medical examiner, police, the attending physician) and to groups or systems (e.g., the school, the family, the church, the juvenile justice system, the team, or subcultures of peers).

❑ *Unfinished business* often emerges because a death or a tragic loss often creates the potential for revisiting unresolved conflicts or abuses of the past (especially among high-risk youth).

TABLE 6.1
Some Normal Grief Reactions for Children and Adolescents

Physical	Cognitive	Emotional	Behavioral
1. Numbness	Disbelief	Moodiness	Increased Aggression
2. Stunned Feeling	Denial	Exaggerated Fears	Decline in School Work
3. Anxiety	Pessimism	Numbness	Withdrawal
4. Stomach aches	Confusion	Sadness	Less Social Risk Taking
5. Headaches	Easily distracted	Relief	More Time With Peers
6. Dry Mouth	Forgetfulness	Guilt	Recklessness
7. Restlessness	Short Attention Span	Low Self-Esteem	Regressive Behavior
8. Overactivity	Decline in School Work	Depression	Disruptive Relationships
9. Hollowness in Stomach	Difficulty Organizing	Loneliness	Defiance
10. Fatigue	Fear of Going Crazy	Longing	Increased Risk Taking
11. Uncontrolled Crying	Blames Self for Death	Hostility	Drug & Alcohol Abuse
12. Breathing Difficulty	Apathy	Defiance	Clinging
13. Sleep Disturbances	Difficulty Verbalizing	Shame	Sexual Acting Out
14. Changes in Eating	Fearfulness	Panic	Possessiveness of Others
15. Appetite Disturbances	Suicidal Thoughts	Abandonment	Overactivity
16. Nausea	Philosophical Attitude	Overwhelmed	Searching
17. Episodic Crying	Lowered Self-Esteem	Fearfulness	Identifies w/ Deceased
18. Oversensitivity to Noise	Insecurity	Gladness	Sighing
19.	"If Only" Regrets	Hopelessness	Hides Things of Deceased's
20.	Sense Deceased's Presence	Vulnerability	Lethargy; Hostility
21.	Fears Things Won't Get Better		Apathy

Students' abilities to develop coping strategies for their uncomfortable but normal feelings and their ability to adjust to loss and maintain control over everyday life experiences will ultimately depend their internal strength and the assistance they obtain from caring adults (Kalafat & Underwood, 1989; Kush, 1990; Thompson, 1990, 1993).

FACTORS AFFECTING THE NATURE OF A SUDDEN LOSS

Natural Versus Human-Caused Disasters

Natural losses are illnesses and natural disasters—heart attacks, strokes, earthquakes, hurricanes, or tornados. With natural losses, the resulting anger is directed toward the deceased or some higher being. Human-caused losses include homicide, bombings, or acts of war and may be due to individual hostile actions. In human-caused disasters the survivor's anger can be focused on the responsible person(s). Within this realm, the element of vindictiveness can be present.

The Degree of Intentionality

In accidental deaths there is no clear focus of intentionality. There is a high degree of intentionality with deaths such as homicide. Anger and blame for the death can be directed at a responsible person.

The Degree of Preventability

Illnesses such as a sudden heart attack or a ruptured aneurysm and natural disasters like earthquakes, hurricanes, tornadoes may not be perceived as being preventable. Others, such as homicide, may be highly preventable. When deaths are perceived as preventable, there may be a strong sense of clinging to a self-defeating cycle of "What ifs," that is, "What if I had done this or what if I had done that? Could I have prevented this catastrophe?" One wife, whose husband had a fatal heart attack, lamented, "What if I could have been a better wife?" Preventable deaths are likely to increase a sense of guilt, especially if one feels responsible or feels a sense of anger or if one holds others at fault.

Suffering

With some losses, the death is instantaneous. Immediate death may leave feelings that the person who died had no time to prepare for the death. Many survivors find the knowledge of an instantaneous death to be comforting. In other situations, there is a question whether the deceased suffered pain or anxiety prior to dying. These memories, particularly if a survivor's relative died in extremely distressing circumstances, may dominate the survivor's thoughts, pushing aside memories about the deceased person. This can thwart the survivor's grieving for the deceased person by disrupting the grieving process. Imaginings or memories of the traumatic death may cause so much distress that remembering the person who died may be actively avoided. At this juncture, delayed stress and reactive depression loom hauntingly down the road as barriers to confront, in order to recover from loss and proceed through the grieving process.

Extent

The number of people affected by the loss can affect the intensity of grief. When large numbers of people are involved, as with a devastating hurricane, the ability of others to offer support may be limited, because of the masses of people involved. Conversely, highly public losses such as the September 11th tragedy, the Columbine school shootings, or losses due to war can result in a greater community response and demonstration of support, allowing survivors to bond and grieve together. As the result of such horrific events, there has been a growth and an acceptance of public mourning through makeshift or more sophisticated memorial sites.

The Degree of Expectedness

Certain sudden losses are still somewhat expected, even if just retrospectively. The heart attack of someone at risk or the sudden loss of someone struggling with a life-threatening illness frequently do not come as a total surprise. Other losses, such as accidents or random acts of violence, offer little to no forewarning and are a shock to the survivor.

UNDERSTANDING AND COPING WITH GRIEF

Grief is not a passive process that will simply happen without effort and pain. It is the work that must be done to come to terms with loss. Grief is not a single emotion but rather is a constellation of feelings that can be expressed through a variety of behaviors and thoughts. Because there are many ways to express grief, there are many ways to resolve grief. It should be remembered, then, that children who are grieving may show a variety of physiological symptoms and psychological and behavioral responses. Because there are various theories on the child's concept of death, it is helpful to ask the student for his or her own interpretation of what happened, in order to deal with the issues at the student's most appropriate level of understanding.

THE GRIEF PROCESS

Grief is a natural and normal process. It is a physical, emotional, spiritual, and psychological response. Grieving is a common life process. Grief is the healthiest way to accept a loss and put it into perspective. It helps us to face the reality of loss, to recover, and to grow through the experience. The expression of grief may differ with each individual, yet it follows a broad common framework. It is important to understand the process of grief.

No matter what type of loss is experienced, the same process is generally gone through each time, although the length and the intensity of the experience will differ. The stages of grief are not necessarily in a particular order. An individual may flow back and forth between stages. There is no set time for an individual to spend in each stage. To reach a level of acceptance may take months or years.

Stages of Grief

The description of the grief process that was originally developed by Kubler-Ross (1969) has been expanded from five stages into nine stages.

Although these stages are considered classic for adults, children's grieving is not commonly described with the same adult stages. Rando (1993) uses different descriptors for the stages of grieving for children in her book *Grief, Dying and Death:*

- Avoidance
- Confrontation
- Reestablishment

TABLE 6.2
Stages of Grief

Stage	Type of Behavior
Shock and Denial	<ul><li>Appears inactive, expressionless, numb</li><li>Exhibits denial, disbelief</li><li>Feels disorganized</li><li>Flat emotions</li><li>Loses appetite</li><li>Compliant behavior</li><li>Prone to injury</li><li>Development of real or imaginary illnesses</li><li>Rhythmic movement for emotional release</li><li>Clinging to mementos</li><li>It is hard to believe or accept the impending death.</li></ul>
Bargaining or Magical Undoing—An Internal Process of Self-Talk	<ul><li>Dramatic changes in compliance</li><li>Perfectionism</li><li>Dedication to something the child thinks will correct the reality of what happened</li></ul>
Fear	<ul><li>Feels terror</li><li>Panics in the absence of parents</li><li>Feels helpless</li><li>Fears something will happen to loved one or self</li><li>Develops physical symptoms, sleep disturbances</li></ul>
Anger and Despair	<ul><li>Resents others and self</li><li>Exhibits uncooperative and rude behavior</li><li>May become angry at those trying to help</li><li>The anger is directed at everyone</li><li>The overriding question is "Why me?"</li><li>Defiance and talking back</li><li>Swearing</li><li>Tantrums</li><li>Fighting and hurting others, self, or property</li><li>Regressing in development</li><li>Withdrawal</li></ul>
Guilt	<ul><li>Blames self for loss</li><li>Has lowered self-esteem</li><li>May seek to punish self</li></ul>

TABLE 6.2
Continued

Stage	Type of Behavior
Depression	• Feels empty
	• Appears unhappy and cries excessively
	• Yearns or searches for lost object or person
	• Withdraws, is silent
	• The person revisits unresolved grief issues from the past
	• The person is very sad for those left behind who must confront the reality of the loss
	• Guilt may accompany depression
Reflection	• Has experienced separation or loss and is able to cope
	• Feels hopeful
	• Reorganizes life and focuses on the present
	• Reviews the past life with satisfaction
	• Becomes ready for death with quiet resolution
Resolution and Understanding— A Process of Letting Go of Anger and Guilt	• Relaxed and at ease
	• Improved concentration and focus
	• Talking about the tragedy without becoming agitated
Acceptance, Hope, and Resilience— The Decision to Go on Living	• Has experienced separation or loss and is able to cope
	• Reflecting on the past and drawing strength from it
	• Talking about the future
	• Describing or seeing self in the future

Adapted in part from *The Stages of Processing Grief and Loss*. Modesto, CA: Stanislaus County Office of Education Child and Family Services: 2003. Reprinted with permission.

Rando (1993) also outlines the Six R Processes of Mourning. They are

- **Recognizing** the loss.
- **React** to the missing.
- **Recollect** the missing, the relationship, and the meaning of the relationship.
- **Relinquish** attachments to the world before the loss, including assumptions that no longer hold.
- **Readjust** to a new world without forgetting the old.
- **Reinvest** in the world around you.

FIGURE 6.1
Common Signs of Grieving Children

- Child continually retells events about the loved one and his or her death.
- Child feels the loved one is present in some way and speaks of him or her in the present tense.
- Child dreams about the loved one and longs to be with him or her.
- Child experiences nightmares and sleeplessness.
- Child cannot concentrate on schoolwork.
- Child appears at times to feel nothing.
- Child is preoccupied with death and worries excessively about health issues.
- Child is afraid to be left alone.
- Child often cries at unexpected times.
- Child wets the bed or loses appetite.
- Child idealizes the loved one and assumes his or her mannerisms.
- Child becomes the "class bully" or the "class clown."
- Child rejects old friends, withdraws or acts out.

Source: Goldman, L. (2000). *Life and Loss: A Guide to Help Children With Complicated Grief.* New York: Taylor and Francis. Reprinted with permission.

STAGES OF GRIEF FOR LOVED ONES

There are 10 stages that people usually go through after a loss before they find their way back to the mainstream or daily routine of life. These grief experiences are normal, but not everyone experiences them in the same order or necessarily goes through all stages.

- **Stage 1:** Shock
- **Stage 2:** Expression of emotion
- **Stage 3:** Depression and loneliness
- **Stage 4:** Physical symptoms of distress
- **Stage 5:** Panic
- **Stage 6:** Guilt
- **Stage 7:** Anger and resentment
- **Stage 8:** Resistance
- **Stage 9:** Hope
- **Stage 10:** Affirmation of reality (NOVA, 2001, p. 123). Reprinted with permission.

To progress through the stages, a grieving person has to actively work through tasks, such as,

- **Accept the reality of loss.** The shock of loss is great. There is a tendency to deny that the death occurred or to deny the significance of the loss.
- **Experience the pain of grief.** The pain is physical, social, and emotional. It hurts tremendously. Avoidance and suppression of the pain prolong the mourning process.
- **Adjust to an environment in which the deceased is missing.** Changes in the daily living routine happen after the loss. Excessive dependency on others will foster helplessness.
- **Withdrawal of emotional energy and reinvesting in another relationship.** Past attachment with the deceased is lessened without betraying the memory, and new relationships are formed. The gap may be filled, but grief takes on new meaning. Life goes on.

CHILDREN'S CONCEPTS OF DEATH

This is a commonly accepted description of children's concepts of death at different ages. Children develop at different rates and may not fit these categories exactly. Different cultures vary in their concepts of death, as well as in their methods of grieving.

Ages 3–5

These children do not yet accept death as a permanent process. Death is seen as an ending. They fear separation and abandonment more than they do death. Children may feel mad or sad that someone is not coming home. They often ask questions such as. "When will grandma come back?"

- Has some understanding of death, but thinks it is reversible.
- Has confusion related to a limited concept of time.
- Often connects unrelated events to the death.
- Incorporates "magical thinking" (e.g., "I made this happen. It's all my fault.").
- Exhibits regressive behaviors (thumb sucking, temper tantrums, fear of separation and abandonment).
- Often views death as punishment for bad behavior.
- Acts out feelings through play.

- Asks about the dead person's return.
- Animistic thinking, that is, assumes that everything in the whole world is alive. Preschoolers believe that inanimate objects can move, think, feel, and rest. Thus people are always alive. Death is merely a deep sleep. Children worry about the comfort and the physical care of their bodies. They are concerned that the dead person might be hungry, cold, or lonely.
- Magical thinking attributes power to everyone. Everything is under the control of someone else's will. Within the system, people can die because of another's wish and can return to life just as readily. A prince can turn into a toad, and a dead princess can wake up with a kiss.
- Artificialistic thinking is the belief that things exist for people's convenience. If toys can be fixed upon request, then why not dead people?

Ages 5–9

Children of this age are beginning to understand that death is very concrete and irreversible. They may fear darkness and being alone. They know the body decays but believe the spirit still lives. Talk openly to clear up misconceptions and lessen fears. Reassure children that they will be looked after, and accept that their level of conceptual understanding necessitates a concrete view of death.

- Begins to understand that death is final.
- Can understand a more detailed description as to why or how the person died.
- Views death in a violent sense, often personified as a skeleton or a monster that comes after you.
- May feel that death is contagious.
- Looks for natural explanations.
- Acts as a literal and concrete thinker.
- Has concerns for peers.
- Denies that death happened.
- Fears that other loved ones will die.

Ages 10–14

Children are beginning to understand and accept a mature, realistic explanation of death as final and inevitable. They are developing their independence from parents but are not yet fully established individuals. Consequently, a death, especially of a peer, can cause considerable distress based on a fear for their own security. They may refuse to believe that they are mortal.

- Begins to understand the possibility of his or her own death.
- Sees death as final.
- Feels intense emotions of anger, guilt, or both.
- Displays interest in the physical aspects (biological processes) of dying.
- May express concerns about the future effect of the death on him or her (especially regarding finances and future lifestyle); becomes more future-oriented.
- Withdraws from others and tries to hide his or her feelings.

Ages 15–18

Teens are aware of complex social issues. They are moving to a more abstract level of thinking, and yet their tendency is to react, especially in the death of a person, in a highly dramatic, intense fashion, with a reliance on personalized rituals, symbols, and so on. Their energy can appear to come in great spurts, and their responses can be unpredictable.

- Usually is able to view death on an adult level.
- Sees death as universal, inevitable.
- Develops his or her own abstract thinking related to death.
- Strives to conquer death with an immortal attitude.
- Feels uncomfortable with the intensity of feelings related to death.
- Reacts by trying to take care of others or becomes regressive in behaviors.

The variety of grief response in adults is extensive, largely due to how previous losses have or have not been resolved. It is important to remember that culture plays an important role in how the experience of death is expressed and resolved.

SUGGESTED WAYS TO PROVIDE COMFORT TO A GRIEVING CHILD

- **Act naturally.** Show natural concern and sorrow.
- **Be there**. Spend time with the child, walking, reading, and talking. Spend some time with the child away from the group.
- **Listen**. Be sure to have good eye contact. Use simple, direct words. Let the child be mad or express other feelings.

- **Explain things**. Give information about what's going to happen. Keep promises that you make. Be as predictable as possible.
- **Comfort the child**. Don't assume that a seemingly calm child is not sorrowing. If you can, be a friend to whom feelings can be confided and with whom tears can be shed.

TO COMFORT A GRIEVING ADULT

- **Be there.** Attend the funeral, visit, call, and spend time with those grieving. Particularly after the initial attention subsides, bring food, do errands.
- **Listen.** Grieving people need to talk about the sudden vacuum in their lives. Allow them to know that you wish to hear about their experiences. Don't force conversation; let the grieving person lead. Don't attempt to tell the grieving person how he or she feels. Ask (without probing), but realize that you can only know what you are told.
- Avoid talking about trivia in the presence of the recently grieving person, even if this is done to distract the bereaved.
- Don't take away pictures, clothing, student belongings, or a desk too quickly. Acknowledge the death.
- **Send a note.** Notes can share personal memories, yet are short and simple.
- **Give a gift**. Donate a collection of poems, a book to the library in memory of the deceased, or a gift to a related charity.
- **Extend an invitation**. Consider what the person likes to do. Bereaved people often decline invitations or cancel at the last minute. Don't give up. Ask again. Don't forget the person after time has passed.
- **Encourage the postponement of major decisions**. Whatever can wait should wait until after the period of intense grief.

VARIOUS RESPONSES TO LOSS CAN BE ACUTE TRAUMATIC RESPONSE, ACUTE GRIEF RESPONSE, OR ACUTE STRESS DISORDER

A variety of responses—physical, cognitive, behavioral, and emotional—can be exhibited after experiencing a loss. Different types of loss can precipitate these responses be it a death, a traumatic event, or the break up of a long-standing relationship. A grieving person can undergo both significant and subtle changes that impact his or her physical, mental, emotional, and spiritual states. It is important to understand that these feelings and experiences are a way of coping. These are normal reactions to a major loss. These responses should be viewed as a normal reaction to an abnormal event. It is important to remember that *the acute responses to loss are not unhealthy or maladaptive responses.*

Rather, they are normal responses to an abnormal event. Depending on the perception and experiences of the loss, people may experience one of the following responses or a combination of the following normal responses to this event:

1. Acute Traumatic Response
2. Acute Grief Response
3. Acute Stress Disorder

Which reaction or response is experienced may be determined by which type of health-care professional you might encounter. Trauma responders and emergency room physicians are more familiar with the acute traumatic response. Primary care and family practitioners encounter more often the acute grief response, and mental health workers most frequently see the acute stress disorder (or the more chronic condition post-traumatic stress disorder). The signs symptoms involved in these different reactions to loss are overlapping and interrelated.

The traumatic nature and the magnitude of the events that occurred on September 11, 2001, combined with the vastness of the death and the destruction, the suddenness and senselessness of the attack, make it more likely those who witnessed the events will have some response to this abnormal event.

People may respond differently to the same loss or traumatic event. People experience stress and respond to it in different ways. Not everyone demonstrates a reaction to a loss. Some people may not appear to be affected. Some have delayed reactions that do not show up for days, to weeks, or even months later. Others never have a reaction at all. Everyone has his or her own coping mechanisms and ways of dealing with death and grief. It is important not to compare our reaction with the reactions of others, or to judge their reactions or even lack of reactions.

The grieving person may experience a variety of physical or body complaints: fatigue, insomnia, pain, gastrointestinal symptoms, chest pressure, palpitations, stomach pains, backaches, panic attacks, or increased anxiety. These potentially serious complaints require a thorough evaluation to exclude potentially serious medical disorders before a traumatic response, a grief response, or a stress disorder can be diagnosed.

Acute Traumatic Response

The acute traumatic response is the response that occurs during or immediately following the traumatic event. The reactions are often noted by trauma

TABLE 6.3
Physical Reactions: Acute Traumatic Response

** Difficulty breathing	* Fainting	Pale appearance
** Shock symptoms	* Headaches	Chills
** Chest pains	* Thirst	Cold, clammy skin
** Palpitations	* Dizziness	Increased sweating
* Rapid heartbeat	* Gastrointestinal upset	Vertigo
* Elevated blood pressure	Flushed face	Hyperventilation
* Fatigue	Muscle tension & pains	Grinding of teeth
		Twitches

** Requires IMMEDIATE medical evaluation.
* May need medical evaluation
Source: Dyer, K. A. (2002). Physical Reactions: Acute Traumatic Response.
http://www.journeyofhehearts.org/jofh/grief/trauma. Reprinted with permission.

responders such as firefighters, police, emergency personnel, and emergency room staff. A variety of "normal responses and symptoms" manifest themselves physiologically, emotionally, cognitively, and behaviorally. These responses can be experienced either during or shortly after a traumatic event. The following physical, emotional, cognitive and behavioral reactions are commonly observed during traumatic exposure. It is important to remember that *these responses are not unhealthy or maladaptive responses. Rather, they are normal responses to an abnormal event.* The key is to know them and recognize them and take time to debrief and process at the end of the day. The universality of common traumatic experiences takes the loneliness out of helping.

Note: Not every response is evidenced by every person.

TABLE 6.4
Emotional Reactions: Acute Traumatic Response

Shock	Helplessness	Irritability
Denial	Emptiness	Depression
Dissociation	Uncertainty	Grief
Panic	Horror	Feelings of guilt
Fear	Terror	Emotional outbursts
Intense feelings of aloneness	Anger	Feeling overwhelmed
Hopelessness	Hostility	

Source: Dyer, K. A. (2002). Emotional Reactions: Acute Traumatic Response.
http://www.journeyofhearts.org/jofh/grief/trauma. Reprinted with permission.

TABLE 6.5
Cognitive Reactions: Acute Traumatic Response

Poor concentration	Forgetfulness	Nightmares
Confusion	Self-blame	Intrusive memories
Disorientation	Blaming others	Flashbacks
Difficulty in making a	Lowered self-efficacy	Questioning religious
decision	Thoughts of losing control	values
A short attention span	Hypervigilance	Feeling as though the
Suggestibility	Perseverative thoughts of	world no longer
Vulnerability	the traumatic event	"makes sense"
		Difficulty remembering
		the event

Source: Dyer, K. A. (2002). Cognitive Reactions: Acute Traumatic Response. http://www.journeyofhearts.org/jofh/grief/trauma. Reprinted with permission.

The acute responses to loss are not unhealthy or maladaptive responses. Rather, they are normal responses to an abnormal event.

Acute Grief Response

Grief can be defined as an adaptive response to loss through the death of or separation from a person, the loss of a material object, the loss of one's livelihood, or the loss of physical abilities as the result of a tragic accident. When a person experiences a loss, he or she is likely to also experience an *acute grief response to that loss.* After a severe loss, these are normal responses that occur. A diagnosis of an acute grief response is likely to be

TABLE 6.6
Behavioral Reactions: Acute Traumatic Response

Withdrawal	Reluctance to abandon	Antisocial behaviors
"Spacing out"	property	Increased alcohol
Noncommunication	Aimless walking	consumption
Changes in speech	Pacing	Inability to attach importance
patterns	Inability to sit still	to anything but this event
Regressive behaviors	Exaggerated startle	Refusing to talk
Erratic movements	response	Feeling that one should not cry
Impulsivity		

Source: Dyer, K. A. (2002). Behavioral Reactions: Acute Traumatic Response. http://www.journeyofhearts.org/jofh/grief/trauma. Reprinted with permission.

made by a person's primary care provider, frequently after extensive medical evaluations are conducted to rule out physiological problems. Many of the symptoms experienced in acute grief are presenting symptoms of medical emergencies. If there is any doubt whether the symptoms one might be feeling in the aftermath of the tragedy are physical or psychological, it's important to seek professional treatment. Acute grief is a definite syndrome characterized by psychological and somatic symptoms, such as

1. Sensations of somatic distress that occur in waves lasting for 20 minutes to an hour, characterized by
   • Tightness in the throat
   • Choking
   • Shortness of breath
   • Sighing
   • An empty feeling in the stomach
   • Lack of muscular strength
   • Intense subjective distress described as tension or pain
2. Intense preoccupation with the image of the deceased, as in waking dreams, accompanied by feelings of vagueness and unreality.
3. Guilt feelings; the survivor reviews his or her behavior before the death for evidence of negligence and failure.
4. Emotional distancing in relationships with others, accompanied by erratic responses of irritability, hostility, and anger.
5. Disoriented behavior, such as restlessness, insomnia, absentmindedness, and an inability to concentrate or to initiate and maintain normal daily activities.

Symptoms of the Acute Grief Response

TABLE 6.7
Physical Symptoms for Acute Grief Response

Fatigue	Diarrhea	Dizziness
Trouble initiating or maintaining sleep	Constipation	Change in appetite— increased or decreased
	Abdominal, stomach pain	
Chest heaviness or pain	Back pain	Weight change
Shortness of breath	Headache	Hair loss
Tightness in the throat	Lightheadedness	Crying, sighing
Palpitations		Restlessness
Nausea		

Source: Dyer, K. A. (2002). Physical Symptoms for Acute Grief Response. http://www.journeyofhearts.org/jofh/grief/trauma. Reprinted with permission.

TABLE 6.8
Emotional Symptoms FOR Acute Grief Response

Sadness	Apathy	Fear
Anger	Numbness	Guilt
Irritability	Abandonment	Longing
Relief	Helplessness	Loneliness
Anxiety	Emotionally labile	Apathy
Panic	Vulnerability	Disbelief
Meaninglessness	Self-blame	Denial

Source: Dyer, K. A. (2002). Emotional Symptoms for Acute Grief Response. http://www.journeyofhearts.org/jofh/grief/trauma. Reprinted with permission.

Acute Stress Disorder

Acute stress disorder consists of the anxiety and behavioral disturbances that may develop within the first month after exposure to an extreme trauma. Usually, the symptoms begin during or shortly following the trauma. Such extreme traumatic events include rape, abduction, severe physical assault, near-death experiences in accidents, witnessing a murder, or participating in uncertain combat. The events of September 11, 2001, and the crisis in the Middle East with suicide bombers are recent examples that meet the criteria for extreme traumatic events.

Common presenting signs and symptoms of acute stress disorder include generalized anxiety and hyperarousal, avoidance of situations or stimuli that elicit memories of the trauma, and persistent, intrusive recollections of the event, such as having flashbacks, dreams, or recurrent thoughts or visual images. The symptom of dissociation (a perceived detachment of the mind from the emotional or one's physical state) is a crucial feature for the diagnosis. Dissociation is also characterized by a sense of the world as a dreamlike or surreal place. It may also be accompanied by poor memory of

TABLE 6.9
Social Symptoms for Acute Grief Response

Overly sensitive	Lack of interest
Dependent	Hyperactive
Withdrawn	Underactive
Avoids others	Relationship difficulties
Lack of initiative	Lowered self-esteem

Source: Dyer, K. A. (2002). Social Symptoms for Acute Grief Response. http://www.journeyofhearts.org/jofh/grief/trauma. Reprinted with permission.

TABLE 6.10
Behavioral Symptoms for Acute Grief Response

Forgetfulness	Feelings of unreality	Assuming mannerisms or
Difficulty concentrating	Feelings of emptiness	traits of the loved one
Slowed thinking	Dreams of the deceased	Needing to retell the story
Sense of unreality	Searching for the	of the loved one's death
Wandering aimlessly	deceased	Preoccupied with one's own
Feeling trancelike	Sense the loved one's	death
	presence	Avoiding talking about loss
	Hallucinations of the	so others won't feel
	deceased, sensing his	uncomfortable
	or her presence	
	(visual or auditory)	

Source: Dyer, K. A. (2002). Behavioral Symptoms for Acute Grief response.
http://www.journeyofhearts.org/jofh/grief/trauma. Reprinted with permission.

the specific events, which in most severe form is known as dissociative amnesia.

Acute Stress Disorder is a diagnosis made by a mental health professional. Specific diagnostic criteria must be met before this diagnosis can be made. The person must have been exposed to a traumatic event in which both of the following were present: the person experienced, witnessed, or was confronted with an event or events that involved actual or threatened death or serious injury, or a threat to the physical integrity of self or others; and the person's response involved intense fear, helplessness, or horror. During or after experiencing the distressing event, the individual has three (or more) of the following dissociative symptoms:

- A subjective sense of numbing, detachment, or absence of emotional responsiveness
- A reduction in awareness of his or her surroundings (e.g., "being in a daze")
- Derealization
- Depersonalization
- Dissociative amnesia (i.e., inability to recall an important aspect of the trauma)
- The traumatic event is persistently reexperienced in at least one of the following ways: recurrent images, thoughts, dreams, illusions, flashback episodes, or a sense of reliving the experience; or distress on exposure to reminders of the traumatic event.
- There is marked avoidance of stimuli that arouse recollections of the trauma (e.g., thoughts, feelings, people, conversations, activities, places).

- There are marked symptoms of anxiety or increased arousal (e.g., difficulty sleeping, irritability, poor concentration, hypervigilance, exaggerated startle response, motor restlessness).
- The disturbance causes clinically significant distress or impairment in social, occupational, or other important areas of functioning or impairs the individual's ability to pursue some necessary task, such as obtaining necessary assistance or mobilizing personal resources by telling family members about the traumatic experience.
- The acute stress disorder lasts for a minimum of 2 days and a maximum of 4 weeks.
- The disturbance is not due to the direct physiological effects of a substance (e.g., a drug of abuse, a medication), and a general medical condition is not present. Table 6.11 clarifies the difference between grief and trauma.

TASKS OF MOURNING AND GRIEF COUNSELING

Accepting the reality of the loss and confronting the fact that the person is dead are two of the most important initial tasks of mourning. Early denial and avoidance are quickly replaced by the realization of the loss, the necessity of feeling the pain of the loss, and working through the grief process.

Special Treatment Issues With Children and Adolescents

- Allow regression and dependency.
- Realize their lack of life experience in handling trauma.
- Allow the expression of feelings such as sorrow, hostility, and guilt.

TABLE 6.11
Grief and Trauma: The Confusion—The Difference

Normal Grief	Bereavement
Neurotic Grief	Traditional Mourning
Inhibited Grief	Distorted Mourning
Acute Grief	Psychoanalytical Mourning
Morbid Grief	Unanticipated Mourning
Complicated Grief	Chronic Mourning
Pathological Grief	Complicated Mourning
Traumatic Grief	Traumatic Mourning

Source: The National Institute on Trauma and Loss in Children, http://www.tlcinst.org. Reprinted with permission.

- Encourage discussion.
- Allow for fluctuations in their maturity level.
- Watch for the emergence of "unfinished business" or unresolved grief issues and conflicts from the past.
- Answer questions and provide factual information.
- Correct distortions.
- Avoid power struggles with adolescents.
- Focus on strengths and constructive adaptive behaviors.
- Address conscious, as well as unconscious, guilt.
- Identify and help resolve adolescents' sense of powerlessness.

Children Suffer Physically, Emotionally, and Spiritually in Response to Losses, Such as the Following:

- Loss of childhood dreams
- Loss of health
- Family moves
- Changing schools
- Loss of personal belongings
- Failure
- Loss of security
- Loss of safety
- Loss of self-esteem
- Loss of a pet
- Parent separation and divorce
- Loss of relationships
- Death of a significant other

THE AFTERMATH OF A CRISIS OR A CRITICAL INCIDENT CAN BE A MEANINGFUL LEARNING EXPERIENCE

In the aftermath of disaster strategy, tragedy, or loss, children and families, schools and communities, counselors and helping professionals reverberate in grief and ramifications of traumatic loss. Creative, powerful tools for group and individual healing can make a significant difference on the long road of creating a new equilibrium, or what some grief workers call a "new normal." These techniques and strategies need to be individually and developmentally tailored to provide each person with a safe and comfortable venue to explore the pain and begin the process of rebuilding his or her life.

Following are many ideas to help people who are mourning a loved one's death. Different kinds of losses dictate different responses, so not all of these ideas will suit everyone. Likewise, no two people grieve alike— what works for one may not work for another. Treat this list as what it is: a gathering of assorted suggestions that various people have tried with success. Perhaps what helped them through their grief will help you. The emphasis here is upon 47 specific, practical ideas to deal with individual loss and grief:

1. ***Talk regularly with a friend.***
   Talking with another about what you think and feel is one of the best things you can do for yourself. It helps to relieve some of the pressure you may feel, it can give you a sense of perspective, and it keeps you in touch with others. Look for someone who's a good listener and a caring soul. Then speak what's on your mind and in your heart. If this feels one-sided, let that be okay for this period of your life. Chances are, the other person will find meaning in what he or she is doing. And the time will come when you'll have the chance to be a good listener for someone else. You'll be a better listener then if you're a good talker now.

2. ***Carry or wear a linking object.***
   Carry something in your pocket or purse that reminds you of the one who died—perhaps a keepsake the person gave you, perhaps a small object he or she once carried or used, or a memento you select for just this purpose. You might wear a piece of the deceased's jewelry in the same way. Whenever you want, reach for or gaze upon this object and remember what it signifies.

3. ***Create a memory book.***
   Compile photographs that document your loved one's life. Arrange them into some sort of order so that they tell a story. Add other elements if you want: diplomas, newspaper clippings, awards, accomplishments, and reminders of significant events. Put all this in a special binder and keep it out for people to look at if they wish. Go through it on your own if you desire. Reminisce.

4. ***Recall your dreams.***
   Your dreams often have important things to say about your feelings and about your relationship with the one who died. Your dreams may be scary or sad, especially early on. They may seem weird or crazy to you. You may find that your loved one appears in your dreams. Accept your dreams for what they are and see what you can learn from them. No one knows that better than you.

5. ***Tell people what helps you and what doesn't.***
   People around you may not understand what you need. So tell them. If hearing your loved one's name spoken aloud by others feels good, say

so. If you need more time alone, assistance with chores that you're unable to complete, or an occasional hug, be honest. People can't read your mind, so you'll have to speak it.

6. *Ask for a copy of the memorial service.*

    If the funeral liturgy or the memorial service held special meaning for you because of what was spoken or read, ask for a copy of the words. Whoever participated in that ritual will feel gratified that what they prepared was appreciated. Turn to these words whenever you want. Some people find that these thoughts provide even more help weeks and months after the service.

7. *Plant something living as a memorial.*

    Plant a flower, a bush, or a tree in memory of the one who died. Or plant several things. Do this ceremonially if you wish, perhaps with others present. If you do this planting where you live, you can watch it grow and change day by day, season by season. You can even make it a part of special times of remembrance in the future.

8. *Spend time in your loved one's space.*

    If it's what you want to do, you may sit in the other's favorite chair, lie in his or her bed, or just stand in the deceased's room or among the person's possessions. Do this if it brings you comfort. But don't do it if it feels too awkward. You'll know quickly enough what's right for you.

9. *Journal.*

    Write out your thoughts and feelings. Do this whenever you feel the urge, but do it at least several times a week, if not several times a day. Don't censor what you write—be just as honest as you can. In time, go back through your writings and notice how you're changing and growing. Write about that, too.

10. *Purchase something soft to sleep with.*

    A teddy bear is a favorite choice for some, but there are other options. Select something that feels warm and cuddly. Then, whatever your age, cuddle it.

11. *Write to the person who died.*

    Write letters or other messages to your loved one, thoughts you wish you could express if he or she were present. And who knows if the person is not present in some way? Preserve what you write in your journal, if you wish, or on stationery or your computer. Or, if you wish, discard what you've written after a while. You'll find that this urge to write to the other will eventually leave you, but for a while it can be a real release for you, as well as a real connection.

12. *Consider a support group.*

    Spending time with a small group of people who have undergone a similar life experience can be very therapeutic. You can discover how natural your feelings are. You can learn from the experiences and the ideas of others. You can find backing as you make the changes you must. Support groups are not for everyone, of course. But many people have come to trust them. You won't know unless you try. Make sure the person who is leading the support group is a licensed counselor or someone who has some specialized training in processing grief and loss. You want to grow and progress through this life transition, not ruminate in it.

13. *Light a candle at mealtime.*

Especially if you eat alone, but even if you don't, consider lighting a taper at the table in memory of your loved one. Pause to remember the person as you light it. Keep the loved one nearby in this time of sustenance. You might light a candle at other times as well—for instance, as you sit alone in the evening, for instance.

14. *Create a memory area at home.*

In a space that feels appropriate, arrange a small tableau that honors the person: a framed photograph or two, perhaps a prized possession or an award, or something the person created or loved. This might be placed on a small table, a mantel, or a desk. Some people like to use a grouping of candles, representing not just the person who died but others who have died as well. In that case, a variety of candles can be arranged, each representing a unique life.

15. *Use your hands.*

Sometimes there's value in doing repetitive things with your hands, something you don't have to think about very much because it becomes second nature. Knitting and crocheting are like that. So are carving, woodworking, polishing, solving jigsaw puzzles, painting, braiding, shoveling, washing, and countless other activities. This type of action gives you some control in your present situation. You can see things change, and you can produce a product.

16. *Begin your day with your loved one.*

If your grief is young, you'll probably wake up thinking of that person anyway. So why not decide that you'll include her or him from the start? Focus this time in a positive way. Bring to your mind fulfilling memories. Recall lessons this person taught you, gifts he or she gave you. Think about how you can spend your day in ways that would be in keeping with your loved one's best self and with your best self. Then carry that best self with you through your day.

17. *Invite someone to be your telephone buddy.*

If your grief and sadness hit you especially hard at times and you have no one nearby to turn to, ask someone you trust to be your telephone buddy. Ask the person's permission for you to call whenever you feel you're at loose ends, day or night. Then put the person's number beside your phone and call if you need to. Don't abuse this privilege, of course. And know that someday it will be payback time—some day you'll make yourself available to help someone else in the same way you've been helped. That will help you accept the care you're receiving.

18. Structure alone time.

You may have your full share of alone time, in which case you'll want to ignore this suggestion. But if you're often among family, friends, and colleagues, make sure you also have time all by yourself. A large part of the grieving process involves what goes on inside yourself—your thoughts, your feelings, your memories, your hopes and dreams. So allow yourself the opportunity to go inside so you can grow inside.

19. Listen to music.

Choose music you believe will help you at a given moment, whether it's contemporary or ancient, instrumental or vocal, secular or religious. Let the sounds surround you and soothe you. Take this music with you, if you wish, as you go about your day.

20. Do something your loved one would enjoy.

Remember the one who died in your own unique way. One widowed woman has a special sauerkraut meal once a year. She doesn't like this tangy dish herself, but it was her husband's favorite, and she finds solace in remembering him in that way. There are probably a hundred different things you could do that once brought meaning or satisfaction to the one you loved. The meaning and satisfaction don't have to end with the death of that person.

21. Screen your entertainment.

Some TV shows and movies are best not viewed when you're deep in grief. The same goes for certain books or articles. If you have any questions, do a bit of research before you find yourself in the midst of an experience that brings up too many feelings for you to handle comfortably. For example, if your loved one recently died of cancer, you can do without reliving that experience on a 30-foot movie screen.

22. Engage your soul.

You'll want to do this your own way. Some people meditate, some pray, and some spend time alone in nature. Some worship with a congregation, and others do it on their own. Many grieving people begin to sense that all of the dead and us living are connected on a spiritual level in a way that defies easy understanding. Include your soul as you grow through your grief.

23. Change some things.

As soon as it seems right, alter some things in your home to make it clear that this significant change that has occurred. Rearrange a room, replace a piece of furniture, or give away certain items that will never again be used in your home. This does not mean removing all signs of the one who died. It does mean not treating your home or your loved one's room as a shrine that cannot be altered in any way.

24. ***Allow yourself to laugh.***
Sometimes something funny will happen to you, just like it used to. Sometimes you'll recall something hilarious that happened in the past. When that happens, go ahead and laugh if it feels funny to you. You won't be desecrating your loved one's memory. You'll be consecrating the person's love of life, and your own, too.

25. ***Allow time to cry.***
Crying goes naturally with grief. Tears well up and fall even when you least expect them. Subdued sniffles can become racking sobs on a moment's notice. It may feel awkward to you, but this is not unusual for a person in your situation. A good rule of thumb is this: If you feel like crying, then cry. If not, then don't. Also, understand that some grieving people seldom cry—it's just their way.

26. ***Talk to the other one.***
If it helps, you might talk with the one who died as you drive along in your car, as you stand beside the grave, or as you need the courage to make an important decision. This talking might be out loud or under your breath. Either way, it's the same; you're simply wishing that the other was with you that so you could talk things over, and for the moment you're doing the best you can to continue that conversation. This inclination to converse will eventually go away, when the time is right.

27. ***Create or commission a memory quilt.***
Sew or invite others to sew with you. Or hire someone to sew for you. However you get it completed, put together a wall hanging or a bedroom quilt that remembers the important life events of the one who died. Take your time doing this. Make it what it is: a labor of love.

28. ***Read about how others have responded to a loved one's death.***
You may feel that your own grief is all you can handle, but if you'd like to look at the ways others have done it, try C. S. Lewis's *A Grief Observed*, Lynn Caine's *Widow*, John Bramblett's *When Good-Bye Is Forever*, or Nicholas Wolterstorff's *Lament for a Son*. There are many others. Check with a counselor or a librarian.

29. ***Take a day off.***
When the mood is just right, take a one-day vacation. Do whatever you want, or don't do anything. Travel somewhere or stay inside by yourself. Be very active or don't do anything at all. Just make it your day, whatever that means for you.

30. ***Invite someone to give you feedback.***
Select someone you trust, preferably someone familiar with the workings of grief, to give you his or her reaction when you ask for it. If you

want to check out how clearly you're thinking, how accurately you're remembering, how effectively you're coping, go to that person. Pose your questions, and then listen to their responses. What you choose to do with that information will be up to you.

31. *Monitor signs of dependency.*
Although it's normal to become more dependent upon others for a while immediately after a death, it will not be helpful to continue in that role long term. Watch for signs that you're prolonging your need for assistance. Congratulate yourself when you do things for yourself.

32. *Give yourself rewards.*
Be kind to yourself in your grief. Do those things for yourself that you really enjoy, perhaps at the end of a long day or in the midst of a lonely time. Treat yourself to a favorite meal or a delicacy. Get a massage. Buy some flowers. Do something frivolous that makes you feel good. Then soak up those moments as fully as you can.

33. *Do something to help someone else.*
Step out of your own problems from time to time and devote your attention to someone else. Offer a gift or your service. Do this for yourself as much as for the other. Feel good about your worth.

34. *Write down your lessons from your experiences.*
Your grief experience will have much to teach you. From time to time, reflect upon what you're learning. State it as plainly as you're able. Carry those lessons with you as you go about your days. (Source: Jim Miller @ Willowgreen Grief Tips, http://www.opn.com/willowgreen/gtips.html. Reprinted by permission.)

35. *Do a web page*.
If you don't have the expertise, but you really want to do a memorial and/or personal page, hire a teenager. Others can share in your loss and provide words of encouragement.

36. *Surf the web*.
There are so many resources for help with grief. Never give up learning what you ache to know.

37. *Make a treasure box.*
Take an old shoebox and wrap it in decorative paper. Wrap the lid separately so that you can get in and out of the box as desired. Put things in the box that remind you of your loved one. You can live your loved one's life for him or her through the treasure box.

38. *Sing!*
Surely, there is a hymn or a song that is uplifting to your heart. In your moments of despair, hum or sing a song that puts you in a good mood. Maybe you think there is nothing to sing about, but there is! You are still alive and your loved one is watching over you from the most glorious existence of heaven and you will someday reunite with him or her.

39. *Volunteer.*

   Hospitals need compassionate and understanding help. Who can understand another person's pain better than one who has experienced it oneself or has seen a loved one go through it? Don't be afraid to cry *with* someone who needs to cry *to* someone. We need each other, and we heal better from our pain when serving others because we don't think of our own problems

40. *Endowment Funds and Scholarships.*

   Many universities and their students could use financial help. A person could give, in the loved one's name, directly to the university of his or her choice in the form of an endowment, or set up a scholarship fund in your child's name through the university.

41. *Become a "Santa" for a child in need.*

   Use money you would have spent on a loved one for Christmas and buy presents for the needy.

42. *Find a way to preserve your loved one's memory through his or her possessions.*

   If your loved one enjoyed the Christmas holidays, buy a Christmas wreath and decorate it with all of her favorite jewelry, or his favorite fly-fishing creations. Then put it in a shadow box and hang it in the dining room every Christmas.

43. *Create stationary and letterheads with your child's picture or artwork on it.*

   As mentioned earlier, technology makes anything possible. The local technical schools usually have printing classes, and they might be happy to help you with your printing and designing needs for a small fee. Also, local printers will give excellent suggestions for your project.

44. *Use a deep frame box to display special items.*

   Check out the hobby stores for the deep inset frames, or build one yourself. Make it deep enough to put in the special items your loved one enjoyed. How about some fabric from the first prom dress your daughter wore, a favorite toy that was especially liked, or your son's first pair of glasses. There is a lot of room for imagination. For example, siblings in the family could add an item they most remember their brother or sister for. This makes the frame box even more meaningful when it's ready to be hung.

45. *Attend a Survivor's of Suicide (SOS) group.*

   Look in your local paper for the locations of these groups. Many times, they are coordinated with a hospice house or a chaplain. Communicating feelings and developing listening skills in the family are encouraged.

*46. **Attend The Compassionate Friends (TCF) chapter meeting.***

You will find, after attending TCF, that it doesn't matter how or what caused your child's death, *the loss of your child left a big hole in your heart*, an experience shared by everyone else in the group. Compassion and understanding for others will help you deal with your own loss.

*47. **Write your child's life history.***

Sit down as a family and talk about your loved one and the fun things you did together, and if your child was very young. Your grandchildren deserve to remember the memories of your loved one.

(Source:http://www.jaredstory.com/dealing_with_grief104.html. Reprinted with permission.)

TALKING TO CHILDREN ABOUT GRIEF

- Stay physically close to your children. Hugs and cuddling are in order.
- Be honest, but limit their exposure to grim news on television.
- Reassure them of their safety. Ask what they need from you to feel safer.
- Keep communication open between parent and child.
- Be a good listener.
- Talk about feelings and provide outlets for expression: drawing, writing, and talking.
- Share your own feelings and let children offer help to you in your depression and grief.
- Although there is plenty to worry about, keep adult fears for other adults.
- Ask whether children are hearing words they don't know the meaning of; explain these.
- When children ask difficult questions, it's okay to say you don't know the answer.
- Some examples: Why? Is he still alive? Did she suffer? Why didn't God protect him? Answers should reflect your own beliefs, be truthful, and be geared to the child's age level.
- If a child asks a question that really throws you, simply say: "That is a really good question. Let me think about it for a while." Or ask the child what he or she thinks is the answer. This may lead to a good discussion.
- Watch for physical symptoms or unusual behavior: angry outbursts or total passivity.
- Maintain daily routines as much as possible.

- Try to spend extra time with your children, reading, playing games before bed.
- Protect their health; try to see that they get appropriate sleep and exercise.
- Watch for post-traumatic stress disorder, possibly reflected in recurring nightmares, or intense anxiety over a period of time.

Give children something positive to think about, some reason to carry on in spite of the terrible losses that you and they have endured. Example: discuss the way the whole country has become united in grief.

Source: Fitzgerald, H. (2003). American Hospice Foundation, Washington, DC.

STRENGTHS CHILDREN NEED TO LEARN

Information

- There are many types of loss.
- Significant loss makes us grieve.
- Grief is a normal process that takes time.
- There is no timetable for resolving loss.
- Grieving is personal.
- Working through grief is difficult.
- Anger, sadness, loneliness, guilt, frustration, and numbness are normal feelings.
- Grief can be expressed through pictures, talking to others, or writing a poem.
- Expect emotional highs and lows.
- Take breaks from grieving by spending time with friends, listening to music, and doing healthy things.

Sharing Feelings

- Share feelings in discussions and in pictures.
- Ask for help.
- Share your grief.
- Realize that painful feelings do not last forever.

Sharing Beliefs

- Share beliefs about loss and death to help children recognize the power that their thoughts play in affecting feelings and action.
- Challenge irrational beliefs and replace them with rational thoughts and more responsible action.

Taking Action

- Teach that taking action reduces stress.
- Include children in cooking a meal, delivering food, planning part of the service, selecting flowers, or sending cards.
- Emphasize the importance of connecting with the deceased through pictures, mementos, and memories.

Explanations that Don't Help

Children are very literal in their thinking. If an adult says:

- "Grandpa died because he was too old and tired," the child may wonder when he, too, will be too old? and when he is tired, "What is tired enough to die?"
- "Daddy went on a long trip and won't be back for a long time." Then the child may wonder why Daddy didn't say good-bye, or did he do something to cause Daddy to leave?
- "Uncle John was sick and went to the hospital, where he died." Then the child may be afraid to go to the hospital. Also, it's important to explain little illness versus big illness.
- "Grandma will sleep in peace forever." Then the child may be fearful of going to bed or to sleep.
- "It is God's will. God took him because he was so good." The child may decide to be bad so that God won't take him.

Characteristics That Require More Individualized Assistance

1. Bizarre behavior such as self-destruction, hurting animals, giving away possessions, playing with knives
2. Frequent panic attacks; in a state of shock over the loss
3. Socially inappropriate delinquent behaviors, stealing, or vandalism

4. Refuses to socialize with other children
5. Is assessed as suicidal

CONCLUSION

Perhaps nothing in life is more painful than experiencing the loss of a friend or a loved one. Even though most people experience varying degrees of loss, the grief cycle is not fully understood until it comes closer to the heart. When sudden death comes with no time for anticipation, many additional feelings are involved in the grief process. The grief work normally will be longer, lonelier, and more debilitating to lasting emotional stability because of the intensity of the anguish experienced when a loved one is taken suddenly or senselessly. Grief work is not a set of symptoms but rather a process of suffering that marks a transition from an old lifestyle to a new one, punctuated by numbness, denial, anger, depression, and eventually recovery. Different kinds of losses dictate different responses, so not all of these ideas will suit everyone. Equally, no two people grieve alike, in other words, what works for one may not work for another.

**A Parent's Guide for Assisting Young Children
Through Trauma and Loss**

Possible Reactions by Children Under Age 6
Disruption of family routines can make children irritable, angry, and confused or quiet and withdrawn. They long for things to be as they were. Some behaviors include whining, wetting themselves, asking to be fed or dressed, not allowing parents out of their sight, being terrified of crowds, and needing to be continually held.

Children who cling to their parents are expressing fears of separation in a very natural way. Because their security has been threatened (trauma; loss-death, separation, a move), they are trying to prevent anything from disrupting their feeling of being safe and protected. Attaching to special blankets, animals, and so on, or habits such as thumb sucking and nail biting, provide security and comfort.

How You Can Help
- Understand that your child's regressive behavior is normal and is usually temporary.
- Try not to overreact. Relax. Overconcern, nagging, and punishment often cause undesirable behaviors to last longer.
- Acknowledge, encourage, and praise appropriate and positive behavior.
- Spend extra time with your children. Show them they are understood and loved and that you aren't upset by their regressive behavior.
- Clinging children need to know that you will come back. Be patient. Leave when necessary, but don't go without telling them where you are going and that you will return. Give lots of extra praise, love, and attention.
- Keep the family together, especially in the early days after a traumatic event such as disaster or loss. It is natural to want to protect your children and send them away from unpleasant situations, but this may add to their fears, not lessen them. Children need their parents or familiar adults around them as much as possible.
- In the case of disasters, including your children in the cleanup helps to give them needed activity.
- Return to regular family routines as soon as possible. This includes the reestablishment of bedtime schedules and having playmates over. Familiar routines are comforting for a child.

Possible Reactions by Children Ages 6 to 11
At this age, fears and anxieties are based on an increasing awareness of real danger. Loss of prized possessions, especially pets, seems to hold special meaning. Imaginary fears that seem unrelated to the loss may appear as well. Regressive behavior may appear, such as bed-wetting, clinging, and nightmares, sometimes to a marked degree. Where the loss is associated with a disaster, such as a fire, a flood, and so on, weather conditions (thunder, lightning, heavy

**FIGURE 6.2
Fact Sheet for Parents of Elementary Students**

winds) may trigger fears that the disaster will recur. Other reactions can include irritability, disobedience, depression, headaches, and visual or hearing problems.

How You Can Help
- Take your children's fears seriously. A child's fear doesn't have to make sense. A child who is afraid is truly afraid. Don't be angry or make fun. Don't say, "It's silly to be afraid." Rather, say, "I can see you are afraid." or "It is a scary feeling when you think you're all alone." Being told that it is normal to feel afraid is reassuring.
- Listen to what your children tell you. Knowing their fears will help you understand the situation.
- Don't force your children to be brave or to face what frightens them. Help by easing them out of the fear. The stronger the fear, the greater the need to confront it gradually and the longer it will take to overcome. Help by providing a night-light, gradually moving it away; a flashlight by the child's bed; or a friend to sleep overnight.
- Explain the situation as best you can. Situations that are not understood cause the greatest fear. Information helps to normalize the event.
- Provide an atmosphere in which children can talk freely about their fears. Often parents are reluctant to talk, due to the belief that this keeps painful memories alive and harms children. Children who think that their parents don't understand their fears feel ashamed, rejected, unloved, and, consequently, even more afraid.
- Although it is important to demonstrate strength and control to your children, it will not harm them to let them know that you experience fear. Put their feelings into words, such as, "It is a scary feeling when it rains/thunders (etc.)." This encourages children to talk about their own experiences.

Understanding Children's Nighttime Fears
Children may refuse to go to their rooms or be reluctant to sleep by themselves. When they go to bed, they may have difficulty falling asleep. Once asleep, they may awaken frightened, crying, screaming, or shaking with reexperienced terror. Once awake, they may insist on sleeping with their parents or having someone stay near them. They may also express fears of darkness.

Traumatic events and loss naturally increase a child's fear of separation from the parents. It is normal for a child to seek the comfort of a parent's presence. Nightmares provide a way for children to work through strong emotions. The frightening creatures and events encountered are as real as daily life.

To calm your child, differentiate what is real from what is fantasy. To do this, you need to hear what the nightmare was about. Listen without interruptions. Do not deny the fear by saying, "There's nothing to be afraid of." Validate the experience by saying, "That sounds like a frightening experience. I don't blame you for hiding/crying/screaming." Give reassurance that you are near. Allowing the child to sleep on a mattress in your bedroom or in another child's room on a temporary basis might help.

(Continued)

FIGURE 6.2. *Continued*

If a child is having increasing numbers of nightmares or is extremely upset, seek the help of a school counselor, a family doctor, or a public health nurse.

How You Can Help
- Spending increased time with your children during waking hours will help them feel more secure at night.
- Providing opportunities for exercise and vigorous play helps burn off excess tension and creates needed fatigue.
- Providing a comforting bedtime routine (quiet play, telling a story, snuggly toys) contributes to a sense of well-being that is needed to reduce stress. This time also enables children to share anxieties and fears with their parents.
- If your children get out of bed, lead them calmly back, reassuring them of your presence: "I'm here and I love you, but it's time to go to sleep now."
- If your children call to you or cry after being put to bed, go and offer hugs of reassurance. Acknowledge their fear of separation, "It can be scary when you are by yourself." Reassure them of your presence: "We are here. We will protect you and make sure that no harm comes to you." It can be helpful to have a night-light on and the door left open.
- If your children wake up frightened, go to them at once and provide comfort. Try not to turn on a light or talk in a loud voice. Acknowledge the fear, "You must have had a very scary dream."

A Difficult Time
The events of recent days have, no doubt, been upsetting for you and your child. Traumatic events shake the world that we had considered safe and predictable. These events also create a high level of confusion and apprehension. Discussion in the news and on the playground often adds to the disruption.

Children exposed to a loss or a sudden violent event experience intense feelings, including anxiety and fear. These feelings are very normal responses. Children fear injury, death, being separated from their family, and loss. These fears are very real to the child and should be accepted at face value by parents. This isn't to say that these reactions won't be upsetting or confusing, but remember, a wide range of reactions to a loss is normal.

We all recognize the expressions of the crying child, but we aren't always able to recognize the signs and needs of the angry child or the withdrawn child. Sometimes we don't connect certain behavior to the tragedy. This advice is intended to help you, as a parent, to understand and help your children through this difficult time.

Other Sources of Help
Loss and disaster wound many, even those who seem not to be touched by what occurred. There is no shame in expressing your pain, as well as the pain felt by your children. There is also no shame in seeking help from people in the community. School counselors, counseling clinics, Health Department personnel, the clergy, and so on, are just some of the resources available to assist you and your family.

FIGURE 6.2. *Continued*

A Parent's Guide for Assisting Teens Through Trauma and Loss

Assisting Teenagers Through Loss

The loss of people we care for is very painful and confusing. We recognize pain that is expressed by tears, but pain evidenced by withdrawal, hopelessness, and anger can be harder to detect. Sometimes we see pain and grief as short term, so that when certain behaviors appear, we wonder what is behind them.

Adolescents often present an image of strength. Unfortunately, this results in a tendency for emotions to be buried, only to be resurrected later, sometimes in less healthy ways.

The need not to reveal weakness often causes much pain and grief to go unnoticed. These coping strategies may be unwittingly rewarded with comments such as, "You are handling things very well." Though this may appear to be the case, it is often an illusion.

How You Can Help

Although most helping responses occur in the first few weeks after a traumatic event, grief usually lasts longer than anticipated. The effects of grief are often revisited long after the event. These delayed, seemingly unrelated, responses to grief can be baffling. It is important to keep this in mind when dealing with behavior that is uncharacteristic.

- Be a listener. Teens are most helped by genuine concern that is expressed by others listening rather than people seeking to give the "right" piece of advice. Tell teens that grieving lasts longer than anyone expects, although the intensity usually subsides. Certain events, such as birthdays and holidays may result in a "revisitation" of grief.
- Do not avoid talking about the person or the event because you feel that it might reawaken the pain. Avoidance of the topic conveys a lack of caring, rather than the more likely fact that you do not know what to say. Usually, your teenager will want to talk, although it may not come in the fashion or at the time you had planned. Follow the teen's lead and be a listener.
- Try not to make any unnecessary changes during this time of grief and loss. This is not the time to be making an important decision. Attempt to keep the situation as normal as possible.

Perhaps the greatest challenge that you, as a parent, have is to encourage and allow the teen's admission and healthy expression of grief.

(Continued)

FIGURE 6.3
Fact Sheet for Parents of an Adolescent

What to Watch For
Trouble signs to watch for in adolescents following a loss may include

- withdrawal and isolation
- physical complaints (headache, stomach pain)
- emotional concerns (depression, sadness, tension, suicidal thoughts, confusion)
- antisocial behavior (stealing, acting out, aggression, substance abuse)
- school problems (avoidance, disruptive behavior, academic failures)

Most of these are temporary. Teenagers who appear to be withdrawn and who isolate themselves from family and friends may be experiencing emotional difficulties. The need to appear competent may work against their reaching out to others for assistance. Most grief reactions are normal responses to disaster or loss; however, it is imperative that suicidal thinking be treated seriously and that help be sought.

Loss and disaster can thrust teenagers into an adult role. Regardless whether these results occur, it is important that teens give themselves permission to grieve.

Understanding the Grief Process
Although the following stages commonly occur in the grief experience, it is important to remember that grief does not follow a defined pattern. These stages may be experienced repeatedly, in different sequences, and with various intensities.

- **Denial**, such as a person's unwillingness to talk abut the loss, is a shock absorber that temporarily reduces the full impact of the crisis. In the early stages, denial isn't wrong; however, problems can occur if it continues. Give the teenager permission to feel the feeling.
- **Anger or guilt** often occur, due to a person's feeling of powerlessness over the loss. Questions include: How could he or she do this to me? Why would God allow it? How could this happen to someone at our school? Blaming others can also be a common response. It is important to admit the anger, identify the real source of the anger, and understand that is okay to be angry. Seek healthy ways to express it, such as strenuous physical activity, keeping a journal, sketching, or talking with people you trust.
- **Sorrow and depression** are evidenced by some or all of the following: crying, isolation, silence, a loss of energy, and an inability to sleep. Allow and encourage expressions of grief. Emphasize that crying is not a sign of weakness; rather, it is facing and acknowledging a loss. Recording thoughts in a journal can also be very healing. Activity is helpful for depression, although sometimes depression is so deep that even activity seems too difficult. Referral to the family physician is encouraged for depression that persists.

FIGURE 6.3. *Continued*

- **Bargaining** is a means of trying to regain control or to make sense of what has occurred. This often takes the form of a promise to God that things will change if only He does something. The question "Why?" is very naturally asked through all stages but is perhaps most prevalent in the anger and the bargaining phases. The real problem cannot be faced until the "why" is abandoned and the person looks at "who, when, where, and how" things happened. The reality of what has happened cannot be changed.

- **Acceptance and admission** of our powerlessness in the situation are not quickly or easily reached. Having grieved, we can move on with life. Emphasize that acceptance is not a matter of forgetting the person or minimizing the pain. In fact, it is a full acceptance that the loss was real, significant, and painful.

A Difficult Time

The events of recent days have, no doubt, been upsetting for you and your teenager. Traumatic events shake the world that we had considered safe and predictable. These events also create a high level of confusion and apprehension. Discussion in the news and at the school often adds to the disruption.

The experience of a loss or a sudden violent event can produce intense anxiety and fear. These feelings are very normal. Suffering, loss, and death have shattered the teenager's sense of invincibility and immortality. Teenagers often present an image of strength and other forms of "best face forward." Unfortunately, this results in a tendency for emotions to be buried, only to be resurrected later, sometimes in less healthy ways.

The need not to reveal weakness often causes much pain and grief to go unnoticed. These coping strategies may often be unwittingly rewarded with comments such as, "You are handling things very well." Although this may appear to be the case, it is often an illusion.

This advice is intended to help you, as a parent, to understand and help your teenager through this difficult time.

Other Sources of Help

Loss and disaster wound many, even those who seem not to be touched by what occurred. There is no shame in expressing your pain, as well as the pain felt by your teenager. There is also no shame in seeking help from people in the community. School counselors, mental health clinics, Health Department personnel, the clergy, and so on, are just some of the resources available to assist you and your family.

FIGURE 6.3. *Continued*

Chapter 7

Debriefing Survivors After a Crisis, a Disaster, or a Critical Incident

PROCESSING TRAUMA, GRIEF AND LOSS

Debriefing

Trauma essentially overwhelms a person's sense of security, stability, control, connection, and meaning in life. It promotes a sense of fear, helplessness, and isolation in all those affected. For children and adolescents, trauma may directly affect the growth and the development of appropriate responses in a child's brain. It disrupts a child's ability to develop a sense of balance or equilibrium with the world. It compromises the child's sense of safety and security and hinders the developmental process of establishing an identity. If trauma and loss are not processed, they may eventually disrupt the formation of future interpersonal relationships and appropriate social interactions.

School-aged youths are most likely to show severe impairment following a traumatic event: In certain studies, 62% of school-aged samples experienced severe impairment, compared to 39% of adult survivor samples (Rose, Brewin, Andrews, & Kirk, 1999). Problems specific to youths include various behavioral problems and separation anxiety among children and deviance and delinquency among adolescent survivors (Pfefferbaum, Seale, McDonald, Brandt, Rainwater, Maynard, & Miller, 2001). Providing comfort, information, and support and meeting peoples' immediate practical and emotional needs are useful in helping them cope with highly stressful events.

Debriefing helps people to manage and come to terms with the traumatic event and its consequences, in order to return to a normal level of functioning. The degree of understanding and support within the post-trauma environment influences the long-term impact of traumatic events. The principal, the lead counselor, and other key personnel need to be aware of the following:

1. The intensity of the trauma and how to minimize its effects;
2. The specific effects that critical incidents may have on individuals or groups (e.g., gangs, minority youths, adults whose child has been murdered or who have found a dead child);
3. Self-management strategies that will lead to recovery;
4. The best ways to provide support to those who have experienced trauma; and
5. Counseling to bring the people affected to their precrisis equilibrium.

People who may be affected by critical incidents include

1. Those directly exposed to the incidents and who suffered intense trauma;
2. Family, friends, and staff who are grieving for the injured and the affected;
3. Recovery personnel who must maintain functional efficiency during the incident and cope with the psychological effects that come with their job. This includes the critical management team, school counselors, administrators, and emergency service personnel;
4. The surrounding community and people indirectly involved, such as feeder schools, people who were spared from harm because of a chance circumstance (e.g., they often experience survivor guilt), and those for whom stress is triggered as the result of the incident such as unresolved grief from the past.

Debriefing following a crisis or a traumatic event provides structure for individual and group interventions and is critical for working through the grief experience. By adults providing an opportunity to review the facts of the trauma, share emotions, validate individual experiences, learn new coping skills, evaluate current symptoms, and prepare for future experiences, children and adolescents will be able to construct meaning from the event and reach their precrisis equilibrium. Three debriefing strategies (Psychological Debriefing, Critical Incident Stress Debriefing, Post-Traumatic Loss Debriefing) and a family intervention strategy, the Family Safety Watch (for suicidal or high-risk youths) plus Critical Incident Stress Management will be outlined in the following sections.

WHAT RESEARCHERS ARE LEARNING ABOUT TRAUMA IN CHILDREN AND ADOLESCENTS

The National Institute of Mental Health (NIMH), a component of the federal government's National Institutes of Health, supports research on the brain and on the wide range of mental disorders, including post-traumatic stress disorder (PTSD) and related conditions. Recent research findings include the following:

- Some studies show that counseling children very soon after a catastrophic event may reduce some of the symptoms of PTSD. A study of trauma/grief-focused psychotherapy among early adolescents exposed to an earthquake found that brief psychotherapy was effective in alleviating PTSD symptoms and preventing the worsening of co-occurring depression (Everly, Flannery, & Mitchell, 2000).
- Parents' responses to a violent event or a disaster strongly influence their children's ability to recover. This is particularly true for mothers of young children. If the mother is depressed or highly anxious, she may need to get emotional support or counseling in order to be able to help her child (Fullerton, Ursano, Vance, & Wang, 2000).
- Either being exposed to violence within the home for an extended period of time or exposure to a one-time event, like an attack by a dog, causes PTSD in a child (Bisson, McFarlane, & Rose, 2000).
- Community violence can have a profound effect on teachers, as well as students. One study of Head Start teachers who lived through the 1992 Los Angeles riots showed that 7% had severe post-traumatic stress symptoms, and 29% had moderate symptoms. Children also were acutely affected by the violence and anxiety around them. They were more aggressive and noisy and less likely to be obedient or get along with each other (Pynoos, Goenjian, Tashjian, Karakashian, Manijikian, & Manoukian, 1993).
- Research has demonstrated that PTSD after exposure to a variety of traumatic events (family violence, child abuse, disasters, and community violence) is often accompanied by depression (Bryant, Harvey, Guthrie & Moulds, 2000). Depression must be treated along with PTSD, and early treatment is best.
- Inner-city children experience the greatest exposure to violence. A study of young adolescent boys from inner-city Chicago showed that 68% had seen someone beaten up and 22.5% had seen someone shot or killed. Children and adolescents who have been exposed to community violence were more likely to exhibit aggressive behavior or depression within the following year (Brewin, Andrews, Rose, & Kirk, 1999).

The NIMH continues to conduct research into the impact of violence and disaster on children and adolescents. It has been focusing on the emotional, social, and academic effects of exposure to violence. It is particularly important to conduct research to discover which individual, family, school, and community interventions work best for children and adolescents.

THE EMOTIONAL EFFECTS OF A TRAUMATIC EVENT

Children and adolescents, as well as adults who care for them, increasingly experience stressful events on a daily basis. Although there are different levels of coping, some events overwhelm almost everyone's ability to cope. These extraordinary "traumatic" events share several commonalities, according to Ehrenreich (2001, 2002):

- The characteristics or the sheer magnitude of the events make them impossible for any one individual to control.
- The events threaten individuals or their loved ones with death or severe injury; and
- The events create feelings of intense fear, helplessness, terror, and horror.

In the first hours or the first days that follow the traumatic event, a variety of emotional reactions may appear. Some survivors many vacillate from one kind of response to another, may not show a "typical" response, or may not seem to show any evident response at all. Reactions include

- Psychic "numbing": Survivors may seem stunned, dazed, confused, and apathetic. Superficial calmness is followed by denial or attempts to isolate themselves from others. Survivors may report feelings of unreality: "This can't be happening." They may respond to helpers in a passive, docile way or may be rebellious and antagonistic as they try to regain a sense of personal control.
- Heightened arousal: Survivors may experience intense feelings of fear, accompanied by physiological arousal: heart pounding, muscle tension, muscular pains, and gastrointestinal disturbances. They may engage in excessive activity and may express a variety of rational and irrational fears.
- Diffuse anxiety: Survivors may show an exaggerated startle response, an inability to relax, and an inability to make decisions. They may express feelings of abandonment, anxiety about being separated from loved ones, a loss of a sense of safety, and yearning for relief.

- "Survivor's guilt": Survivors may blame themselves or feel shame at having survived when others didn't. There may be a preoccupation with thoughts about the disaster and obsessive rumination over their own activities. Could they have acted differently? They may feel responsible for the unfortunate fate of others.
- Conflicts over nurturance: Survivors may be dependent on others, yet suspicious, and may feel that no one can understand what they have been through. Some survivors may feel a need to distance themselves emotionally to maintain their own self-control. They may be irritable in the face of sympathy. Others may feel a strong desire to be with others at all times.
- Emotional and cognitive instability: Some survivors may show sudden anger and aggressiveness or, conversely, apathy, lack of energy, and an inability to mobilize themselves. They may be forgetful or may cry easily. Feelings of vulnerability and illusions about what happened are common.
- Occasionally, survivors appear to be acutely confused. Hysterical reactions and psychotic symptoms, such as delusions, hallucinations, disorganized, speech, and grossly disorganized behavior, may also appear (Ehrenreich, 2002, p. 6).

Many of the immediate reactions to a traumatic event serve as an adaptive response until the mind is ready to accept the reality of the event. Initially, these responses may seem abnormally intense or entirely unfamiliar, but in actuality they are *normal reactions to an abnormal event.*

How Children and Adolescents React to Trauma

The more direct the exposure to the traumatic event, the higher the risk for the survivor experiencing emotional harm. In a school shooting, the student who is injured probably will be most severely affected emotionally. And the student who sees a classmate shot, even killed, probably will be more emotionally affected than the student who was in another part of the school when the violence occurred. The impact is likely to be greater in the child or the adolescent who previously has experienced child abuse or another trauma. But even secondhand exposure to violence can be traumatic. All children and adolescents exposed to violence or a disaster, even if only through graphic media reports, should be watched for signs of emotional distress.

Reactions to trauma may appear immediately after the traumatic event or days and even weeks later. Loss of trust in adults and fear of the event occurring again are responses seen in many children and adolescents who have been exposed to traumatic events. Other reactions vary according to age.

In children 5 years of age and younger, typical reactions can include a fear of being separated from the parent, crying, whimpering, screaming, immobility or aimless motion, trembling, frightened facial expressions, and excessive clinging. Children might return to behaviors exhibited at earlier ages (called regressive behaviors), such as thumb sucking, bed-wetting, and fear of darkness. Children at this age tend to be strongly affected by the parents' reactions to the traumatic event.

Children 6 to 11 years old may show extreme withdrawal, disruptive behavior, inability to pay attention, or any combination of these. Regressive behaviors, nightmares, sleep problems, irrational fears, irritability, refusal to attend school, and outbursts of anger and fighting are also common in traumatized children of this age. The child may complain of stomach aches or other bodily symptoms that have no medical basis. Schoolwork often suffers. Depression, anxiety, feelings of guilt, and emotional numbing or "flatness" are often present as well.

Adolescents 12 to 17 years old may exhibit responses similar to those of adults, including flashbacks, nightmares, emotional numbing, avoidance of any reminders of the traumatic event, depression, substance abuse, problems with peers, and antisocial behavior. Also common are withdrawal and isolation, physical complaints, suicidal thoughts, school avoidance, academic decline, sleep disturbances, and confusion. The adolescent may feel extreme guilt over his or her failure to prevent injury or loss of life and may harbor revenge fantasies that interfere with recovery from the trauma.

DEBRIEFING IN GENERAL

Debriefing in general is based on the basic principals of listening. Effective listening is a skill developed with training, practice and patience. It is based on the principles shown in Figure 7.1.

Pscyhological Debriefing

Psychological Debriefing is a structured group meeting in which participants review the traumatic event they have experienced and their reactions to it. It is highly directive—people are assisted in reviewing the event and their reactions. It is focused on helping people organize their thoughts about what has happened and their reactions, and it has a strong educative

**Figure 7.1
Debriefing in General**

- *Ask questions* only to facilitate the flow of storytelling. Survivors need to retell their stories.

- *Believe* that the speaker's impressions and reactions are the most important concern.

- *Clarify* what is being said.

- *Discern unspoken messages* from speakers in their body language, voice tone, and facial expression. Learn to notice the feelings under the words.

- *Echo* words or phrases that survivors use, to indicate that you are paying attention and following their stories.

- *Find* new alternative words that repeat or enhance the meaning of the speakers, in order to respond affirmatively to their reactions.

- *Give* information that might help survivors understand the situation more clearly, if it might dispel specific concerns, without arguing with them or answering unasked questions.

- *Help* survivors remember what happened by asking them about the chronology of time during which the event took place and a chronology of what has happened since the event, or asking them to describe the contextual nature of the event, such as colors, sounds, sensations, or impressions.

- *Instill* peace through silence by waiting for survivors to decide when they may want to continue their stories.

- *Journey* with survivors through their narratives. If parts of the story are confusing, ask survivors if they can repeat those parts or remember other things that might help you to understand what they are saying.

- *Keep* your personal values, beliefs, biases, and judgments to yourself, and avoid imposing them on others.

component. The aims of Psychological Debriefing include (Hodgkinson & Stewart, 1998):

- Promoting cognitive organization
- Facilitating the screening of those at risk
- Disseminating educational and referral information
- Decreasing the sense of uniqueness and promoting a sense of universality in reactions to the event
- Mobilizing of school and community resources
- Preparing for reactions that might arise as the result of the trauma
- Reducing unnecessary side effects; in other words, those beyond the normal reactions to a traumatic event
- Identifying of further avenues of help

The recommendations for structured Psychological Debriefing (PD) of youths and adults who have experienced a traumatic event were developed by Foa, Terence, and Friedman (2000). Fundamentally, however, it is important to remind the helping professional that these are only guidelines, and that sensitivity to the emotional state of those involved is most important. Specifically, it is crucial that the timing of these questions and interventions occur when the client is receptive. Above all, those working with children and adolescents, as well as adults, must avoid the retraumatization that can occur through mistimed interventions.

Stage 1: The Introduction

The counselor states that the purpose of the meeting is to review the participants' reactions to the trauma, to discuss these, and to identify methods of dealing with them to prevent future problems. The counselor assumes control and specifies his or her own competence, in order to lend confidence to those attending. Three rules are made explicit: (a) Participants are under no obligation to say anything except why they are there and what their role was vis-à-vis the traumatic event; (b) confidentiality is emphasized in groups, and the members understand not to divulge outside the group what others have said; and (c) the focus of the discussions is on the impressions and the reactions of the participants.

Stage 2: Expectations and Facts

The particulars of what actually happened are discussed in considerable detail, without focusing on thoughts, impressions, and emotional reactions. Participants are encouraged to describe their expectations; that is, did they expect what happened? *(This is believed to focus the individuals on their experiences at the time and may help them to understand why they reacted in the way they did. This is felt to be extremely important in certain situations, for example, witnessing unexpectedly violent behavior can magnify the intensity of a traumatic situation.)*

Stage 3: Thoughts and Impressions

When the facts are being described, thoughts and impressions are evaluated by asking questions such as: "What were your thoughts when you first realized you were (or someone was) injured?" and "What did you do?" This information aims to (a) construct a picture of what happened, (b) put individual reactions into perspective, and (c) help with the integration of traumatic experiences. Sensory impressions in all five modalities are elicited, for example, "What did you see, hear, touch, smell, taste?" The aim is to produce a more realistic reconstruction of the trauma.

Stage 4: Emotional Reactions

This is usually the longest stage in Psychological Debriefing. The earlier questions concerning thoughts and impressions lead to answers that reflect emotions. The counselor attempts to aid the release of emotions with questions about some of the common reactions during the trauma, such as fear, helplessness, frustration, anger, guilt, anxiety, and depression. Emotional reactions experienced since the event are also discussed.

Stage 5: Normalization

After the emotional reactions have been expressed, the counselor's goal is to normalize their acceptance. Stressing that the reactions are "normal reactions to an abnormal event" does this. When more than one person is present in the Psychological Debriefing, it is likely that emotions will be shared. This universality of thoughts, feelings, and emotions helps with the normalization process. The counselor stresses that individuals do not have to experience all of the emotions that normally occur after a trauma, but it is normal to react after a critical incident. The counselor also describes common symptoms that individuals may experience in the future: intrusive thoughts and images, distress when reminded of what happened; attempts to avoid thoughts, feelings, and reminders; detachment from others; loss of interest in things that once gave pleasure; anxiety and a depressed mood; sleep disturbance, including nightmares; irritability, shame, guilt, and anger; and increased startle reactions.

Stage 6: Future Planning/Coping

This stage allows the counselor to focus on ways of managing symptoms should they arise and to attempt to mobilize internal support mechanisms (e.g., discussing coping mechanisms) and external support (e.g., family and friends). Emphasis is on the importance of open discussion of feelings with family and friends; the counselor highlights the possibility of needing additional support from them for a while.

Stage 7: Disengagement

In this stage, other topics are discussed. Leaflets or fact sheets describing normal reactions and how to cope with them can be distributed. Information is also given regarding the need for further help and where it may be obtained if necessary. Participants are advised to seek further help if, for example, (a) psychological symptoms do not decrease after 4 to 6 weeks; (b) psychological symptoms increase over time; (c) there is ongoing loss of function and occupation or family difficulties; or (d) others comment on marked personality changes.

CRITICAL INCIDENT STRESS MANAGEMENT

Debriefing is a specific technique designed to assist others in dealing with the physical or psychological symptoms that are generally associated with trauma exposure. Debriefing allows those involved with the incident to process the event and reflect on its impact. Ideally, debriefing can be conducted on or near the site of the event (Davis, 1992; Mitchell, 1983). Defusing, another component of Critical Incident Stress Management (CISM), allows for the ventilation of emotions and thoughts associated with the crisis event. Debriefing and defusing should be provided as soon as possible but typically no longer than the first 24 to 72 hours after the initial impact of the critical event. As the length of time between exposure to the event and CISM increases, the less effective CISM becomes. Therefore, a close temporal (time) relationship between the critical incident and defusing and initial debriefing (i.e., there may be several debriefing sessions) is imperative for these techniques to be most beneficial and effective (Davis, 1993; Mitchell, 1988).

As crises and disasters become epidemic, the need for effective crisis response capabilities becomes obvious. Crisis intervention programs are recommended and even mandated in a wide variety of community and occupational settings (Everly & Mitchell, 1997). Critical Incident Stress Management (CISM) represents a powerful, yet cost-effective, approach to crisis response procedures (Everly & Mitchell, 1997). Critical Incident Stress Management is a comprehensive, integrative crisis intervention system. CISM is considered comprehensive because it consists of multiple crisis intervention components, which functionally span the entire temporal spectrum of a crisis. CISM interventions range from the precrisis phase through the acute crisis phase and into the post-crisis phase. CISM is considered comprehensive, in that it consists of interventions that may be applied to individuals, small functional groups, large groups, families, organizations, and even communities. The seven core components of CISM are defined as follows and are summarized in Table 7.1:

1. Precrisis preparation. This includes stress management education, stress resistance, and crisis mitigation training for both individuals and organizations.
2. Disaster or large-scale incident, as well as school and community support, programs, including demobilizations, informational briefings, "town meetings," and staff advisement.
3. Defusing. This is a three-phase, structured small-group discussion provided within hours of a crisis for purposes of assessment, triage, and acute symptom mitigation.
4. Critical Incident Stress Debriefing (CISD) refers to the "Mitchell model" (Mitchell & Everly, 1996) a seven-phase, structured group discussion, usually provided 1 to 10 days postcrisis and designed to mitigate acute symptoms, assess the need for follow-up, and, if possible, provide a sense of postcrisis psychological closure.
5. One-on-one crisis intervention/counseling or psychological support throughout the full range of the crisis spectrum.
6. Family crisis intervention, as well as organizational consultation.
7. Follow-up and referral mechanisms for assessment and treatment, if necessary.

Critical Incident Stress Debriefing uses a similar process to that used by NOVA (National Organization for Victims Assistance, 2001), but most people using CISD models address trauma by guiding groups through the following phases:

1. Introduction;
2. The facts of the incident;
3. What participants think about the incident;
4. How participants reacted to the incident;
5. What stress symptoms have been experienced;
6. Education about the incident and subsequent stress; and
7. A conclusion and preparation for the group to go back to their lives and their daily routines (NOVA, 2001, p. 284).

TABLE 7.1
Seven Core Components of Critical Incident Stress Management

Intervention	Timing	Activation	Goals	Format
1. Precrisis preparation	Precrisis phase	Anticipation of crisis	Set expectations Improve coping Stress management	Group Organization
2. Demobilization & staff consult (rescuers); group info. briefing for civilians, schools, and businesses	Postcrisis; or shift disengage-ment	Event-driven	To inform, consult. Allow psychological decompression, stress management.	Large group organization
3. Defusing	Postcrisis (within 12 hrs)	Usually symptom-driven	Symptom mitigation. Possible closure. Triage.	Small group
4. Critical Incident Stress Debriefing (CISD)	Postcrisis (1 to 7 days)	Usually symptom-driven; can be event-driven	Facilitate psychological closure. Symptom mitigation. Triage.	Small group
5. Individual crisis intervention (1:1)	Anytime Anywhere	Symptom-driven	Symptom mitigation. Return to function, if possible. Referral, if needed.	Individual
6. Family CISM organization consultation	Anytime	Either symptom-driven or event-driven	Foster support, communications. Symptom mitigation. Closure, if possible. Referral, if needed.	Organizations
7. Follow-up; referral	Anytime	Usually symptom-driven	Assess mental status. Access higher level of care.	Individual family

(From: Everly, G., & Mitchell, J. T. (1997). *Critical Incident Stress Management (CISM). A New Era and Standard of Care in Crisis Intervention*. Ellicott City, MD: Chevron Publishing.) Re-printed with permission.

CISM is a form of psychological "first aid" and should be used as part of initiatives by the Critical Incident Management Team. Prior training should be a key component of this initiative. This system's approach underscores the importance of using multiple interventions, combined in such a manner as to yield maximum impact to achieve the goal of crisis stabilization and symptom mitigation. The CISD intervention has always been conceived of as one component of a larger functional intervention framework. The effectiveness of CISM programs has been empirically validated through thoughtful qualitative analyses, as well as through controlled investigations and even meta-analyses (Dyregrov, 1997; Everly & Boyle, 1997; Everly & Mitchell, 1997; Flannery, 1998; Mitchell & Everly, 1996). Although the CISM approach to crisis intervention is continuing to evolve, current investigations have clearly demonstrated its value as a tool to reduce human suffering. Future research should focus upon ways in which the CISM process can be made even more effective to those in crisis. Although the roots of CISM can be found in the emergency services professions, dating back to the late 1970s, CISM is now becoming a "standard of care" in many schools, communities, and organizations well outside the field of emergency services (Everly & Mitchell, 1997).

CRITICAL INCIDENT STRESS DEBRIEFING (MITCHELL, 1988A, 1988B)

Critical Incident Debriefing, sometimes called CID or Critical Incident Stress Debriefing (CISD) in the literature, has been developed as a structured intervention to help groups that have been affected by a critical incident. Jeffrey Mitchell of the Department of Emergency Health Services, University of Maryland, developed the Critical Incident Stress Debriefing for use with fire and other emergency response workers who experience traumatic events in their work.

Sometimes an entire class, a staff, or a whole school community is affected as a group by a critical incident. The death of a student or a staff member, a natural disaster occurring during school hours, witnessing of a violent crime, child abuse by a staff member, and other traumatic events can present the need for a group intervention. An adapted form of Mitchell's debriefing method can be used to deal with such situations. Such debriefings are not a substitute for professional counseling or psychotherapy but are an opportunity for the group, whether students or staff members, to sort out the events and to deal with the crisis.

Mitchell's work describes debriefings as structured group discussions that allow individuals to express their reactions to the critical incident and to develop understanding of the event and their own emotions. This process helps the individual to increase his or her own feeling of personal control. Research has indicated that ongoing support is still needed by people who have experienced trauma, even if Critical Incident Stress Debriefing does have a positive short-term effect.

Suggestions for Leading a School Group

The school counselor or sometimes a skilled classroom teacher will be the leader of a debriefing for students. The purpose of a debriefing discussion is not therapy, but rather education that goes beyond what is provided in the classroom when students were first informed of the critical incident. The key actions involve the establishment of ground rules, exploration of facts, sharing of feelings, and learning about future possibilities. If no staff person in the school is trained in critical incident debriefing techniques, then the school Critical Incident Team should find a counselor or another experienced person from outside the school to assist in the group. The style of the leader can vary, but the qualities of warmth, acceptance, and a non-threatening nature, combined with the ability to quietly control the group process, are particularly helpful.

Ground Rules

The leader should set the ground rules for the debriefing session or the discussion. Alternatively, the ground rules may be developed by the group, in order to make members feel more comfortable. These rules may vary, but some commonly used ones include the following:

- Maintain confidentiality. ("What is said here stays here.")
- No put-downs
- No interruptions
- Speak only for yourself

In making any assurance of confidentiality, the leader should remind the group of any limits to confidentiality, such as the duty to report child abuse or endangerment. It is not uncommon for the feelings of trauma after a critical incident to create a climate for disclosure of other traumatic events.

Discussion Format

During group discussion, the leader will need to ensure that each individual has an opportunity to contribute. For example, during the facts and feelings portions of a debriefing, individuals are invited to share what they saw when they experienced the incident, what they have heard about it, and what they have felt. Using the word *felt* can confirm the ambiguity of sensations versus the validity of feelings. Relating the material in a group round robin can allow the reality of the experience to emerge and gives each person an opportunity to participate. The leader will have to decide whether to allow open discussion or keep it controlled. Care must be taken that each individual has an opportunity to share but is not coerced by the group or the leader. If a student appears to need further support, the teacher should immediately refer that person to the school or district counselor or principal.

Managing the appropriate timing for discussion is another decision the leader must make. If the session becomes dominated by an individual or digresses into unproductive discussion, it should be ended. As long as it is focused and constructive, it should go on.

Connections to Past Incidents

As the group members discuss the critical incident and their own responses, students may need to talk about similar incidents they have experienced or heard about in the past. This is normal behavior, as part of the process of sorting out the present experience. The present critical incident may be less serious than a past one, such as the death of a student whom one didn't know bringing up feelings about the death of one's parent.

Children may disclose facts about abuse or family violence in the atmosphere following a critical incident, so group leaders need to ensure that they are knowledgeable about the protocol for reporting abuse and protecting the child. The facilitator will also need to be sensitive to underlying social issues related to the critical incident and feel comfortable discussing them in a frank and honest manner. The leader may need to provide clarification and a balanced understanding of the current crisis in the context of larger issues affecting young people in our society.

1. Introductory Stage

The choice of a facilitator will depend on the nature of the group. In the case of a school staff, the facilitator might be the principal, the school counselor, or a trained community person. For a class of students, the leader will usually be their regular teacher. The person leading the session should be the first to present the facts or any new information about the incident and should also set the basic rules for participation, in order to provide security for the group.

Talking about disturbing events is difficult. Providing a clear structure and an assurance of confidentiality is important. The group needs to be protected from fear of social judgment so that members can risk expressing their feelings. The facilitator sets the tone for the entire session during the introductory phase.

The rules for the session should be stated: (a) No one is required to speak, although people are encouraged to do so; (b) judgment or blaming others will not be allowed; (c) everyone must listen to the others and let them have their say; (d) participants should speak for themselves, not for others; and (e) if anyone is very upset, he or she should still try to stay in the group. If people have to leave to recompose themselves, they may accompanied by one of the counselors, if two are leading the group), but they should return promptly. The proceedings are confidential: no one can talk about what others said outside the group (i.e., no "gossiping").

2. Narrative Stage

In this phase, the aim is sharing facts and collectively creating a picture of what happened. "Tell us who you are and what happened from your perspective. Who would like to start?" Include everyone's account of what happened to him or her (although, again, participants can pass if they choose to). Refrain from focusing on psychological reactions at this point. If participants begin to talk about their reactions, gently steer them back to the "facts."

The participants then discuss the sequence of events surrounding the critical incident and the role each person may have played in the incident or in responding to the incident. During this phase, everyone should have an opportunity to describe the incident from his or her perspective. By the end of this phase, all participants should feel clear about the events and realize that they are not alone in the experience and in their emotional responses to the incident. From this, a shared perspective of the incident will begin to emerge.

3. Reaction Stage

During this stage, members of the group or class are encouraged to explore their feelings in a supportive context. Each person is given an opportunity to share his or her feelings without pressure. Some individuals can still benefit from listening, even if they are not comfortable expressing their feelings in the group. The facilitator needs to ensure that the participants all understand that feelings are not right or wrong; they just are.

Go around the room and ask about people's cognitive reactions at the time of the incident.

1. "What were your first thoughts?
2. "What did you think next?"
3. "What did you do then?"

Then turn to reactions in the aftermath of the events.

1. "What did you think when the event was over?"

Next, shift to reports of feelings, rather than of thoughts. Ask participants to describe their feelings, linking these to their thoughts and appraisals of the situation.

1. "How did you feel then?"
2. "What was the worst thing about the experience for you?"
3. "What aspect of the events caused or causes you the most pain?"

Ask about subsequent reactions (e.g., "that night" or "the next day "). Ask about both physical reactions and emotional symptoms.

Finally, shift back from emotions and explore coping strategies.

1. "How did you deal with it?
2. "How are you dealing with it?"
3. "What do you usually do when you feel this way?"
4. "What has helped you at other times to cope with problems?"
5. "What could you do to help yourself next time you feel this way?"
6. "Were there any positive aspects of the experience?" (With relief workers, helping them identify positive or hopeful memories is especially important, because it may help them return to their relief work).

4. Teaching or Education Stage

During the session, the helping professional teaches or reviews for the group the nature of normal reactions to a critical incident, as well as anticipated reactions. The group learns about post-traumatic responses, so that members can validate the normalcy of their individual experiences. Misconceptions are cleared up and the group is informed of other resources, such as the school counselors or employee assistance services. Summarize the session, bringing together the narratives and the responses (thoughts, actions, feelings).

Warn participants that their symptoms may not subside instantly and that new symptoms may appear. Recognize the potential for some difficult times. Hold out the expectation that this will be for a limited time. Be realistic, though, because it can take months or even a year or more for symptoms to subside. *At the same time, teach participants that symptoms are not universal and that a lack of symptoms is just as "normal" as having symptoms. Teach techniques of stress management (e.g., relaxation exercises).*

Emphasize the importance of getting rest, having a good diet, getting exercise. Encourage talking with others. Encourage identifying concrete steps they need to pursue. *Identify those who need immediate help (e.g., desensitization of phobic symptoms). Arrange for follow-up or referral.* Community resources, beyond the school district, can be discussed. A list of community resources should be made available to students, parents, and staff.

5. Closure Stage

A debriefing can be a significant event in the lives of the staff or the class members and can affirm group cohesiveness and the school's sense of community. In the final phase of the meeting, the group may decide to devise some plan of action to regain a feeling of at least partial control over fate. The facilitator should invite the group or individuals to a further discussion at a later date so that they will know that support can continue past this session.

The group's sense of security needs to be established by a return to a normal routine at the end of the debriefing session. The critical incident has been a disruption, and changes in routine that were made to deal with the critical incident further disrupt people's lives. Plans designed to provide support can themselves become unsettling. A sense of hope and continuity will be provided by a return to the normal daily routine. The facilitator should firmly lead the group back to the normal routine and at the same time be sensitive to people who are not ready and need immediate support from a mental health professional or a counselor.

POST-TRAUMATIC STRESS DEBRIEFING

Post-traumatic stress debriefing offers a therapeutic structure to "work through" the experience of traumatic loss and the accompanying stress. Talking about the death and related anxieties in a secure environment provides a means to work through the experience and serves to prevent destructive fantasy building. Because loss is so painful emotionally, however, our natural tendency (personally or professionally) is to deny loss or to avoid coming to terms with it. Inherently, loss is a process that extends over time and, more often than not, has a lifelong impact. The tasks of mourning and grief counseling include the following:

- To accept the reality of the loss and to confront the fact that the person is dead. Initial denial and avoidance are replaced by the realization of the loss.
- To experience the pain of grief. It is essential to acknowledge and to work through this pain, or it will manifest itself through self-defeating behavior(s).

- To adjust to an environment in which the deceased is missing. The survivor(s) must face the loss of the many roles the deceased person filled in his or her life.
- To withdraw emotional energy and reinvest it in another relationship. Initial grief reaction to loss may be to make a pact with oneself never to love again. One must become open to new relationships and opportunities.
- To accept the pain of loss when dealing with the memory of the deceased.
- To express sorrow, hostility, and guilt overtly and to be able to mourn openly.
- To understand the intense grief reactions associated with the loss, for example, to recognize that such symptoms as startle reactions, restlessness, agitation, and anxiety may temporarily interfere with one's ability to initiate and maintain normal patterns of activity.
- To come to terms with anger, which often is generated toward the one who has died, toward the self, or toward others—to redirect the sense of responsibility that somehow one should have prevented the death.

10 Ways to Recognize Post-Traumatic Stress Disorder

Post-traumatic stress disorder (PTSD) is in many ways a normal response to an abnormal situation. Clearly, the tragedies that occurred on September 11, 2001, were unprecedented. After a tragic event, it is likely that many will experience a variety of symptoms and emotions. Sometimes, however, these symptoms surface several weeks or months after the tragedy. This is called post-traumatic stress disorder. Recognizing these symptoms is the first step toward recovery and finding appropriate treatment. Symptoms include

1. Reexperiencing the event through vivid memories or flash backs
2. Feeling "emotionally numb"
3. Feeling overwhelmed by what would normally be considered everyday situations and having diminished interest in performing normal tasks or pursuing usual interests
4. Crying uncontrollably
5. Isolating oneself from family and friends and avoiding social situations
6. Relying increasingly on alcohol or drugs to get through the day
7. Feeling extremely moody, irritable, angry, suspicious, or frightened
8. Having difficulty falling or staying asleep, sleeping too much, or experiencing nightmares

9. Feeling guilty about surviving the event or being unable to solve the problem, change the event, or prevent the disaster
10. Feeling fear and a sense of doom about the future

With chronic PTSD, anxiety and depression are also prevalent. The particular pattern of the emotional reaction and the type of response will differ with each survivor, depending on the relationship with the deceased, circumstances surrounding the death, and coping mechanisms of the survivors. Grinspoon (1991) provided 16 suggestions that counselors can utilize when dealing with a client who is experiencing PTSD:

• Provide a safe environment for confronting the traumatic event.
• Link events emotionally and intellectually to the symptoms.
• Restore identity and personality.
• Remain calm while listening to horrifying stories.
• Anticipate one's own feelings or responses and coping skills—dread, disgust, anger at clients or people who had hurt them, guilt, anxiety about providing enough help.
• Avoid overcommitment or detachment.
• Avoid identifying with the client or seeing oneself as a rescuer.
• Tell the client that change may take some time.
• Introduce the subject of trauma to ask about terrifying experiences and about specific symptoms.
• Moderate extremes of reliving and denial while the client works through memories of trauma.
• Provide sympathy, encouragement, and reassurance.
• Try to limit external demands on the client.
• During periods of client numbing and withdrawal, pay more attention to the traumatic event itself.
• Help the client bring memories to light by any means possible, including dreams, association, and fantasies.
• Use photographs, and old medical records (for children, play therapy, dolls, coloring books, and drawings).
• Employ special techniques, systematic desensitization, and implosion to eliminate conditioned fear of situations that evoke memories and to achieve catharsis.
• Facilitate group therapy.

POST-TRAUMATIC LOSS DEBRIEFING (THOMPSON, 1990, 1993)

Post-traumatic loss debriefing provides immediate support for survivors of violence, suicide, homicide, or sudden loss. School counselors, administrators, and mental health professionals need to develop systematic strategies to intervene with survivors. Diminished responsiveness to one's immediate environment with "psychic numbing" or "emotional anesthesia" usually begins soon after the traumatic event. Sometimes the stress reactions appear immediately after the traumatic event, or a delayed reaction may occur weeks or months later.

The sudden, unexpected death of someone by suicide or the sudden loss from an accidental death often produces a characteristic set of psychological and physiological responses among survivors. People exposed to traumatic events such as suicide or sudden loss often manifest the following stress reactions: *irritability, sleep disturbance, anxiety, startle reaction, nausea, headache, difficulty concentrating, confusion, fear, guilt, withdrawal, anger, and reactive depression.*

The ultimate contribution of suicide or sudden loss intervention with survivor groups is to create an appropriate and meaningful opportunity to respond to suicide or sudden death.

Post-traumatic loss debriefing is a structured approach toward understanding and managing physical and emotional responses of survivors and their loss experiences. It creates a supportive environment to process blocked communication, which often interferes with the expression of grief or feelings of guilt, and to correct distorted attitudes toward the deceased as well as to discuss ways of coping with the loss. The purpose of the debriefing is to reduce the trauma associated with the sudden loss, to initiate an adaptive grief process, and to prevent further self-destructive or self-defeating behavior. Allowing for a ventilation of feelings and an exploration of symbols associated with the event, as well as enabling mutual support, will accomplish the goals.

Post-traumatic loss debriefing is composed of six stages: introductory stage, fact stage, feeling stage, reaction stage, learning stage, and closure stage. Post-traumatic loss debriefing is a structured approach to the management of the acute emotional upset that affects one's ability to cope emotionally, cognitively, or behaviorally to the crisis situation. Successful resolution and psychological well-being are dependent upon interventions that prepare individuals for periods of stress and help survivors return to their precrisis equilibrium.

A debriefing should be organized 24 to 72 hours after the death. Natural feelings of denial and avoidance predominate during the first 24 hours. The debriefing can be offered to all people affected by the loss. The tone must be positive, supportive, and understanding.

I. Description of Introductory Stage

This stage includes brief introductions to the debriefing process and an establishment of rules for the process.

- Acting as caregiver-as-facilitator, define the nature, limits, roles, and goals within the debriefing process.
- Clarify time limits, the number of sessions, confidentiality, possibilities, and expectations to reduce the unknowns and anxiety for survivors.
- Encourage members to remain silent outside the group regarding details of the debriefing, especially details that could be associated with a particular individual.
- Assure participants in a debriefing that the open discussion of their feelings will in no way be utilized against them under any circumstances.
- Give reassurances that the caregiver-as-facilitator will continue to maintain an attitude of unconditional positive regard. Reduce the survivors' initial anxieties to a level that permits them to begin talking.

II. Description of Fact Stage

This stage includes the warm-up, gathering information, and recreating the event. During the fact phase, participants are asked to recreate the event for the therapist. The focus of this stage is on facts, not on feelings. Encourage individuals to engage in a moderate level of self-disclosure statements, such as, "I didn't know. . . . Could you tell me what that was for you?" Try to achieve an accurate sensing of the survivor's world and communicate that understanding to him or her.

Be aware of the survivors' choices of topics regarding the death to gain insight into their priorities for the moment. Help survivors to see the many factors that contributed to the death, to curtail self-blaming. Ask group members to make a brief statement regarding their role, relationship with the deceased, how they heard about the death, and circumstances surrounding the event. Have group members take turns in adding details to make the incident come to life again. This low initial interaction is a nonthreatening warm-up and naturally leads into a discussion of feelings in the next stage. It also provides a climate to share the details about the death and to intervene to prevent secrets or rumors that may divide survivors.

III. Description of Feeling Stage

This stage includes the expression of feelings surrounding the event and an exploration of symbols. At this stage, survivors should have the opportunity to share the burden of feelings that they are experiencing and to be able to do so in a nonjudgmental, supportive, and understanding environment. Survivors must be permitted to talk about themselves, to identify and to express feelings, to reveal their own behavioral reactions, and to relate to the immediate present—that is, the "here and now."

An important aspect of this stage is for the caregiver-as-facilitator to communicate acceptance and understanding of the survivor's feelings. Acceptance of the person's feelings often helps him or her to feel better immediately. It also can serve as a developmental transition to a healthier coping style in the future. Thoughtful clarification of or reflection on feelings, rather than self-depreciation and self-pity, can lead to growth and change.

Each person in the group is offered an opportunity to answer these and a variety of other questions regarding his or her feelings. Often survivors will confront the emotion of anger and where the feeling is directed. It is important that survivors express thoughts of responsibility regarding the event and process the accompanying feelings of sadness.

At this stage, care is to be taken to assure that no one gets left out of the discussion, and that no one dominates the discussion at the expense of others. At times, the therapist has to do very little. Survivors have a tendency to start talking, and the whole process goes along with only limited guidance from the therapist. People will most often discuss their fears, anxieties, guilt, frustration, anger, and ambivalence. All of their feelings—positive or negative, big or small—are important and need to be listened to and expressed. More important, however, this process allows survivors to see that subtle changes are occurring between what happened then and what is happening now.

IV. Description of Reaction Phase

This stage includes an explanation of cognitive and physical reactions and of the ramifications of the stress response. This stage explores the physical and cognitive reactions to the traumatic event. Acute reactions can last from a few days to a few weeks. Inherently, the survivor wants to move toward some form of resolution and articulates that need in terms such as "I can't go on like this anymore"; "Something has got to give"; "Please help me shake this feeling"; or "I feel like I'm losing my mind." Typical anxiety reactions are a sense of dread, fear of losing control, or the inability to focus or to concentrate.

- The caregiver-as-therapist asks such questions as "What reactions did you experience at the time of the incident or when you were informed of the death?" and "What are you experiencing now?"
- The caregiver-as-therapist encourages clients to discuss what is going on with them in their peer, school, work, and family relationships.
- To help clarify reactions, the caregiver-as-therapist may provide a model for describing reactions, such as the focus of "ownership plus feeling word plus description of behavior." For example, "I am afraid to go to

sleep at night since this has happened," or "I feel guilty about not seeing the signs that he was considering suicide."

V. Description of Learning Stage

This stage includes the understanding of post-traumatic stress reactions to loss. This stage is designed to assist survivors in learning new coping skills to deal with their grief reactions. It is also therapeutic to help survivors realize that others are having similar feelings and experiences. The caregiver-as-therapist assumes the responsibility to teach the group members something about their typical stress response reactions. The emphasis is on describing how typical and natural it is for people to experience a wide variety of feelings, emotions, and physical reactions to any traumatic event. It is not unique but is a universally shared reaction. Crucial to this stage is being alert to danger signals, in order to prevent negative destructive outcomes from a crisis experience and to help survivors return to their precrisis equilibrium and interpersonal stability.

This stage also serves as a primary prevention component for future self-defeating or self-destructive behaviors, by identifying the normal responses to a traumatic event in a secure, therapeutic environment with a caring, trusted adult.

VI. Description of the Closure Stage

The closure stage includes a wrap-up of loose ends, questions and answers, final reassurances, action planning, referrals, and follow-up. Human crises that involve post-traumatic stress often, if debriefed appropriately, serve as catalysts for personal growth. This final stage seeks to wrap-up loose ends and to answer outstanding questions.

THE FAMILY SAFETY WATCH

The Family Safety Watch is an intensive intervention strategy to prevent the self-destructive behavior of a family member (e.g., a suicidal adolescent). The safety watch can also apply to such problems as depression, self-mutilation, eating disorders, and drug or alcohol abuse. The procedure is as follows:

☑
❑ Family members conduct the watch. They select people to be involved in the watch from among their nuclear family, extended family, and network of family friends.

❏ An around-the-clock shift schedule is established to determine what the youth is to do with his or her time over a 24-hour period, that is, when the youth will sleep, eat, attend class, do homework, play games, view a movie, and so on, according to a structured, planned schedule.

❏ The case manager consults with the family in:
  • Determining what the family resources and support systems are;
  • Figuring out ways to involve these support systems in the effort (e.g., "How much time do you think Uncle Harry can give to watching your son or daughter?");
  • Designing a detailed plan for the safety watch; and
  • Figuring out schedules and shifts so that someone is with the at-risk child 24 hours per day.

❏ A back-up system is also established so that the person on watch can obtain support from others if he or she needs it. A cardinal rule is that the child be within view of someone at all times, even while in the bathroom or when sleeping.

❏ The family is warned that the at-risk youth may try to manipulate situations to be alone for example, pretend to be fine—and that the first days will be the hardest.

❏ A contractual agreement is established that if the watch is inadvertently slackened or compromised, and the at-risk youth makes a suicide attempt or tries to challenge the program in some way, the regime will consequently be tightened. This is a therapeutic move that reduces the family's feeling of failure should a relapse occur.

The primary goal of the watch is to mobilize the family members to take care of their "own" and to feel competent in doing so. With tasks surrounding the watch, the family, the youth, and helping professionals team up to collaborate in determining what the adolescent must do in order for everyone to relax and ultimately terminate the watch. Task issues should focus around personal responsibility, age-appropriate behavior, and handling of family and social relationships, such as the following:

☑

❏ Arise in the morning without prompting.
❏ Complete chores on time.
❏ Substitute courteous and friendly behavior for grumbling and sulking.
❏ Talk to parents and siblings more openly.
❏ Watch less TV and spend more time with friends and significant others.

The decision to terminate the watch is made conjointly by the family and the therapeutic team. It is contingent on the absence of self-destructive behavior, as well as on the achievement of an acceptable level of improvement in the other behavioral tasks assigned to the adolescent. If any member of the therapeutic team feels there is still a risk, the full safety watch is continued.

This approach appeals to families because it makes them feel empowered and useful and reduces the expense of an extended hospital program. It also reestablishes the intergenerational boundary, opens up communication within the family, reconnects the nuclear and the extended families, and makes the youth feel cared for and safe. In addition, it functions as a "compression" move that pushes the youth and the family members closer together and holds them there, while awaiting the rebound or disengagement that almost inevitably follows. This rebound is often a necessary step in bringing about appropriate distance within enmeshed subsystems, opening the way for a more viable family structure—a structure that does not require a member to exhibit suicidal or self-destructive behavior to get someone's needed attention

WHEN A STUDENT DIES: GUIDELINES FOR CLASSROOM DISCUSSION

1. Review the facts and dispel rumors.
   Possible discussion question: "What have you heard and what have people said?"
2. Share your own reactions with the class and encourage students to express their reactions in a way appropriate for them, noting that people react in many ways and that is okay.
   Possible discussion question: "What was it like for you when you first heard the news?"
3. Inform students of locations for grief support; reassure students that any adult in the building is available for support.
   Possible discussion question: "How can you students help each other through this?"
4. Listen to what students have to say. It is important not to shut off discussion.
   Possible discussion question: "I think talking about this today is more important than our scheduled lesson. Let's just talk and see how everyone is feeling."
5. Talk with students about their concerns regarding "what to say" to other bereaved students and to the family of the deceased. If applicable, share information about the deceased's culture (beliefs and ceremonies) that will help students understand and respond comfortably to the affected family.
   Possible discussion question: "If you were a member of (the student's) family, what do you think you would want at a time like this?"

6. If the student died of an illness and it is appropriate to do so, discuss the illness. This is especially useful for younger children, who may need to differentiate between the illness of the child who died and any medical problems of other people the child knows.
   Possible discussion question: "So and so had this illness for a long time. What do you know (want to know) about it?"

7. If a suicide occurs, discuss facts and myths about suicide.
   Possible discussion question: "What do you know about the facts and myths about suicide?"

8. Allow students to discuss other losses they have experienced. Help them understand that this loss often brings up past losses; this is a normal occurrence.
   Possible discussion question: "You know, whenever I hear about someone dying I think of my past losses, is anyone experiencing the same thing?"

9. Encourage students to discuss their feelings with their parents and families.

Source: Schuurman, D., & Lindholm, A. B. (2002). Teens and Grief. *The Prevention Researcher,* 9(2), p. 5.

CONCLUSION

The effects of trauma in childhood can be found both immediately and after a long period of time. Trauma changes those involved. Knowing what to look for in children can lead caring adults to seek professional assistance. Postvention should be a key part of your critical incident management plan. If not processed, many children will manifest such behaviors as acute anxiety, separation anxiety, and school phobia. Acknowledging and processing after a traumatic event can reclaim schools as a safe place to work and learn. It is important, too, to revisit the variety of stages following a trauma that children go through so that adults can better understand them emotionally after the crisis or the critical incident.

Chapter 8

Activities for Children
and Adolescents
to Process Loss and Grief

BEHAVIORS AND REACTIONS ADULTS CAN EXPECT
FROM THEIR STUDENTS

The manner in which children and adolescents react to crisis situations is dependent on many variables, such as personal history, personality, severity of and proximity to the event, level of social support, and the type and the quality of intervention (the component that is the most neglected because of our reluctance to process grief and loss). The following are often seen as immediate reactions to a significant crisis:

- Shock, numbness
- Denial or inability to acknowledge that the situation has occurred
- Dissociative behavior—appearing dazed, apathetic, expressing feelings of unreality
- Confusion
- Disorganization
- Difficulty making decisions
- Suggestibility (Learner & Shelton, 2001)

It is important to clarify that most children will recover from the effects of a crisis or a critical event with adequate support from family, friends, and school personnel. However, some children and adolescents may not get the support from their families that they need because many come from single-parent homes, foster care, or skip-generation parents, where their primary needs are physical and safety needs (i.e., to survive). Nonetheless, their response to a crisis can still be viewed as "a normal response to an abnormal event." Although the emotional effects of the crisis can be significant and can potentially influence functioning for weeks to months, most children will have a full recovery. It is the responsibility of every classroom teacher, regardless of grade level, to be prepared for all situations. Inevitably, death will enter the classroom, affecting students and their learning, as well as teaching. Following are descriptions of responses likely to be observed in children and adolescents ((Learner & Shelton, 2001):

- **Increased Fears and Anxiety.** Children and adolescents may again become afraid of situations they mastered long ago. They may become fearful of the dark and refuse to go to bed alone. A school phobia may emerge, in which the child refuses to go to school for fear of something bad happening or fear of leaving his or her parents. Children may openly verbalize their fear of the crisis occurring again in the school. It's important that parents do not allow children to remain home as a means of dealing with their anxiety. This will result in the anxiety increasing once the child needs to return to school. Due to the increase in fears, additional demands will be made for parent attention and support. Adolescents may experience a more generalized anxiety and not the specific types of fears seen in younger children. If they lack coping skills, adolescents may begin self-medicating with alcohol.
- **Decreased Academic Performance and Poor Concentration.** Given the increase in anxiety and the disruption that a crisis can have on children's sense of safety and security, there is a decrease in the amount of mental energy and focus that is available for them to learn and complete assignments.
- **Increased Aggression and Oppositional Behavior, and Decreased Frustration Tolerance.** Children who have been exposed to a crisis can experience difficulty in controlling their anger and frustration. Situations that would have caused a heightened emotional response prior to the crisis can result in an aggressive response, an expression of frustration, or both. Adolescents may also exhibit an increase in oppositional behavior, refusing to live by the rules and regulations of the home and the school or to meet their responsibilities (e.g., chores, academic assignments). Some adolescents may resort to antisocial behavior (e.g., stealing).
- **Increased Irritability, Emotional Liability, and Depressive Feelings.** Children can also exhibit stronger and more variable emotional responses to situations. There could be symptoms of depression that include a general sense of sadness, difficulty falling and remaining asleep or sleeping more than normal, a change in eating habits, a loss of interest in activities once enjoyed, social withdrawal, mental and physical fatigue,

suicidal ideation, or any combination of these. In younger children there may be an increase in irritability and moodiness.

WHAT CLASSROOM TEACHERS CAN DO TO ADDRESS THEIR STUDENTS' CRISIS REACTIONS

Teachers are unavoidably on the "front lines" during a crisis or a critical situation, and students often take cues from them as to how to react. Teachers have spent the most time with their students and often know them better than anyone else does in the school. Therefore, if prepared, teachers are in the optimal position to provide early and ongoing intervention. This is often difficult because they must remain composed and in control for the benefit of their students at a time when they themselves may be experiencing a flood of emotions in response to the crisis. Following are interventions that teachers can provide to address the reactions of their students to a crisis situation:

- After obtaining the facts regarding the crisis, classroom teachers should accurately and honestly explain what has happened to their students. Their students should be given the information in a manner that they can understand.
- Teachers, can—and, most of the time, should—consult with school counselors who are trained in crisis response and crisis intervention about how to most effectively address their students' reactions to the crisis.
- It is often helpful when teachers model appropriate expressions of feelings for their students and let students know that they have permission to verbalize what they are experiencing. It is important that teachers remain in control of their own emotions while dealing with their students, an enormous task that may be difficult, given that teachers themselves may have been significantly affected by the crisis.
- Education of students regarding likely responses to the crisis is essential. Students should not feel that they are "abnormal" or that they are "going crazy." Explaining to students that they will likely have a "normal reaction to an abnormal situation" can be helpful for them.
- Students need to be warned that they may experience waves of strong emotions and should be coached on how to effectively deal with these (e.g., by talking to others, looking to others for support).
- Classroom teachers should be vigilant for students who are experiencing significant difficulty in comparison to their peers and who may require additional and more individualized crisis intervention.
- It is imperative that students, as a group, be given the opportunity to discuss their feelings and reactions to the crisis situation. The world as

they know it is under constant threat, and their security is undermined. This can lead to a form of existential depression. They need to be able to discuss these feelings and know that others similarly share their fears and reactions.

- When students discuss their feelings, teachers need to listen in a noncritical and nonjudgmental manner, with empathy, compassion, and support. It is important that teachers communicate to the students that they understand the students' feelings. Students who are hesitant to verbalize their feelings should be encouraged to do so, but demands to verbalize should be avoided.
- Students should be given the opportunity to express themselves through other modes of communication (e.g., writing, drawing, or music), especially those students who have difficulty expressing feelings.
- Teachers can structure classroom activities and assignments and homework assignments that address students' feelings regarding the crisis or the critical incident. Assignments that are a catalyst for group discussions are best and may facilitate empowerment and a shared learning experience when many individuals feel a sense of hopelessness, helplessness, and despair.
- During these initial conversations, try to understand what the children think about divorce or death. Do they have a view of an afterlife? Do they place the blame for a divorce on one party or another? The more you understand how the children think about death or divorce, the easier it will be for you to talk about these topics in a meaningful way.
- If children sense that you are upset by the loss, they may not bring up the topic even when they want to. Be a good role model, showing children how to express emotions in a healthy and nondisruptive fashion. It can be very helpful for children to know that you have been affected by the event and that you are willing to talk about how you feel.
- Help the children understand how devastated their grieving classmate feels. Explain that this child may be more tired than usual, more irritable, and less interested in playing. Advise them that their classmate may want to talk about the loss, and encourage them to listen.
- Tell the children that this is a completely out-of-bounds topic for teasing. You can teach the children to respect the grieving process and to avoid the emotional tender spots of a child. Also, help children understand that this will be a long process and a major challenge for their classmate.

GENERAL GUIDELINES FOR PROCESSING LOSS IN THE CLASSROOM

- Gather as many facts as possible after the death occurs, be prepared to stop rumors, and be truthful about the death.

- Share your own feelings of loss and grief.
- Be open and honest—if the answer to children's questions is unknown, tell them so.
- Explain funeral rituals, customs, and services.
- Be understanding of students' feelings of anger, fear, and guilt.
- Expect children to function in the classroom—encourage them to try to complete their work.
- Be flexible with schedules, assignments, and schoolwork; children who are grieving have short attention spans and may have difficulty concentrating on tasks.
- Be patient with children who talk constantly about the person who died.
- Remember that grieving takes time and children often fluctuate between stages of grief.
- MOST IMPORTANT: Be available when children need to talk—encourage open communication and acceptance.
- Discuss and prepare for the funeral (what to expect, people's reactions, what to do, what to say).
- Encourage mutual support.
- Discuss ways to cope with traumatic situations.
- Discuss the stages of grief.
- Encourage students to keep a journal of events and of their reactions, especially in an ongoing situation.
- Respect the preferences of children who do not want to participate in class discussions about the traumatic event. Do not force a discussion or repeatedly bring up the catastrophic event; doing so may retraumatize children.
- Hold in-school sessions with entire classes, with smaller groups of students, or with individual students. These sessions can be very useful in letting students know that their fears and concerns are normal reactions. Many counties and school districts have teams that will go into schools to hold such sessions after a disaster or an episode of violence. Involve mental health professionals in these activities, if possible.
- Be sensitive to cultural differences among children. In some cultures it is not acceptable to express negative emotions, and the child who is reluctant to make eye contact with a teacher may not be depressed but may simply be exhibiting behavior appropriate to his or her culture.
- Encourage children to develop coping and problem-solving skills and age-appropriate methods for managing anxiety.
- Hold meetings for parents to discuss the traumatic event, their children's response to it, and how they and you can help. Involve mental health professionals.

Honor the deceased by:

- Writing a eulogy
- Writing stories about the victim
- Placing a collection box in school for notes to the family
- Designing a yearbook page commemorating the deceased
- Composing and practicing a song in memory of the deceased
- Supporting a cause the deceased supported
- Collecting and displaying memorabilia
- Planting a tree, building a sculpture, or painting a mural
- Starting a new school activity, such as a SADD (Students Against Drunk Drivers) unit if a child was killed by a drunk driver

Possible Classroom Activities after a Loss

- Use journal writing to help children work through their feelings: students may record their memories of the person or describe their feelings about death.
- Dedicate and decorate a bulletin board in the school to the memory of the deceased student or faculty member.
- Draw or paint pictures of the deceased or of a remembered activity with that person.
- Display a deceased student's work.
- Help students create a memorial book that contains writings, pictures, letters, or small mementos connected to the person who died.
- Make a collage of pictures or words cut from magazines that reminds students of the person who died.
- Create a special art project, such as a mural, pottery, or weaving, in memory of the deceased.
- Reach out to the family members of the deceased person by talking with them about the person who died.
- Use journal writing to help children and adolescents work through their feelings about death
- Start a fund in honor of the student or the faculty member who died. Use the money to purchase books for the school library. Inside each book bought with the money, place a bookplate that honors the person who died.
- Write letters, stories, and poems about the deceased person to send to the family.
- Have a memorial service at the school so that faculty and students can honor the deceased.
- Read books about death and grief.
- Writing a reaction paper.

- Discuss historical precedents about issues related to the crisis.
- Write a "Where I was when it happened" report.
- Investigate laws governing similar incidents.
- Conduct a mock trial if laws were broken.
- Debate controversial issues.
- Read books about loss.

Other Therapeutic Interventions

Storytelling

Oral or written storytelling is among the methods that can be used to help children reenact their experiences in a constructive manner. Encouraging group discussion after each child relates his or her story allows the children to assist each other.

Write a story about the frightening event. It might start with: "Once upon a time, there was a terrible____and it scared us all. This is what happened:_____" Be sure to end with, "And now we are safe."

Art Projects

Encouraging children to draw what they have felt, wished, or dreamed after a disaster allows them to express their feelings. Like storytelling, the drawings can be shared during a period of group discussion. Nonverbal activities promote the sharing of feelings and the beginning of grieving. Encourage children to draw or paint pictures of how they feel about their experiences. Hang these at the child's level to be seen easily.

Group Projects

In a discussion led by their teacher, children can talk about what they could do to assist with the recovery efforts. Examples include gathering books and toys for the relief effort or working together on a clean-up project, especially in schools that have been seriously affected. During the disaster and during recovery, there are many concerns about child care. Where are children safe? Who can watch them while parents are busy "fighting the disaster" or assisting with a clean-up?

Some possibilities are churches, clergy/members, child-care facilities, relatives, certain high school students, or older people in the community. Check for afterschool or summer school activities; this would give the child a meaningful place to be and would free your time for dealing with the crisis. Other ideas include library programs, foster grandparent agencies, the 4-H Club, church youth groups, and child-care centers.

TABLE 8.1
Traumatic Symptoms and Therapeutic Interventions

Preschool through Second Grade

Traumatic Symptoms	Therapeutic Interventions
Helplessness and passivity	Provide support, rest, food, activities, and drawing.
Generalized fear	Reestablish adult protective shield.
Mental confusion about the event	Give repeated concrete clarification of events.
Difficulty identifying what is bothering them	Provide emotional labels for common re-actions.
Lack of verbalization; traumatic play	Help verbalize feelings, complaints, and loneliness.
Attributing magical qualities to the trauma	Separate what happened from physical reminders.
Sleep disturbances; nightmares	Encourage them to let their parents/teachers know.
Anxious attachment; separation anxiety	Provide constant caretaking and assurances of your return.
Regression symptoms (e.g., thumb sucking)	Tolerate regressive symptoms for a short time.
Anxieties about death; fantasy for fixing the dead	Give explanations about the physical reality of death.

Third through Fifth Grade

Traumatic Symptoms	Therapeutic Interventions
Preoccupation with their actions during the event Issues of responsibility and guilt emerge	Help them to express their secretive imagining re: the event.
Specific fears triggered by traumatic reminders	Help them to articulate traumatic reminders and anxieties.
Retelling and replaying of the event (traumatic play)	Talk/act it out; address distortions; acknowledge normal feelings.
Fear of being overwhelmed by their feelings	Encourage expressions of fear, anger, sadness.
Impaired concentration and learning	Tell them to let adults know when thoughts and feelings interfere with learning.
Sleep disturbances	Provide information on why we have bad dreams.
Concern about their own and other's safety	Share worries; reassure with realistic information.
Altered and inconsistent behavior	Help cope with impulse control and angry feelings.

TABLE 8.1
Continued

Traumatic Symptoms	Therapeutic Interventions
Somatic complaints	Identify the physical sensations they felt during the event.
Close monitoring of parent's responses and recovery	Let parents know how children are feeling.
Concern over victims and their families	Encourage constructive activities for deceased and injured people.
Feeling disturbed, confused, and frightened about their grief responses	Help children retain positive memories.

Sixth Grade and Up

Traumatic Symptoms	Therapeutic Interventions
Detachment, shame, and guilt	Discuss the event, feelings about it, and realistic expectations of what could have been done.
Self-consciousness about their fears, sense of vulnerability; fear of being labeled abnormal	Clarify the adult nature of these feelings; encourage peer understanding and support.
Life-threatening reenactment; self-destructive or accident-prone behavior	Address the impulse toward reckless behavior in the acute aftermath; link impulse control problems w/violence.
Post-traumatic acting-out behavior (drug use, delinquent behavior, sexual acting out)	Explain that acting-out behavior is an effort to numb their responses and voice their anger over the event.
Abrupt shifts in interpersonal relationships	Discuss the inevitable strain on relationships with family and peers.
Desires and plans to take revenge	Elicit their actual plans of revenge; address the realistic consequences of their actions; encourage constructive alternatives that lessen the traumatic sense of helplessness.
Radical changes in life attitudes, which influence identity formation	Link their attitude changes to the event's impact.
Premature entrance into adulthood (e.g., leaving school or getting married) or reluctance to to leave home	Encourage postponing radical decisions, in order to allow time to work through their responses the event and to grieve.

Source: Crisis Management Manual, developed by the Crisis Management Task Force under the auspices of the Mental Health Association of Greater San Antonio and the United Way of San Antonio and Bexar County. Reprinted with permission.

Guided Free Play

Traumatized children will often automatically use toys to reenact their trauma and their concerns. If caregivers have a range of toys available in a special box, on a shelf, or in a bag, children can pick and choose their favorite mode of expression. Young children will run to the toys or immediately ask what is in the bag so that they can start to play as soon as possible. Caregivers can observe children begin to play without prompting, while doing preparatory things such as putting out refreshments, or hanging up coats. Join the children by asking neutral questions such as "That looks interesting, what are you doing?" Toys that are often helpful storytellers are: building blocks, cars, trucks, airplanes, human figures, dolls, stuffed animals, and simple puzzles of people or people's faces.

Stimulating Discussion

For children who are articulate and verbal, discussions can have a healing effect similar to that experienced by many adults who retell their stories and "talk out their concerns and reactions." Caregivers can help children begin to discuss the trauma by showing photographs of the deceased; showing a video story about death and trauma; reading a short story, a poem, or a parable relating to death and trauma; or presenting a news story or a media article about the event to provide information and promote reflection.

Creative Writing

Children and adolescents sometimes find it helpful to write about what concerns them. Disturbed children often give clues about their pain in drawings and writings. Outlets for creative writing include journals, letters to loved ones, prose, poetry, articles, or memory books. Caregivers can suggest titles for pages in the memory books that may help children express powerful feelings. One suggestion is to have the child write a deceased child's name, that is, "Mary's down the side of a page, and attach a word to each letter that spells Mary's name or finish open-ended sentences, such as the following:

- The thing I loved most about Mary is . . . "
- The happiest thing I remember about Mary is . . . ."
- The saddest thing I remember about Mary is . . . ."
- The things I can no longer do with Mary are . . . "
- If you had been able to say good-bye to Mary, what would you have said?

Dramatic Enactments

Most children like to role-play, particularly if props, costumes, or makeup are available to enable them to become totally involved in being another person. Puppets can also be used. Young children may use the opportunity to reenact funerals or portions of the trauma stories because of their curiosity and lack of real-life experiences. Older children and adolescents may also find playing parts or reading scripts from classic and modern tragedies helpful in expressing their concerns over death. Adolescents can empower peers with prevention and awareness plays regarding the dangers of drinking and driving during high-risk activities such as the prom and graduation.

Descriptions of Stories and Metaphors

Stories and metaphors can facilitate the expression of threatening emotions with a minimum of risk to the child. One method that the counselor may find useful is the mutual storytelling technique (Gardner, 1986). Gardner developed this technique to communicate with children using their own language and to gain insight into their behavior and interactions. In the mutual storytelling technique, the counselor tells the children that they are going to do a Make-Up-a-Story television program. To start this television program, the child must tell a story, with a beginning, a middle, and an end. The child invents the characters, the setting, the themes, and the plot of the story. The counselor listens to the story, attempting to grasp the symbolic meaning of the setting, the characters, and the plot. Then the counselor chooses one or two important ideas from the original story and tells a different story, using the same setting and characters. The characters in the counselor's story, however, should resolve their differences in a more mature, adaptive way than do the characters in the original story (Kottman, 1990). In the creative characters technique, Brooks (1987) uses stories to represent different aspects of a child's interpersonal life, such as self-esteem, relationships, beliefs, values, feelings, learning style, and coping style. The counselor audiotapes the beginning of the story before the counseling session. The counselor establishes the characters, the setting, and some general themes in the beginning story. Each story contains significant characters that represent the child and significant others in the child's life. The counselor takes on the active role of key character (such as "wise owl" or "superhero") to communicate with the child about the dynamics of the problem situation and about possible alternative solutions to difficulties (Brooks, 1987). After the initial segment of the story, in which the structure for the setting and characters is established, the child becomes the storyteller, responsible for the plot and the themes from his or her point of view. Many times, simply by listening to the child describe various significant others, the counselor can generate metaphors that "will resonate with client's inner world and a significant level of understanding will be established" (Brooks, 1985, p. 765). Kottman (1990) maintained that "communication through metaphors allows children to experience and express threatening emotions directly. This sanctioned distancing may help decrease some of the stress involved in the counseling process and convert resistance to co-operation" (Kottman, 1990, p. 142).

Music

Listening to music, as well as playing music or singing, can be a wonderful release for children. It provides a reconnection to the sense of rhythm. Certain musical instruments may also echo sounds of grief reactions: anger might be expressed through the sound of drums or a blaring trumpet; reed and string instruments might remind children of weeping or feelings of loneliness; drum rolls and cymbals may reflect tensions, anxieties, and fears; harps, flutes, and piccolos often sound like spirits talking. Death-related lyrics are found in virtually all types of music.

Bibliotherapy

According to many experts, it is believed that the most effective way to reach children on the subject of death is through bibliotherapy. Biblio-therapy is the use of literature to help children cope with changes in their lives. The goals of bibliotherapy are:

1. To provide information about problems;
2. To provide insight into problems;
3. To simulate discussion about problems;
4. To communicate new values and attitudes;
5. To create awareness that others have dealt with similar problems; and
6. To provide solutions to problems.

Selection criteria for choosing an effective book for children to read about death and grief:

1. Can children identify with the plot, the setting, the dialogue, and the characters?
2. Does the book use the correct terminology and psychologically sound explanations and portray events accurately?
3. Are the origins of emotional reactions revealed and inspected?
4. Does the book reflect an appreciation for individual differences?
5. Are good coping strategies modeled for the child?
6. Does the book present the crisis in an optimistic, surmountable fashion?

Classroom Activities

Many teachers respond to disasters with creative classroom activities to assist their students in ventilating and integrating their experiences. Some of these activities are appropriate for various age groups. They are meant to be vehicles for expression and discussion for your students, important steps in the healing process. These are examples of what can be done. They can be used to stimulate your own ideas and can be adapted to meet your own students' needs and the teacher's teaching style.

Preschool Activities

1. Having a variety of toys available that **encourage play reenactment** of children's experiences and observations during the disaster can help children to integrate these experiences. These might include fire trucks, dump trucks, rescue trucks, ambulances, and building blocks or playing with puppets or dolls, as ways for children to ventilate and act out their own feelings about what has occurred. Emotions and thoughts expressed in play provide an important window into understanding how a child is processing the trauma and the disaster.

2. Play structured games that involve physical touch among children. Children need **close physical contact** during times of stress to help them reestablish ego boundaries and a sense of security. Some examples might be:
   a. Ring Around the Rosie
   b. London Bridge
   c. Duck, Duck, Goose

3. Providing extra amounts of finger foods, in small portions, and fluids is a concrete way of supplying the emotional and physical nourishment children need in times of stress. Oral satisfaction is especially necessary, as children tend to revert to more regressive behavior in response to feeling that their survival or security is threatened.

4. Have the children **create a mural** on long paper, with topics such as "What happened in your house (school or neighborhood) when the big storm/flood/earthquake/tornado hit?" This is recommended for small groups, with a discussion afterward facilitated by an adult.

5. Let the children **dictate short stories** to an adult on a one-to-one basis, on such topics as "What I do and don't like about the rain." This activity can help the child verbalize his or her fears, as well as to perhaps get back in touch with previous positive associations toward the disruptive phenomena.

6. Have the children **draw pictures about the disaster** and then discuss the pictures in small groups. This activity allows them to vent their experiences and to discover that others share their fears.

7. Create a **group collage**. This normalizes feelings, and children get a sense that their peers have been feeling the same way they do.

Primary School Activities
1. For younger children, the availability of toys **that encourage expressive play reenactment** of their experiences and observations during the disaster can be helpful in their integrating these experiences. These might include ambulances, dump trucks, fire trucks, building blocks, and dolls. Playing with puppets can provide ways for the older children, as well, to ventilate their feelings.
2. Help or encourage the children to **develop skits or puppet shows** about what happened in the disaster. Encourage them to include anything positive about the experience, as well as those aspects that were frightening or disconcerting.
3. Stimulate group discussion about disaster experiences by showing your own feelings, fears, or experiences during the disaster. It is very important to **legitimize children's feelings** and to help them feel less isolated.
4. Have the children **brainstorm on their own classroom or family disaster plan**. What would they do? What would they take if they had to evacuate? How would they contact parents? How should the family be prepared? How could they help the family? Encourage them to discuss these things with their families.
5. Encourage class activities in which children can organize or build projects (scrapbooks, replicas, etc.), thus giving them a sense of mastery and control over events.
6. Have the children **color the pictures** in "The Awful Rain and How It Made Me Feel" (or similar material appropriate to the disaster). *Encourage the children to talk about their own feelings* during and after the disaster.

Junior High and High School Activities
1. Facilitating group discussion of their experiences of the disaster is particularly important among adolescents, who need the opportunity to vent, as well as to normalize the extreme emotions that come up for them. A good way to stimulate such a discussion is for the teacher to share his or her own reactions to the disaster. Adolescents may need considerable reassurance that even extreme emotions and "crazy thoughts" are normal in a disaster. It is important to end such discussions on a positive note (e.g., What heroic acts were observed? How can we be of help at home or in the community? How could we be more prepared for a disaster?). Such a discussion is appropriate for any course of study, in that it can facilitate a return to more normal functioning.

2. Break the class into small groups and have them **develop a disaster plan for their home, school, or community.** This can be helpful in repairing a sense of mastery and security, as well as having practical merit. The small groups might then share their plans in a discussion with the entire class. Encourage students to share their plans with their families. They may wish to conduct a "Family Disaster Preparedness" meeting and invite family members and disaster-preparedness experts to participate. This gives students both a sense of ownership and a sense of empowerment.

3. Conduct a class discussion or support a **class project on how the students might help the community rehabilitation effort—or do both.** It is important to help students develop concrete and realistic ways to be of assistance. This helps them to overcome the feelings of helplessness, frustration, and "survivor's guilt" that are common in disaster situations.

4. **Classroom activities that relate the disaster to course study** can be a good way to help the students integrate their own experience or observations while providing specific learning experiences. In implementing the following suggestions or similar ideas of your own, it is very important to allow time for the students to discuss feelings that are stimulated by the projects or issues covered.

Journalism

Have the students write stories that cover different aspects of the disaster. These might include the impact on the community, lawsuits that result from the disaster, human interest stories from fellow students, geological impact, and so on. Issues such as the accurate reporting of catastrophic events versus sensationalism might be discussed. The stories could be compiled into a special student publication.

Science

Cover scientific aspects of the disaster, for example, discuss climate condition, geological impact, and so on. Assign projects about stress: physiological responses to stress and methods of dealing with it. Discuss how flocks of birds, herds of animals, and so on, band together and work in a threatening or emergency situation. What can be learned from their instinctive actions?

English Composition

Have the students write about their own experiences in the disaster. Such issues as the problems that arise in conveying a heavy emotional tone without being overly dramatic might be discussed.

Literature

Have students report on natural disasters in Greek mythology, in American and British literature, and in poetry.

Psychology

Have the students apply what they have learned in the course to the emotions, behaviors, and stress reactions they felt or observed in the disaster. Cover post-traumatic stress syndrome. Have a guest speaker from the mental health professions who was involved in disaster work with survivors, and so on. Have students discuss (from their own experience) what things have been most helpful in dealing with disaster-related stress. Have students develop a mental health education brochure discussing emotional and behavioral reactions to the disaster and things that are helpful in coping with disaster-related stress. Have students conduct a survey among their parents or friends: What was the most dangerous situation in which you ever found yourself? How did you react psychologically?

Peer Counseling

Provide special information on common responses to disaster; encourage the students' helping each other to integrate their own experiences.

Health

Discuss emotional reactions to disaster, the importance of taking care of one's own emotional and physical well-being, and so on. Discuss health implications of the disaster—for example, water contamination, food that may have gone bad due to lack of refrigeration, and other health precautions and safety measures. Discuss the effects of adrenaline on the body during stress and danger. A guest speaker from the Public Health Department or a mental health field might be invited to the class.

Art

Have the students portray their experiences of the disaster in various art media. This may be done individually or as a group effort (e.g., making a mural).

Speech/Drama

Have the students portray the catastrophic emotions that come up in response to a disaster. Have them develop a skit or a play on some aspects of the event. Conduct a debate: Women are more psychologically prepared to handle stress than men (or vice versa).

Math

Have the class solve mathematical problems related to the impact of the disaster (e.g., build questions around gallons of water lost, cubic feet of earth that moved in a mud slide).

History

Have students report on natural disasters that have occurred in your community or geographic area and what lessons were learned that can be useful in preparing for future disasters.

Civics/Government

Study governmental agencies that are responsible for aid to survivors, how they work, how effective they are, and their political implications within a community. Examine the community systems and how the stress of the disaster has affected them. Have students invite a local governmental official to class to discuss disaster precautions, warning systems, and so on. Have students contact the California Seismic Safety Commission or state legislators regarding recent disaster-related bills passed or pending. How will this legislation affect your community and other areas or the state? Visit local emergency operating centers and learn about their functions.

(*Source:* http://www.ces.ncsu.edu/depts/fcs/humandev/disas3.html. NC State University Cooperative Extension.)

STRUCTURED SENSORY INTERVENTIONS FOR TRAUMATIZED CHILDREN, ADOLESCENTS, AND PARENTS

Intervention Strategies for School Counselors

Steele and Raider (2002) developed Structured Sensory Interventions for Traumatized Children, Adolescents and Parents (SITCAP). Their premise is that survivors desperately want to, and are capable of, sharing the details of their experience—to make us a witness to that experience. To be a witness, we must be involved in the child's telling of the story by being curious about all that happened. For us to engage this "witness" role, the intervention must be very concrete and literal in response to all the elements of the story, its details, and the visual representations provided by the child, the adolescent, or the parent.

Part of becoming a witness is seeing how the survivors now view themselves and the world around them following the trauma. To see what the survivor sees is to understand and know what will be helpful. Because trauma is a sensory experience, the memory is often stored symbolically. Images—how one looks at oneself and the world around one—define what that trauma was like. Even adults rarely have words to adequately describe what their experience was like, but they can show us. Presenting that visual representation must be done in a structured fashion. Boundaries provide the structure that promotes a "sensory" safety. Boundaries in drawing involve the use of 8½" × 11" paper and fine point pens, color pencils, or felt markers. Drawing activities are structured versus unstructured. They direct themselves to helping the survivor describe how specific sensations or themes of trauma, like fear, revenge, and hurt, are now impacting their lives.

Focus on Themes, Not Behavior

SITCAP focuses on 10 major sensations or themes: fear, terror, worry, hurt, anger, revenge, accountability, safety, power, and throughout the process shifting from victim thinking to survivor thinking. This process, therefore, does not direct itself toward attempting to treat behavior but rather toward the sensations (themes) that fuel and drive the behavior. One 7-year-old boy, for example, at age 3 saw his father kill his mother. He was later kidnapped by his father, who had posted bail. For the next 6 months his father held him captive. He was left alone for long periods of time and witnessed his father beat several women. There was a 4-year period from the time this boy was rescued to the time SITCAP was initiated. During that time, two primary behaviors resulting from his trauma surfaced. The first was that he slept on the floor every night, and the second was that he would seldom leave his grandmother's side. He even followed her into the bathroom at times, making it difficult for her to have any privacy without a struggle.

Sleeping on the floor was a way of being in a state of readiness for any danger that might come his way. Following his grandmother into the bathroom was rooted in the sensation of fear. His behaviors were helping, at a sensory level, to create the sensation of safety. SITCAP did not directly address this boy's behavior but his fears and worries. In a process of helping him reexperience the sensation of safety, his levels of fear and worry were reduced and the behavior changed. Following the restoration of the sense of safety, he began to cognitively alter his responses.

In another example, Robert, an 11-year-old boy, was facing his second suspension from school for fighting. One year earlier his older sister was brutally raped and murdered by a serial killer. He was not a witness to the killing but was certainly traumatized by his sister's murder and all the exposure from the media that followed. Fighting had not previously been a problem. His mother reported that it was totally unlike her son. Attempts at peer mediation and conflict resolution, which frequently focus on behavior and seek resolution through cognitive approaches, simply failed. At a sensory level, this youngster was terrified. His "fighting response" was an attempt, at a sensory level, to not feel afraid. It was a way for him to overpower his fear; to communicate to others and to himself, "No one is going to do to me what was done to my sister." SITCAP helped him to "recapture," at a sensory level, a sense of power and safety that helped to diminish the fighting response. Help the survivor with the sensations of trauma, and behavior will change accordingly.

Details

Part of telling the story is asking questions to elicit details. Obtaining details is another very important component of the SITCAP process. For the survivor, details can provide a sense of control, as well as a sense of relief. For the intervention, details can point the way toward helping the client find relief. The structure of SITCAP keeps the child focused on details as a way of being able to later "see" the experience differently, to cognitively reframe it in a way that is now manageable. Details can also provide information that helps children to make sense out of what happened and may still be happening to them.

When asked where he felt the hurt the most, Robert, the 11-year-old boy whose sister was brutally murdered 1 year earlier, said, "All over my body when I was told. It was like I was in shock and then I got a big headache." He continued to experience the headaches when he thought of his sister. While this topic was pursued with him, he told the story of how, on the same night his sister was discovered missing, his friend was in a car accident. His friend's head went through the windshield, and he died. Given the high profile of the murder, no one ever dealt with this second traumatization, which seemed minimal compared to the murder. Only when Robert was given the opportunity to tell the entire story and all the details of what happened at the time of the incident did this second trauma reveal itself as a source of some of the headaches he was experiencing. He in essence had two stories to tell. All too often, it is the events following the primary trauma that trigger trauma reactions.

Type of Incidents

SITCAP addresses Type I and Type II incidents (Steele & Raider, 2002). Type I refers to a single trauma-inducing incident. Type II trauma refers to a single incident, like sexual abuse, repeated over a period of time, or multiple traumas (different incidents). By addressing the major themes of trauma, SITCAP is beneficial for both Type I and Type II incidents. It addresses those incidents that are assaultive and violent, such as murder, physical or sexual abuse, domestic violence, armed assault, and suicide. It also addresses incidents of a nonassaultive origin, such as terminal illness, critical injury, natural disasters, car fatalities, house fires, drownings, divorce, or separation from parents.

Age, Gender and Ethnicity

It is important to remember that trauma has very few boundaries when it comes to culture, ethnicity, gender, or age. Whatever an adult can experience in trauma, a child can also experience. Whatever a child can experience in trauma, an adult can also experience.

A 27-year-old woman's brother was shot and killed just outside her home. As she told her story, she described hearing the gunshot and immediately knowing it was her brother who was shot. It was a random killing, in this case. There was no gang or drug history. When she ran outside, her fear was confirmed. She said that as she approached his body, she wanted to touch him, but she knew that if she "touched him, he would die." She could not touch him.

This woman's response is an example of "magical thinking." Magical thinking is a reaction generally assigned to young children, who believe it was something they thought, said, or wished for that caused the death of a family member or a friend. Whatever a child can experience, however, an adult in trauma can experience. A 42-year-old nurse's teenage son was shot and killed outside her home. Telling her story, she talked about looking at that spot 24 hours a day. She went on to say that at times, she would be cooking something on the stove and would forget she was cooking. The close physical proximity to the trauma, among other elements, has kept her in the hyperarousal state. Forgetting that she was cooking is a short-term memory loss associated with the mid-brain arousal response that is experienced by children, as well as adults. It manifests itself in traumatized children who seem "not to be listening" because they cannot remember what they were asked to do just 5 minutes earlier.

SITCAP intervention adjusts activities for developmental differences, but its focus on major sensations or themes versus behavior allows it to help reduce symptoms across age levels. Its primary intervention processes of exposure, trauma narrative, and cognitive reframing remain the processes for preschool-aged children, elementary-aged children, adolescents and adults.

Structured Sensory Intervention Is Unique in Several Ways

- Intervention can be initiated for either violent or nonviolent trauma incidents of the type detailed earlier.
- Intervention addresses children of preschool age, children 6 to 12 years old, adolescents, and adults.
- Activity worksheets accompany each session and are designed to facilitate a focus on the major themes of trauma.
- The interventions are so structured, trauma-focused, and client-oriented that clinicians who follow the format are afforded little opportunity to inappropriately respond.
- Field-tested in schools, as well as agency settings, the model and its interventions meet the many limitations placed on school counselors, social workers, and clinicians.
- Rather than address symptoms, the model focuses on the themes of trauma—fear, terror, worry, hurt, anger, revenge, accountability, safety, power, and being a survivor versus a victim.
- Given the reality that parental involvement is frequently minimal, the model encourages a minimum of two sessions with parents. These are specifically structured and designed to obtain necessary information and support, and to provide the opportunity to make the parent a witness to the ways the trauma has impacted the child, so as to increase the likelihood that parental response to the child is the most supportive.
- The parent component also addresses those parents whose child's trauma has triggered reactions from their own person history or parents who themselves experienced a trauma not involving their child but that is creating problems for them in their role as a parent.
- Exposure is accomplished by drawing activities. Developing the trauma narrative is accomplished through asking trauma-specific questions, and cognitive reframing is structured to speak to the major sensations of trauma.
- Resource materials for the child and parent ensure that they receive the information (education) they need about the differences between grief and trauma as well as the course the intervention will take. These are also included in a structured booklet format to ensure that the interveners are, in fact, covering the important issues.
- The model is outcome-driven. An assessment tool is available to identify current reactions and their severity levels. It provides a baseline to compare initial levels of severity to final outcomes. It is clinically based, so it serves as a diagnostic tool to support third-party insurance requirements for approved treatment and, if needed, continuation beyond the short-term period.

- The components of SITCAP are also designed to assist the school or the community's response to critical incidents. In school environments, certain events like school shootings, car fatalities, and the sudden death of a staff member dictate a specific series of interventions from the first day through several weeks. The SITCAP model provides these interventions.

8 to 10 Sessions

Structured Sensory Intervention for Traumatized Children, Adolescents and Parents is an 8- to 10-session intervention. The attention span of preschool-aged children varies from 15 to 25 minutes. It therefore takes 10 sessions to cover the major themes of trauma for that age group. Children, adolescents, and adult/parent intervention involve eight structured sessions, which address the major themes of trauma in a sequential manner. Activities vary to some degree with different age levels, but the primary intervention processes and the focus on major trauma sensations and themes are used with all age levels.

Participants in SITCAP may not need all eight sessions, as levels of severity and reactions will vary. Some participants may need additional intervention. SITCAP lends itself to identifying those reactions (themes) that may need additional attention. Additional intervention, if necessary, can therefore be very focused and specific to the client's needs. Overall reactions, for example, may be reduced, but safety remains a primary worry. Additional intervention would then concentrate on safety issues. Some individuals may also see major reductions in all three *DSM-IV* subcategories yet might need "first aid" following additional exposure or when entering different developmental periods.

The goals of SITCAP are

- Stabilization (return to the previous level of functioning or the prevention of further dysfunction)
- Identification of PTSD reactions
- The opportunity to revisit the trauma in the supportive, reassuring presence of an adult (professional) who understands the value of providing this opportunity
- An opportunity to find relief from trauma-induced terror, worry, hurt, anger, revenge, accountability, powerlessness, and the need for safety
- An opportunity to reestablish a positive "connectiveness" to the adult world
- Normalization of current and future reactions
- Support of the heroic efforts to become a survivor, rather than a victim of their experience

- When appropriate, assistance for parents in resolving those reactions triggered by their child's traumatization
- Replacement of the traumatic sensory experience with positive sensory experiences
- Identification of additional needs and recognition of the role that parents can take to help meet those needs
- The provisioning of parents with ways to respond to their traumatized child's reactions

Education

Structuring statements at intake clearly identify how the process works, what will be expected, and what outcome can be anticipates. SITCAP also structures itself to teach the survivor the difference between grief and trauma. Information about trauma lessens anxiety. Normalizing the trauma reactions helps people to make sense out of what happened, while supporting the fact that what is being experienced is quite normal. This helps to decrease anxiety.

Drawing

- Drawing is a psychomotor activity. Because trauma is a sensory experience, not a cognitive experience, intervention is necessary to trigger those sensory memories. Drawing triggers those sensory memories when it is trauma-focused. It provides a safe vehicle to communicate what children, even adults, often have few words to describe.
- Drawing engages the child and the adult in an active involvement with their own healing. It takes them from a passive to an active, directed, controlled externalization of that trauma and its reactions.
- Drawing provides a symbolic representation of the trauma experience in a format that is now external, concrete, and therefore manageable. The paper acts as a container of that trauma.
- Drawing provides a visual focus on details that encourage the client, via trauma-specific questions, to tell his story, to give it a language so that it can be reordered in a way that is manageable.
- Drawing also provides for the diminishing of reactivity (anxiety) to trauma memories through repeated visual reexposure in a medium that is perceived and felt by the client to be safe.

Trauma-Specific Questions

In addition to drawing, trauma-specific questions are used to help in telling the story and detailing what reactions were experienced. Questions are directed to trauma themes and focus on trauma sensations and are also directed to the details of the trauma incident itself. Following are some examples:

- "What do you remember seeing or hearing?" relates to the overall sensory imploding of detailed components of the trauma.
- "Do you sometimes think about what happened even when you don't want to?" deals with intrusive thoughts.
- "Do certain sounds, sights, smells, and so on, sometimes suddenly remind you of what happened?" refers to startle reactions.
- "What would you like to see happen to the person (or thing) that caused this to happen?" deals with anger and revenge.
- "Do you sometimes think it should have been you instead?" is an accountability (survivor's guilt) question.

Throughout the process, questions are specific to the theme being addressed. Their concreteness keeps the child focused on the specific theme, encourages the narrative (story) to be told for each theme, and encourages the attention to detail. Details, as discussed earlier, are critical to helping establish a sense of control and provide information needed to help the child find relief.

Multiple questions are asked because the specific trauma reference may be worry, not anger or revenge. The child's trauma reference may be about the hurt experienced at a sensory level, not at the physical level. It may be accountability for some, fear for others. SITCAP encourages the systematic presentation of all questions and attention to all themes to give the survivor the opportunity to make us a witness to his specific trauma reference.

Example

It was New Year's Eve. A high school senior was ushering at a movie complex where several movies ran concurrently. He was slated to graduate in the spring and had been accepted into the police academy. Also a football player, he was physically quite strong and stood over 6 feet tall. Several kids in the movie he was assigned to were causing trouble. He attempted to get control but was unable to do so. He sought out the manager for help, but the manager had a full house and told him he would just have to handle it on his own. The situation did not change. In this complex, movies were scheduled so that several let out at the same time. There was a "common" area that the theaters opened into, so that everyone was moving into this area simultaneously.

The teen took his post across the common area outside the doors of the movie he was responsible to monitor. When the youths he had trouble with came out of the movie and into the common area, they spotted him, rushed him, knocked him down, and began beating on him. They broke his nose and several ribs. About a month later his parish priest, who was trying to help this teen, called for assistance. The boy was skipping school and not attending the youth activities at church, which was not at all like him.

"What was the worst part for you?" was one of the trauma-specific questions that helped to encourage this youngster's telling of the story and focusing on specific details. When this case was presented in trainings and participants were asked to anticipate what the "worst part" must have been, their numerous responses rarely identified what the worst part was for this teenager. Responses ranged from the anger he felt at the manager for leaving him on his own, the embarrassment and shame that he couldn't help himself, and the pain he felt during the beating. The point is, what we often as observers consider to be the worst part is not necessarily experienced by the trauma survivor. Only by giving the individual the opportunity to make us a witness can we truly know his experience as he knows it.

The teen's response was as follows: *"I can see it as if it is happening all over again. I'm on the ground and they're kicking me. As they are kicking me, I can see between their legs. [This kind of detail is unique to trauma, in which events seem to happen almost in slow motion so that such details emerge.] As I'm looking between their legs, I see all these people standing around and no one is helping me."*

At that moment in time, he experienced complete abandonment, betrayed by the adults in his world. Without appropriate intervention, this could have easily triggered very self-defeating, even destructive responses. He had already begun to isolate himself, was missing school, and was putting his future in jeopardy. If he had gone much longer without help, it would not have been unusual for him to start carrying a weapon, join a gang, or even actively seek out the kids who beat him with the intent of getting revenge. Being unable to trust the adult world was the worst part of his experience and one that often leads to destructive behavior and identifying with the aggressor. By asking this one trauma-specific question, the specialist was able to help this teen work through the abandonment he experienced, a focus that likely would have otherwise gone untreated.

Cognitive Reframing

Cognitive reframing is scripted in SITCAP to ensure that the individual is provided with a "survivor's" way of making sense of the trauma experience. The goal is to help move the person from "victim thinking" to "survivor thinking," which leads to empowerment, choice, active involvement in his or her own healing process, and a renewed sense of safety and hope.

Activities also assist in supporting the reframing of the experience. The high school senior in our earlier example, who was beaten on New Year's Eve and had lost trust in the adult world, withdrew. By having him draw what his fears looked like and later giving them a name, he realized that he was responding as a victim to his own fear that if the police academy found out, it would never allow him to start his training. This was irrational, but not from a "victim's" viewpoint. A sense of shame also emerged, as his view of self was not being able to take care of himself. When asked why the standard operating procedure of the police was to always work with a partner, he was able to refocus on the reality that when one is alone, even in the midst of bystanders, protection and help are not always given. Working in pairs, he realized, dealt with the reality that even police could find themselves suddenly overwhelmed. At a cognitive level, he was then able to reframe that what happened to him was not his fault and that as a police officer he would be doing for others what others could not do for him—help. In this sense, cognitive framing allowed him to reorder his experience in a way that gave his future new meaning.

Parent Involvement

A good deal of research has concluded that parents are critical to their child's ability to recover from trauma. (Nader, Pynoos, Fairbanks, & Frederick, 1990; Rustemeli, & Karanci, 1996) cited parents as the single most important support for school-age children following a disaster. McFarlane (1988) reported that studies after World War II showed that the level of upset displayed by the adult in the child's life, not the war itself, was the single most important factor in predicting the emotional well-being and recovery of the child. We see the same relationship today.

An unstable parent creates an unstable child. A traumatized adult will find it difficult to help his or her traumatized child. Adults (parents), more frequently than children, experienced the greatest distress when presented with a trauma. Most children are amazingly resilient, as long as they have caregivers who are emotionally available. When a child has been traumatized, his or her parents also experience extreme distress and often are unable to adequately respond to their traumatized children without appropriate intervention. Learning about trauma helps parents who themselves have been traumatized, especially when their experience is brought back to life (triggered) by their child's traumatic experience. Education is an essential, necessary component to help parents become aware of how their own unresolved fears block their ability to allow their child to openly tell his or her story. The child needs a parent who is not terrified and emotionally overwhelmed. Parents with their own history often discover that their child's experience threatens to bring all the terror of their own experience back to life. Unknowingly, they reject their child's cry for help or minimize the child's terror in hopes of calming the child.

CONCLUSION

Children and adolescents need a variety of venues from which to process their grief and loss, to prevent acute stress disorder and post-traumatic stress disorder. The percentage of those exposed to a traumatic stressor who then develop post-traumatic stress disorder (PTSD) can vary, depending on the nature of the trauma and the child's or the adolescent's previous life experiences and coping resources. At the time of a traumatic event, many people feel overwhelmed with fear; others feel numb or disconnected. Most trauma survivors will be upset for several weeks following an event but recover to a variable degree without treatment. With traumatic exposure as the foundation, other risk factors that have been shown to contribute to the development of PTSD include the magnitude, the duration, and the type of traumatic exposure. Variables such as earlier age of onset and lower education are also associated with increased risk for developing PTSD.

Chapter 9

Sample Policies to Prevent Legal Liability and to Use for Assessments and as Screening Instruments

The sample policies are provided as guidelines to prevent legal liability as the result of a crisis, a critical incident, or a traumatic event. Sample policies address confidentiality, abuse and neglect, sexual harassment, and imminent risk of suicide or self-harm. Assessment and screening instruments are also included for potential referral to resources outside of the school.

Professional ethics are the principles of right or professional conduct. The professional school counselor has ethical responsibilities to protect the safety, needs, confidentiality, and interests of students, parents, staff, colleagues, self, and the profession. The counselor should know and follow the ethical standards of professional associations: ACA Code of Ethics and Standards of Practice (Online, http://www.counseling.org) and Ethical Standards in ASCA Membership Services Guide (Online, http://www.schoolcounselor.org/).

AVOIDING ETHICAL PITFALLS

(ASCA Ethics Committee. Doing the Right Thing: Ethics and the Professional School Counselor 1996–97. http://www.edge.net/asca/)

1. Clarify the right to privacy, complying with all laws, policies, and ethical standards pertaining to confidentiality.
2. Respect the rights of parents and families.

3. Inform parents of the counselor's role, with emphasis on the confidential nature of the counseling relationship.
4. Understand and refrain from dual relationships.
5. Inform the student counselee of the purposes, goals, techniques, and so on, under which she or he may receive counseling assistance.
6. Adhere to laws and local guidelines when assisting parents.
7. Understand the primary obligation and loyalty to the student.
8. Establish and maintain a cooperative relationship with faculty, staff, and administration to facilitate the provision of services.
9. Provide parents with accurate, comprehensive, relevant information in an ethical manner.
10. Share information about a counselee only with the people properly authorized to receive such information.

ADMINISTRATIVE POLICY AND SCHOOL LAW: MANDATES FOR DUTY TO WARN REGARDING SUICIDE IDEATION AND SELF-HARM

Crisis intervention and management procedures are often supported by administrative directives or school board policy or mandated by state law. To provide maximum care when a student verbalizes suicide ideation, the school counselor and helping professionals should use the following steps, outlined by administrative policy, regarding a potential suicide threat:

22.1–272.1, related to suicide prevention in public schools, the Code of Said State was amended by adding a section as follows:

§22.1–272.1. Responsibility to contact parent of student at imminent risk of suicide; notice to be given to social services if parental abuse or neglect; Board of Education, in cooperation with the Department of Mental Health, Mental Retardation and Substance Abuse Services and the Department of Health, to develop guidelines for parental contact.

A. Any person licensed as administrative or instructional personnel by the Board of Education and employed by a local school board who, in the scope of his/her employment, has reason to believe, as a result of direct communication from a student, that such student is at imminent risk of suicide, shall, as soon as practicable, contact at least one of such student's parents to ask whether such parent is aware of the student's mental state and whether the parent wishes to obtain or has already obtained counseling for such student. Such contact shall be made in accordance with the provisions of the guidelines required by subsection C.
B. If the student has indicated that the reason for being at imminent risk of suicide relates to parental abuse or neglect, this contact shall not

be made with the parent. Instead, the person shall, as soon as practicable, notify the local department of social service of the county or city wherein the child resides or wherein the abuse or neglect is believed to have occurred or the state Department of Social Services' toll-free child abuse and neglect hotline, as required by §62.1-248.3. When giving this notice to the local or state department, the person shall stress the need to take immediate action to protect the child from harm.

C. The Board of Education, in cooperation with the Department of Mental Health, Mental Retardation and Substance Abuse Services and the Department of Health, shall develop guidelines for making the contact required by subsection A. These guidelines shall include, but need not be limited to:

1) Criteria to assess the suicide risks of students,
2) Characteristics to identify potentially suicidal students,
3) Appropriate responses to students expressing suicidal intentions,
4) Available and appropriate community services for students expressing suicidal intentions,
5) Suicide prevention strategies which may be implemented by local schools for students expressing suicidal intentions,
6) Criteria for notification of and discussion with parents of students expressing suicidal intentions,
7) Criteria for making contact with the parents,
8) Appropriate sensitivity to religious beliefs, and
9) Legal requirement and criteria for notification of public service agencies, including, but not limited to, the local or state social services and mental health agencies.

These guidelines may include case studies and problem-solving exercises and may be designed as materials for in-service training programs for licensed administrative and instructional personnel.

CONFIDENTIALITY

The professional responsibility of school counselors is to fully respect the right to privacy of those with whom they enter counseling relationships. Counselors must keep abreast of and adhere to all laws, policies, and ethical standards pertaining to confidentiality. The counselor, except where there is clear and present danger to the student, other persons, or both, must not abridge this confidentiality.

Counselors have a responsibility to protect the privileged information received through confidential relationships with students, with the student's parent or guardian, and with staff. The counselor reserves the right to consult with other professionally competent persons when this is in the best interest of the student. In the event of possible judicial proceedings, the

counselor should initially advise the school administration and the counselee, and, if necessary, consult with legal counsel.

It is the responsibility of the counselor to provide notice to students
regarding the possible necessity for consulting with others. This confidentiality must not be abridged by the counselor except where there is a clear
and present danger to the student, to other persons, or both.

The counselor and the student should be provided with adequate physical facilities to guarantee the confidentiality of the counseling relationship.
With the enactment of the Family Educational Rights and Privacy Act, P.L.
93-380 (the Buckley Amendment), which speaks to the rights and the privacy of parents and students, great care should be taken with recorded
information. All counselors should have a copy of the complete law. Counselors must adhere to P.L. 93-380. Counselors must be concerned about
individuals who have access to confidential information. It should be the
policy of each school to guarantee adequate working space for secretaries
so that students and school personnel will not come into contact with confidential information, even inadvertently. Counselors should undertake a
periodic review of information requested of their students. Only relevant
information should be retained. Counselors will adhere to ethical standards
and local policies in relating student information over the telephone.

A counseling relationship requires an atmosphere of trust and confidence between student and counselor. A student has the right to privacy
and to expect confidentiality. The responsibility to protect privileged communication extends to the student's parent or guardian and to staff members in confidential relationships. Counselors must adhere to P.L. 93-380.

(Reprinted with permission from the American School Counselor Association, 1999.)

CONFIDENTIALITY IN THE SCHOOL SETTING

Confidentiality is an ethical duty to the student and the parent not to reveal
to people, other than the parent, information that was disclosed during a
private counselor–student interaction. The legal rights of minors to provide
consent to enter counseling or release information about counseling generally reside in the custodial parent or the guardian as a matter of common
law and statutes.

Counselors have an ethical duty to preserve client confidentiality; however, no teacher, counselor, administrator, or other school staff member has
an unlimited right to confidentiality when dealing with minor students. Although counselors and other staff members may be of assistance to students
who need an adult with whom to discuss personal concerns, the staff is

responsible for knowing and conforming to established guidelines when entering into such discussions.

Students have a right to know the limitations of confidentiality before they disclose information in what they may believe is a confidential relationship. Except as exempted by law, this regulation defines limitations of confidentiality and the responsibilities of staff members with respect to information disclosed by students. Those authorized to provide counseling in the school should comply with the confidentiality guidelines within the ethical standards of their profession, except where such guidelines may conflict with their district regulations, school division policies, or other laws.

Parents are also considered responsible for students under the age of 18 and retain the right to have information about them. Parents may access records that contain information disclosed by minor students. This does not include records held for the sole use of their author. Moreover, a school staff member has an obligation to notify parents or others when certain information is disclosed, except as prohibited by law. Counselors should check local district regulations.

- If the student is involved in illegal activity, parents, authorities, or both must be notified.
- If the student has experienced child abuse or neglect, the Department of Social Services must be notified.
- If the student or others may be at risk of harm, the parents, authorities, or both must be notified in accordance with local school district regulations.

If the risk of harm may be considered imminent, the police department, emergency services personnel, or both should be contacted. If the counselor is unable to determine the degree of risk or the appropriate response, that counselor should confer with a supervisor or an administrator or consult with a colleague on a confidential basis. When consultation is necessary, the identity of the student should not be revealed unless required for the welfare of the student or others.

Parents shall be notified unless such notification would increase the risk of harm to the student, for example, with child abuse. In such cases, the counselor is advised to consult with a supervisor or an administrator to determine the appropriate action. Whenever it is necessary to notify authorities outside the school, the principal or the designee should be consulted, unless urgent notification is required to avoid harm to the student or others.

Under no circumstances should confidential information be discussed openly in the presence of others or with those who do not have a legitimate need to know. Information disclosed by students, parents, or others in the context of their professional relationship with the staff, whether identified as confidential or not, should not be used in casual conversation or in ways that are not consistent with this regulation or the advice of a supervisor or administrator.

DROPOUT PREVENTION AND STUDENTS AT RISK

Professional school counselors at all levels make a significant, vital, and indispensable contribution toward the mental wellness of "at-risk" students. School counselors work as members of a team with other student service professionals, including social workers, psychologists, and nurses, in liaison with staff and parents, to provide comprehensive developmental counseling programs for all students, including those identified as being potential dropouts or "at risk."

Any student may at any time be "at risk" with respect to dropping out of school, becoming truant, performing below academic potential, contemplating suicide, or using drugs. The underlying reasons for these behaviors often deal with personal and social concerns, such as poor self-esteem, family problems, unresolved grief, neglect, or abuse. Students experiencing these concerns can be helped by professional school counselors. The decision to drop out of school can carry with it devastating lifelong implications. The school counselor, in conjunction with other school staff members, identifies potential dropouts and other students considered at risk and works closely with them to help them stay in school or find alternative means of completing their education.

The school counselor provides consultation in defining and identifying "at-risk" students. The goal is to identify and intervene before they move through a continuum of self-destructive behavior. The school counselor provides responsive programs, including short-term individual, group, family, and crisis counseling; provides programs for individual planning to meet academic, educational, and career counseling needs; provides curriculum programs to strengthen personal/interpersonal skills (choice, self-acceptance, feelings, beliefs and behaviors, problem solving, decision making); identifies suicidal students, counsels them, and refers them to appropriate outside agencies; provides in-service support presentations to staff; provides referrals for additional specialized support services within the district and from other community resources; and provides consultation with and support for parents/guardians of "at-risk" students. The school counselor works as a member of a team with other student service professionals.

(Reprinted with permission from the American School Counselor Association)

MANDATED REPORTERS

Code § 63.2-1509(A) defines who is a mandated reporter.

Code § 63.2-1509(A). The following persons who, in their professional or official capacity, have reason to suspect that a child is an abused or neglected child, shall report the matter immediately, except as hereinafter provided, to the local department of the county or city wherein the child resides or wherein the abuse or neglect is believed to have occurred or to the Department of Social Services' toll-free child abuse and neglect hotline:

1. Any person licensed to practice medicine or any of the healing arts;
2. Any hospital resident or intern, and any person employed in the nursing profession;
3. Any person employed as a social worker;
4. Any probation officer;
5. Any teacher or other person employed in a public or private school, kindergarten, or nursery school;
6. Any person providing full-time or part-time child care for pay on a regularly planned basis;
7. Any duly accredited Christian Science practitioner;
8. Any mental health professional;
9. Any law-enforcement officer;
10. Any mediator eligible to receive court referrals pursuant to §8.01-576.8;
11. Any professional staff person, not previously enumerated, employed by a private or state-operated hospital, institution, or facility to which children have been committed or where children have been placed for care and treatment;
12. Any person associated with or employed by any private organization responsible for the care, custody, or control of children; and
13. Any person who is designated a court-appointed special advocate pursuant to Article 5 (9.1-151 et seq.) of Chapter 1 of Title 9.1.

FAILURE BY MANDATED REPORTER TO REPORT ABUSE OR NEGLECT

Code § 63.2-1509(C). Any person required to file a report pursuant to this section who fails to do so within seventy-two hours of his first suspicion of child abuse or neglect shall be fined not more than $500 for the first failure and for any subsequent failures not less than $100 or more than $1,000. If a person required to report fails to do so, that person can be charged with a misdemeanor. If found guilty, the fine for failure to report suspected abuse or neglect is up to $500 for the first incident and between $100 and $1,000 for any subsequent incidents. If the local department becomes aware of an incident involving a mandated reporter who failed to report pursuant to §§ 63.2-1509(A) and 63.2-1509 (B) of the Virginia Code, the local department must report the incident to the local Commonwealth's attorney.

Types of Physical Abuse

- Asphyxiation
- Bone fracture
- Brain damage/skull fracture/subdural hematoma
- Burns/scalding
- Cuts, bruises, welts, abrasions
- Internal injuries
- Poisoning
- Sprains/dislocation
- Gunshot/stabbing wounds
- Munchausen syndrome by proxy
- Bizarre discipline
- Battered child syndrome
- Shaken baby syndrome

Physical Neglect

- Abandonment
- Inadequate supervision
- Inadequate clothing
- Inadequate shelter
- Inadequate personal hygiene
- Inadequate food
- Malnutrition

Medical Neglect

Mental Abuse

Failure to Thrive

Sexual Abuse

- Sexual exploitation
- Sexual molestation
- Intercourse and sodomy

SEXUAL HARASSMENT: ENDURING PRINCIPLES

It continues to be the case that a significant number of students, both male and female, have experienced sexual harassment, which can interfere with a student's academic performance and emotional and physical well-being. Preventing and remedying sexual harassment in schools are essential to ensuring a safe environment in which students can learn. As with the 1997 guidance, the revised guidance applies to students at every level of education. School personnel who understand their obligations under Title IX, that is, understand that sexual harassment can be sex discrimination in violation of Title IX, are in the best position to prevent harassment and to lessen the harm to students if, despite their best efforts, harassment occurs.

One of the fundamental aims of both the 1997 guidance and the revised guidance has been to emphasize that in addressing allegations of sexual harassment, the good judgment and the common sense of teachers and school administrators are important elements of a response that meets the requirements of Title IX.

A critical issue under Title IX is whether the school recognized that sexual harassment has occurred and took prompt and effective action calculated to end the harassment, prevent its recurrence, and, as appropriate, remedy its effects. If harassment has occurred, doing nothing is always the wrong response. However, depending on the circumstances, there may be more than one right way to respond. The important thing is for school employees or officials to pay attention to the school environment and not to hesitate to respond to sexual harassment in the same reasonable, commonsense manner as they would to other types of serious misconduct.

Finally, we reiterate the importance of having well-publicized and effective grievance procedures in place to handle complaints of sex discrimination, including sexual harassment complaints. Nondiscrimination policies and procedures are required by the Title IX regulations. In fact, the Supreme Court in *Gebser* specifically affirmed the department's authority to enforce this requirement administratively, in order to carry out Title IX's nondiscrimination mandate (524 U.S. at 292). Strong policies and effective grievance procedures are essential to let students and employees know that sexual harassment will not be tolerated and to ensure that they know how to report it.

Office of Civil Rights (OCR) has identified a number of elements in evaluating whether a school's grievance procedures are prompt and equitable, including whether the procedures provide for

- Notice of the procedure to students, parents of elementary and secondary students, and employees of the including where complaints may be filed;
- Application of the procedure to complaints alleging harassment carried out by employees, other students, or third parties;

- Adequate, reliable, and impartial investigation of complaints, including the opportunity to present witnesses and other evidence;
- Designated and reasonably prompt time frames for the main stages of the complaint process;
- Notice to the parties of the outcome of the complaint; and
- An assurance that the school will take steps to prevent recurrence of any harassment and to correct its discriminatory effects on the complainant and others, if appropriate. (*Source:* http://www.ed.gov/offices/OCR/shguide/.)

ASSESSMENT AND DIAGNOSIS

The following assessment tools and diagnostic protocols are provided to assess and support intervention needs. They are included to provide the school counselor and other mental health workers with a guide for the purpose of assessment, intervention, and referral to more therapeutic resources.

FIGURE 9.1
Severity of Psychosocial Stressors Scale: Children and Adolescents

Code	Term	Examples of Stressors	
		Acute Events	**Enduring Circumstances**
1	None	No acute events that may be relevant to the disorder	No enduring circumstances that may be relevant to the disorder
2	Mild	Broke up with boyfriend or girlfriend; change of school	Overcrowded living quarters; family arguments
3	Moderate	Expelled from school; birth of sibling	Chronic disabling illness in parent; chronic parental discord
4	Severe	Divorce of parents; unwanted pregnancy; arrest	Harsh or rejecting parents; chronic life-threatening illness in parent; multiple foster home placement
5	Extreme	Sexual or physical abuse; death of a parent	Recurrent sexual or physical abuse
6	Catastrophic	Death of both parents	Chronic life-threatening illness
0	Inadequate information, or no change in condition		

American Psychiatric Association. (1987). *Diagnostic and statistical manual of mental disorders* (3rd ed., rev.) *DSM-III-R*. Washington, DC: Author. Reprinted with permission.

FIGURE 9.2
School Counselor Documented Action Plan

Support Resources Identified by Student	Support Resources Identified by Counselor
Lethality of Method	_____High _____Medium _____Low
Availability of Means (pills, gun, etc.)	_____High _____Medium _____Low
Specificity of Plan	_____High _____Medium _____Low

Action to Be Taken

Date: _____   **Time:** _____ **Crisis Team**

Consultation _____

Action	Yes	No	N/A	Person Responsible	Date Completed
Notify administration					
Contact parents					
Consult with school/community mental health practitioner					
Is it safe to let student go home alone?					
Is the student in need of 24-hour supervision?					
Was the student provided with a contact person and a phone number?					
Should Child Protective Services be notified?					
Should the youth services officer (police liaison) be contacted? Other (specify)					

Source: Thompson, R. A. (1988). Crisis intervention. In D. Capuzzi & L. Golden, *Preventing adolescent suicide* (p. 399). Muncie, IN: Accelerated Development. Reprinted with permission.

FIGURE 9.3
Suicidal Tendencies
Examples of Evaluation Questions for Children and Parents

Child Questions

- ❑ It seems things haven't been going so well for you lately. Your teachers have said you seem sad or depressed. Most children your age would feel upset about that.
- ❑ Have you felt upset, maybe some sad or angry feelings you've had trouble talking about? Maybe I could help you talk about these feelings and thoughts.
- ❑ Do you feel like things can get better or are you worried (afraid, concerned) things will just stay the same or get worse?
- ❑ Other children I've talked to have said that when they feel that sad, angry, or both they thought for awhile that things would be better if they were dead. Have you ever thought that? What were your thoughts?
- ❑ What do you think it would feel like to be dead?
- ❑ How do you think your father and mother would feel? What do you think would happen with them if you were dead?
- ❑ Has anyone that you know attempted to kill himself or herself? Do you know why?

- ❑ Have you thought about how you might make yourself die? Do you have a plan?
- ❑ Do you have (the means) at home (available)?
- ❑ Have you ever tried to kill yourself before?

- ❑ What has made you feel so awful?

Parent Questions

- ❑ Has any serious change occurred in your child's or your family's life recently (within the last year)?

- ❑ How did your child respond?

- ❑ Has your child had any accidents or an illness without a recognizable physical basis?

- ❑ Has your child experienced a loss recently?

- ❑ Has your child experienced difficulty in any areas of his or her life?
- ❑ Has your child been very self-critical or have you or his or her teachers been very critical lately?

- ❑ Has your child made any unusual statements to you or others about death or dying? Any unusual questions or jokes about death or dying?
- ❑ Have there been any changes you've noticed in your child's mood or behavior over the last few months?
- ❑ Has your child ever threatened or attempted suicide before?
- ❑ Have any of his or her friends or family, including you, ever threatened or attempted suicide?
- ❑ How have these last few months been for you? How have you reacted to your child (anger, despair, empathy, etc.)?

Words and phrasings should be changed to better fit the child, the interviewer, or both. Two things need to be accomplished during this questioning: (1) to gather more information about the child and (2) to try to evaluate the parents in terms of their understanding, cooperation, quality of connection with their children, energy to be available to a child in crisis.

Source: Davis, J. M. (1985). Suicidal crises in schools. *School Psychology Review, 14*(3), 313–322. Reprinted with permission.

FIGURE 9.4
Suicide Warning Signs

Warning signs can be organized around the word *FACT*

Feelings	❏ Hopelessness— *"It will never get any better." "There's nothing anyone can do." "I'll always feel this way."*
	❏ Fear of losing control, going crazy, and harming self or others
	❏ Helpless, worthless— *"Nobody cares." "Everyone would be better off without me."*
	❏ Overwhelming guilt, shame, self-hatred
	❏ Pervasive sadness
	❏ Persistent anxiety or anger
Action or Events	❏ Drug or alcohol abuse
	❏ Themes of death or destruction in talk or written materials
	❏ Nightmares
	❏ Recent loss through death, divorce, separation, broken relationships, or loss of job, money, status, self-esteem
	❏ Loss of religious faith
	❏ Agitation, restlessness
	❏ Aggression, recklessness
Change	❏ In personality—more withdrawn, tired, apathetic, indecisive, or more boisterous, talkative, outgoing
	❏ In behavior—can't concentrate on school, work, routine tasks
	❏ In sleep pattern—oversleeping or insomnia, sometimes with early waking
	❏ In eating habits—loss of appetite and weight or overeating
	❏ Loss of interest in friends, hobbies, personal grooming, sex, or other activities previously enjoyed
	❏ *Sudden* improvement after a period of being down or withdrawn
Threats	❏ Statements (e.g., *"How long does it take to bleed to death?")*
	❏ Threats (e.g., *"I won't be around much longer.")*
	❏ Plans (e.g., putting affairs in order, giving away favorite things, studying drug effects, obtaining a weapon)
	❏ Gestures or attempts (e.g., overdosing, wrist cutting)

Kalafat, J. (1990). Adolescent suicide and the implications for school response programs. *The School Counselor, 37*(5), 11–17. Reprinted with permission.

TABLE 9.1
Loss Inventory for Youth

Directions
1. Read the losses listed on this table.
2. If you have experienced a listed loss, place an "x" in the appropriate "time factor" box.
3. When you have completed the entire inventory of losses, tally each loss as follows: *Multiply "impact factor" by "time factor" and enter the answer in the far right column. Add "total" column vertically for your total score.*
4. See score impact information at the end of this inventory.

The Loss Inventory for Youths assists the helping professional to determine the cumulative effect that loss events may have on young people. Reading and completing the inventory can help them understand feelings related to the loss.

Loss Inventory for Youth	Impact Factor	Time Factor			Impact "x" Time Factor
		0–6 Months	6 mos.–1 year	1 year–4 years	
		X 5	X 3	X 1	
Death of parent	10				
Death of brother/sister	10				
Divorce of parents	10				
Extended separation of parents (no divorce)	10				
Diagnosed terminal illness self/parent/sibling	10				
Death of close relative	9				
Moving to new city	9				
Major personal injury or illness (loss of limb, etc.)	9				
Abortion	9				
Rape	9				
Marriage/remarriage of parent	8				
Unplanned job loss—self/parent (fired, laid off)	8				
Retirement—parent	8				
Unwanted pregnancy	8				
Changing to new school	8				
Major change in a family member (health, behavior)	8				
Moved or kicked out of home before age 18	8				
Expulsion from school	8				
Gaining new family member (birth, adoption, relative)	7				
Change in financial status of family (better/worse)	7				
Love relationship breakup	7				
Death of a friend	7				
Diagnosed illness	6				

Sample Policies to Prevent Legal Liability

Loss Inventory for Youth	Impact Factor	Time Factor			Impact Time Factor
		0–6 Months	6 mos.–1 year	1 year–4 years	
		X 5	X 3	X 1	
Loss of harmony (conflicts) with parents, teachers, friends	6				
Brother/sister leaving home (marriage, college, run-away)	6				
Mother beginning work or going back to school	6				
Class/teacher/schedule change	5				
Sporadic school attendance	5				
Moving within city	5				
Beginning/end of school	5				
Taking new job after school	5				
Temporary separations within family (military, business)	4				
Change in physical appearance (pimples, glasses, etc.)	4				
Violations of the law (drugs, speeding)	4				
Trouble in school (teacher/principal)	4				
Change in living conditions (sharing a room, remodeling)	3				
Christmas/Easter/vacations	3				
Daily success loss (A to B on paper, didn't make team)	3				
Argument with friend	3				
				Composite Score	

Under 150: You probably have not faced major losses within the last year. It is not that your life is without loss; however, you have probably adjusted to the losses that have occurred.

150–300: You are experiencing an average amount of loss in your life. More than likely, you have experienced no or very few major losses within the last year. The losses you experienced did cause a change in your life and warranted some adjustment from you. However, there may not have been great confusion or pain with this adjustment.

300–400: You may have experienced several high level losses in the last four years, or one major loss in the last year. The losses may have caused a degree of confusion and pain, and readjustment may have been difficult and prolonged.

400 and up: You probably have experienced multiple high-level losses within the last year. These losses more than likely have affected you physically and emotionally. Adjusting to the losses has been painful and confusing, and there have been major interruptions with which you have had to deal.

Source: Babensee, B. A., & Pewuette, J. R. (1982). *Perspectives on loss: A manual for educators.* P.O. Box 1352, Evergreen, CO.

FIGURE 9.5
Crisis team Member's

Suicide Risk Assessment Scale and Referral Record

Student Name_____ Date: _____

School_____

Person Making Assessment (Please print) _____

A. *Assessment Scale*

The crisis team member making the initial suicide risk assessment of a student should develop either an affirmative YES or a negative NO answer to each of the following questions. The answers should be recorded only after an in-depth interview, for which notes are kept. There should be no "maybes." The crisis team member should probe using all available nonstructured or structured interview techniques until reasonably satisfied with the answer her or she records below. The basis for the YES answers should be recorded separately on interview notes and attached to this scale if a student is referred for being "at risk" of suicide.

YES NO

1. Is the student currently thinking or has recently thought about committing suicide? ___ ___

2. If the answer to question 1 is NO, skip to question 6.
   If the answer to question 1 is YES, does the student have some plan in mind for committing suicide, regardless of how vague he or she might be about the plan? ___ ___

3. Does the student indicate **when** he or she might commit suicide? When? ___ ___

4. Has the student indicated **where** he or she might commit suicide? Where? ___ ___

5. Does the student have the means or the resources to carry out his or her plan? ___ ___

6. Has the student previously attempted suicide? ___ ___

7. Is the student currently using mind-altering substances on either an intermittent or a chronic basis? ___ ___

8. Has the student recently and chronically experienced loss of friends, relationships, status, or self-esteem? ___ ___

9. Has the student recently experienced failure in attempts to achieve desired relationships with others, gain status or material things? ___ ___

10. If so, has there been a chronic pattern of such failure? ___ ___

11. Is the student currently experiencing abuse at home? ___ ___

12. Is the student currently experiencing turmoil at home? ___ ___

13. Is the student currently experiencing turmoil or abuse from peers? ___ ___

14. Is there a history of suicide in the student's family? ___ ___

15. Have friends of the student committed suicide? ___ ___

16. Are parents or other family members unwilling and unable to provide needed emotional support to the student? ___ ___

17. Are peers willing and able to provide needed emotional support to the student? ___ ___

18. Does the student refuse help from others? ___ ___

19. Does the student exhibit poor impulse control? ___ ___

B. Determination of Risk
- If there are one or more YES answers to questions 1–5, the student should be considered an "at-risk" student (Column A below), and referral made. If there are no YES responses to questions 1–5, the student should be noted as showing no discernible risk (Column B below) but may be referred as discussed under Item 4 below.
- Next, enter the totals of YES answers for questions 6–19 in the appropriate column.

	A At Risk	B No Discernible Student Risk
Number of YES responses to questions 1–5:	___ ___	___ ___
Number of YES responses to questions 6–19:	___ ___	___ ___
TOTAL:	___ ___	___ ___

- Please indicate any general concern you may have for the student:
- For an "at-risk" student, the higher the total score, the more at risk the student is of committing suicide.
- Please retain copies of your notes regarding the student's comments or behavior that are relevant to your assessment.

Referral Record
- Any student determined to be "at risk" should be referred for assistance in accord with school policies. The student's family should be informed.
- For a student who shows no discernible risk of committing suicide, the higher the score, the more likely that the student will eventually become an "at-risk" student. Therefore, those students who are not assessed as currently being at risk of committing suicide, but who show several signs of potentially becoming at risk, should be referred to school counselors or school social workers for monitoring. Of course, any student who indicates that he or she is being abused should be immediately referred to the proper office, in accord with legal and school policy requirements.

Student Is Referred To:
External Mental Health Service
Agency_____ Contact Person_____
Phone_____ Date_____Time_____
Parents
Name_____ Phone_____
Date_____ Time_____
Student's Counselor or
School Social Worker
Name_____ Phone_____
Date_____ Time_____
Principal's Office
Name_____ Phone_____
Date_____ Time_____
_____ Phone_____
Person completing assessment (signature)

Source: http://www.bellingham.k12.ma.us/district/Crisis%20Mgmt/riskassessment.html

Homicide Checklist

Initially

( ) Communicate with the police liaison for clarification and instructions.

( ) Notify the superintendent.

( ) Quell rumors.

( ) Notify building counselors, psychologist, social worker, or any combination of these.

( ) Convene the Crisis Team and assign duties.

Principal or Designee Will

( ) Inform the closest relatives and friends of the deceased and provide support (with police approval).

( ) Prepare a formal announcement or a written statement.

( ) Identify students, staff, and parents who are likely to be most affected by the news.

( ) Make an official announcement.

( ) As needed, assign staff members to monitor the grounds; notify parents, support staff, and feeder schools; provide support to the staff; collect student's belongings and withdraw the student's name from school rolls.

( ) Announce the time and the place of an emergency faculty meeting.

( ) Assess the need for additional community resources.

The Critical Incident Team Will

( ) Provide grief support to students.

( ) Review and distribute discussion questions to teachers. (See Resources.)

( ) Stand in for absent/affected/substitute teacher.

( ) Distribute lists of community resources.

( ) Hold an emergency faculty meeting.

( ) Provide follow-up services as needed.

( ) Assess and debrief.

FIGURE 9.6
For Parents—A Depression Checklist

The following checklist will help you assess and document *your child's feelings* and behavior. This information will help you to provide your physician or therapist with a fairly good picture of your child's emotional state.

Instructions: Be as objective and thorough as possible. Use additional paper if you need more space to share your observations or give examples.

Signs of Possible Depression *(Check all that apply.)*	Description *(How long, how often, give examples)*
Feelings. Does your child express the following:	
❑ Sadness ❑ Emptiness ❑ Hopelessness ❑ Guilt ❑ Worthlessness ❑ Not enjoying everyday pleasures	
Thinking. Is your child having difficulty	
❑ Concentrating ❑ Making decisions ❑ Completing school work ❑ Maintaining grades	
Physical Problems. Does your child complain of	
❑ Headaches ❑ Stomach aches ❑ Joint or backaches ❑ Lack of energy ❑ Sleeping problems ❑ Weight or appetite changes (gain or loss)	
Behavioral Problems. Is your child:	
❑ Irritable ❑ Not wanting to go to school ❑ Wanting to be alone most of the time ❑ Having difficulty getting along with others ❑ Cutting classes or skipping school ❑ Dropping out of sports, hobbies. or activities ❑ Drinking or using drugs	
Suicide Risk. Does your child talk or think about	
❑ Suicide ❑ Death ❑ Other morbid subjects	

Source: Dubuque S. E. (1996). *A parent's survival guide to childhood depression.* King of Prussia, PA: Center for Applied Psychology, Inc. Reprinted with permission.

FIGURE 9.7
Suicidal Assessment—Checklist*

Student's Name: _____ Date: _____ Interviewer: _____
(Suggested points to cover with student/parent)

(1) Past Attempts, Current Plans, and View of Death
    Does the individual have frequent suicidal thoughts?   Y   N
    Have there been suicide attempts by the student or significant
        others in his or her life?   Y   N
    Does the student have a detailed, feasible plan?   Y   N
    Has he or she made special arrangements, such as giving
        away prized possessions?   Y   N
    Does the student fantasize about suicide as a way to make
        others feel guilty or as a way to get to a happier afterlife?   Y   N

(2) Reactions to Precipitating Events
    Is the student experiencing severe psychological distress?   Y   N
    Have there been major changes in recent behavior, along with
        negative feelings and thoughts?   Y   N
    (Such changes are often related to the recent loss or threat
    of loss of significant others or of positive status and
    opportunity. They also may stem from sexual, physical, or
    substance abuse. Negative feelings and thoughts are often
    expressions of a sense of extreme loss, abandonment, failure,
    sadness, hopelessness, guilt, and sometimes inwardly directed anger.)

(3) Psychosocial Support
    Is there a lack of a significant other to help the student survive?   Y   N
    Does the student feel alienated?   Y   N

(4) History of Risk-Taking Behavior
    Does the student take life-threatening risks or display poor
        impulse control?   Y   N

*Use this checklist as an exploratory guide with students about whom you are concerned. Each *yes* raises the level of risk, but there is no single score indicating high risk. A history of suicide attempts, of course, is a sufficient reason for action. High risk is also associated with very detailed plans (when, where, how) that specify a lethal and readily available method, a specific time, and a location where it is unlikely that the act would be disrupted. Further high-risk indicators include the student having made final arrangements and information about a critical, recent loss. Because of the informal nature of this type of assessment, it should not be filed as part of a student's regular school records.

Source: Center for Mental Health in Schools, UCLA Dept. of Psychology, P.O. Box 951563, Los Angeles, CA 90095-1563. The center encourages widespread sharing of all resources.

Follow-Through Steps
After Assessing Suicidal Risk—Checklist

____(1) As part of the process of assessment, efforts will have been made to discuss the problem openly and in a nonjudgmental way with the student. (Keep in mind how seriously devalued a suicidal student feels. Thus, avoid saying anything demeaning or devaluing, while conveying empathy, warmth, and respect.) If the student has resisted talking about the matter, it is worth a further effort because the more the student shares, the better off one is in trying to engage the student in problem solving.

____(2) Explain to the student the importance of and your responsibility for breaking confidentiality in the case of suicidal risk. Explore whether the student would prefer taking the lead or at least be present during the process of informing parents and other concerned parties.

____(3) If not, be certain the student is in a supportive and understanding environment (not left alone/isolated) while you set about informing others and arranging for help.

____(4) Try to contact parents by phone to
a) Inform them about your concern
b) Gather additional information to assess risk
c) Provide information about the problem and available resources
d) Offer help in connecting with appropriate resources
Note: if parents are uncooperative, it may be necessary to report child endangerment after taking the following steps.

____(5) If a student is considered to be in danger, release her or him only to the parent or to someone who is equipped to provide help. In high-risk cases, if parents are unavailable (or uncooperative) and no one else is available to help, it becomes necessary to contact local public agencies (e.g., children's services, services for emergency hospitalization, local law enforcement). Agencies will want the following information:
• Student's name/address/birthdate/social security number
• Data indicating that the student is a danger to self (see Suicide Assessment—Checklist)
• Stage of parent notification
• Language spoken by parent/student
• Health coverage plan, if there is one
• Where the student is to be found

____(6) For non–high risks, if phone contacts with parents are a problem, information gathering and sharing can be done by mail.

____(7) Follow up with student and parents to determine what steps have been taken to minimize risk.

____(8) Document all steps taken and outcomes. Plan for aftermath intervention and support.

____(9) Report child endangerment, if necessary.

Source: Center for Mental Health in Schools, UCLA Dept. of Psychology, P.O. Box 951563, Los Angeles, CA 90095-1563. The center encourages widespread sharing of all resources. Reprinted with permission.

FIGURE 9.8
A Crisis Screening Interview

Interviewer_____ Date_____

Note identified problem:

Is the student seeking help? Yes No

If not, what were the circumstances that brought the student to the interview?

_____

Student's Name _____ Age _____ Birthdate _____

Sex: M F Grade _____ Current Placement _____

Born in U.S.? Yes No If No, how long in U.S.?

Ethnicity _____Primary Language _____

> We are concerned about how things are going for you. Our talk today
> will help us to discuss what's going O.K. and what's not going so well. If
> you want me to keep what we talk about confidential, I will do so—
> except for those things that I need to discuss with others in order to help
> you. In answering, please provide as much detail as you can. At times, I
> will ask you to tell me a bit more about your thoughts and feelings.

1. Where were you when the event occurred?
   (Directly at the site? nearby? out of the area?)

2. What did you see or hear about what happened?

3. How are you feeling now?

4. How well do you know those who were hurt or killed?

5. Has anything like this happened to you or any of your family before?

6. How do you think this will affect you in the days to come?
   (How will your life be different now?)

7. How do you think this will affect your family in the days to come?

8. What bothers you the most about what happened?

9. Do you think anyone could have done something to prevent it? Yes No
   Who?

10. Thinking back on what happened,

	not at all	a little	more than a little	very
How angry do you feel about it?	1	2	3	4
How sad do you feel about it?	1	2	3	4
How guilty do you feel about it?	1	2	3	4
How scared do you feel?	1	2	3	4

11. What changes have there been in your life or routine because of what happened?

12. What new problems have you experienced since the event?

13. What is your most pressing problem currently?

14. Do you think someone should be punished for what happened?

       Yes   No   Who?

15. Is this a matter of getting even or seeking revenge?

       Yes   No

    Who should do the punishing?

16. What other information do you want regarding what happened?

17. Do you think it would help you to talk to someone about how you feel about what happened?

       Yes   No   Who?   How soon?

    Is this something we should talk about now?

       Yes   No   What is it?

18. What do you usually do when you need help with a personal problem?

19. Which friends and who at home can you talk to about this?

20. What are you going to do when you leave school today?
    If you are uncertain, let's talk about what you should do.

Source: Center for Mental Health in Schools, UCLA Dept. of Psychology, P.O. Box 951563, Los Angeles, CA 90095-1563. The center encourages widespread sharing of all resources. Reprinted with permission.

CONCLUSION

Schools and communities need policies and procedures to safeguard their liability from legal action. Screening instruments give more structure to assess the student's mental health and well-being. Formal policies also prevent the harassment, the bullying, and the abuse of children and adolescents, which often lead to self-defeating and self-destructive behaviors.

Chapter 10

Compassion Fatigue
The Professional Consequences
of Caring Too Much

THE IMPORTANCE OF DEBRIEFING THE TRAUMA TEAM:
TAKING CARE OF THE CAREGIVER

One category of the most neglected people in the aftermath of a traumatic incident is often the team that went in to work with all the survivors. Team members sometimes fail to recognize the full impact the event has on their own lives. Caregivers spend most of their focus on the people who are directly involved in and impacted by the incident and fail to pay attention to their own needs. Many people have technical skills that are helpful in times of need. However, in dealing with individuals who are traumatized, the first critical factor that comes to the forefront is the mental health of the person who will be a helper. A counselor who has difficulty dealing with the rawness of feelings or who is put off by severe emotional pain is unable to function adequately, let alone effectively, in such circumstances. Therefore, it is crucial that in a crisis situation a counselor be ready physically, mentally, and behaviorally. A counselor who tries to do everything ends up not doing anything worthwhile in the short run and becomes a burden to others. Those who choose to work in crises must quickly build a sense of support through interpersonal relationships with other professionals. Caregivers must make sure that they:

- Are mentally healthy to begin with,
- Interact in positive and professional ways with colleagues,
- Stay flexible and are ready for the unexpected,
- Learn about resources and people within the community to whom they can make referrals,

- Be mindful of the influence of nonverbal actions that lend support to those in need, from giving people tissues to offering them symbols of comfort such as stuffed bears, and
- Take care of themselves through physical exercise, keeping a journal, taking in necessary nourishment, and debriefing regularly.

WHY DEBRIEF CAREGIVERS?

When a trauma response team has finished its work with the people involved in a critical incident, team members are normally tired and ready to return to their own lives. However, they still have one piece of work left to be do—namely, to take a few minutes to debrief themselves. Because they have spent several hours being exposed to the pain of the people involved in the event, they, too, have potentially become affected by it. As a result, members of the team may be having some reactions to the trauma. Through the process of debriefing the response team, three goals should be accomplished:

1. Preventing negative reactions such as vicarious traumatization, cumulative stress, and the effects of negative self-judgment
2. Teaching and reinforcing skills for team members
3. Modeling what is taught to help survivors in the debriefings

By assuring that debriefing the team is a standard operating procedure, the team members will increase their effectiveness and longevity on the team. Debriefing decreases the chances of team members having any negative personal reactions, and it monitors the team for any adverse reactions. It also prepares the team for reentry into the everyday world.

Normally, the debriefing should be done shortly after the team's work is done and before its members disburse. If a team has been involved in a particularly difficult debriefing or a series of defusings/debriefings/demobilizations over a prolonged event response, the debriefing might better be done within a few days. This will allow the team members an opportunity to process some of the event on their own and then to finish the work together. Though the "debriefing the debriefers" process normally takes 15 to 30 minutes for "regular" debriefings, it can be significantly longer for particularly difficult or long situations.

WHO DEBRIEFS THE CAREGIVERS?

Usually, the team leader can lead the "debriefing the debriefers" process. Again, if the debriefing team has been through a particularly difficult or long event, its own debriefing is best accomplished by an experienced member who was not a direct part of the debriefing. This allows all team members to participate in the full experience of the debriefing process.

THE DEBRIEFING PROCESS

The debriefing the debriefers process uses a variation of the International Critical Incident Stress Foundation (ICISF) model. It consists of three phases, REVIEW, RESPONSE, and REMIND.

The Review Phase

The REVIEW phase is essentially a combination of the introduction of the Fact/Thought phase of the regular debriefing. It utilizes questions designed to have members think about and discuss the debriefing and their participation in it. The following questions are examples of this phase:

1. How did it go?
2. How do you think you did?
3. What inappropriate thing(s) did you do?
4. What themes emerged?
5. What was the participation level of the group?

   During this phase, the leader can guide the discussion into teaching what made the debriefing go well or can give examples of other ways to have handled some aspect of the debriefing.

The Response Phase

The RESPONSE phase is a condensation of the Reaction/Symptom phase of the Mitchell model and works to elicit comments on the self-perception of the team members and any concerns they may have about their performance. The following types of questions seem to work well:

1. What did you say that you wish you hadn't?
2. What didn't you say that you wish you had?
3. How has this debriefing affected you?
4. What is the hardest part of this debriefing for you?

   During this phase, the leader guides some group discussion of the members' impressions. What usually follows is reassurance by the team members that no major errors occurred. This is also an opportunity for the team leader and team members to reassure each other that each individual contributed to the process and to offer alternative methods for handling problem issues.

The Remind Phase

The REMIND phase correlates to the Teaching/Reentry phase of the ICISF Model. Questions in this step serve to help the team remember to do the same sort of things that we encourage the debriefed people to do.

1. Is there any follow-up to be done?
2. What are you going to do to take care of yourself in the next 24 hours?
3. What will it take for you to "let go" of this debriefing?

By using this structured approach to debriefing, rauma response teams are maximizing the opportunities for teaching members new skills, minimizing the chances of members returning home distressed or full of self-doubt, and assuring team members that they are valuable assets to the team. Being involved in a trauma response team ought to be a rewarding experience for all team members. It is a responsibility to take care of the caregivers, as well as for caregivers take care of survivors.

THE COST OF CARING FOR HELPING PROFESSIONALS

With the increased incidence of violence in our society, helping professionals will continue to be called upon to process emotionally stressful events. Holaday and Smith (1995) concluded that to protect their emotional well-being, helping professionals would benefit from five categories of coping strategies: social support, task-focused behaviors, emotional distancing, cognitive self-talk, and altruism (p. 360).

Helping professionals who listen to the stories about fear, pain, and suffering of others may feel similar fear, pain, and suffering because they care. Helping professionals in all therapeutic settings are especially vulnerable to "compassion fatigue" and include emergency care workers, counselors, teachers, school administrators, mental health professionals, medical professionals, clergy, advocate volunteers, and human service workers. The concept of *compassion fatigue* emerged only in the last several years in the professional literature. It represents the cost of caring both about and for traumatized people.

Compassion fatigue is the emotional residue of exposure to working with the suffering, particularly those suffering from the consequences of traumatic events. Professionals who work with people who are suffering must contend not only with the normal stress or dissatisfaction of work but also with their emotional and personal feelings for the suffering. *Compassion fatigue* is a state of tension and preoccupation with the individual or cumulative trauma of clients, as manifested in one or more ways, including reexperiencing the traumatic event, avoidance/numbing of reminders of the event, and persistent arousal. Although similar to critical incident stress (being traumatized by something you actually experience or see), with *compassion fatigue,* helping professionals absorb the trauma through the eyes and ears of their clients. It can be thought of as secondary post-traumatic stress.

There are human costs associated with *compassion fatigue.* It reflects a physical, emotional, and spiritual fatigue or exhaustion that takes over a person and causes a decline in his or her ability to experience joy or to feel and care for others. *Compassion fatigue* is a one-way street, in which individuals are giving out a great deal of energy and compassion to others over a period of time, yet aren't able to get enough back to reassure themselves that the world is a hopeful place. This constant outputting of compassion and caring over time can lead to these feelings.

Scalise (2003) revealed that high levels of stress usually result in the release of two key hormones into the bloodstream, adrenaline and cortisol. Both have the potential to produce harmful effects over time. These include an increase in the production of blood cholesterol; a narrowing of the capillaries and other blood vessels leading into and out of the heart; a decrease in the body's ability to flush excessive cholesterol out of its system; and an increase in the depositing of plaque on the walls of the arteries. Like sleep deprivation, the effects of stress and compassion fatigue are cumulative. The ultimate outcome is that the body eventually shuts down all of its systems in fairly rapid succession. A consistent orientation toward compassion can overload the physical, mental, and emotional resources of helping professionals, leading to a dysfunctional lifestyle stress reaction such as the following:

- Developing a preoccupation with stress-producing people or situations
- Overindulging in escape behaviors, such as drugs, alcohol, pornography, or deficit spending
- Avoiding intimacy in personal relationships and seeking fantasy over reality
- Attempting to control everything and everyone as a means of compensation

- Justifying irrational actions by blaming other things, other people, or both
- Escaping behaviors by choosing to leave the profession
- Compromising ethical and professional boundaries

Compassion fatigue comes from a variety of sources. Although it often affects those working in caregiving professions—nurses, physicians, mental health workers, and clergymen—it can affect people in any kind of situation or setting where they're doing a great deal of caregiving and expending emotional and physical energy, day in and day out. *Compassion fatigue* develops over time, taking weeks, sometimes years to surface. Basically, it's a low-level, chronic clouding of caring and concern for others. Over time, the ability to feel and care for others becomes eroded through the overuse of the skills of compassion. Caregivers may also experience emotional blunting, reacting to situations differently than others would normally expect. *Compassion fatigue* happens when caregivers become emotionally drained from hearing about and being exposed to the pain and trauma of the people they are helping. Listed in the following sections is a compilation of self-care strategies that helping professionals should become aware of, to inhibit the fatigue of caring too much.

SCHOOL FACULTY AND STAFF STRATEGIES FOR TAKING CARE OF EACH OTHER

People who are involved with students and their families at school are often survivors of disaster themselves, because on a daily basis they must deal with children who are experiencing stress in the aftermath of a traumatic event. This can be incredibly taxing to teachers and staff, who feel isolated and alone with this burden. Thus, it is critical to help teachers and staff develop ongoing support systems to deal with the issues of compassion fatigue. Some of the following strategies may be helpful:

- **Seek out families who may need assistance,** those who have lost their homes, property, or even loved ones. Help them rebuild and replace lost items. Seek out charities in the community, and coordinate service resources.
- **Be alert to misplaced anger as a result of having firsthand experience with severe trauma.** Sometimes the stress from events or activities that under "normal" circumstances would seem trivial becomes huge, and anyone associated with the event could become the target for anger and frustration. This is inevitable. Administrators, counselors, teachers, and support staff need to expect anger and must learn to diffuse it.

- **Routine visits by mental health professionals to caregivers** and those in leadership positions can be very helpful. These visits can be very casual, innocuous, and unobtrusive.
- **Provide teachers, school staff, and counselors with systematic recognition** for the important support they provided during the traumatic event. Honor their efforts, validate their distress, and give them the support they need. It is often hard to talk about the toil and the stressors that have emerged. The school and the community can initiate and encourage opportunities for recognition and support.
- **Hold informational meetings and debriefings on a routine basis.** Hand out fact sheets on traumatic stress and post-traumatic stress disorder to reinforce that people are having "normal reactions to abnormal events." Many may experience delayed stress and reactive depression as long as 6 months after the traumatic event occurred.
- **Reassure all those involved that there is no ideal way to handle a traumatic event.** Many may feel that they should have been more in control of all situations, and if they had done certain things, people would not have been hurt.
- **Promote counseling support groups.** Provide support groups for children and adolescents, individual counseling in schools, and home visits by mental health professionals. Counseling should be an intricate component of both crisis intervention and Critical Incident Management Plans.

Specific Coping Skills for School Counselors and Other Helping Professionals During a Crisis or a Traumatic Event

Self-Awareness and Self-Care

1. If you are dealing with a community tragedy, learn as much as possible about the event and deal with and articulate the powerful emotions and reactions related to the event.
2. Know your own "triggers" and vulnerable areas, and learn to defuse them or avoid them.
3. Resolve your own personal issues, and continue to monitor your own reactions to others' pain.
4. Be human and allow yourself to grieve when bad things happen to others. Remember that "normal responses to abnormal situations" is true for helpers, as well as for victims.
5. Develop realistic expectations about the rewards, as well as the limitations, of being a helper. Set boundaries for yourself.
6. Become aware of and alter any irrational beliefs about the helping process.

7. Balance your work with other professional activities that provide opportunities for growth and renewal.

Ask For and Accept Help from Other Professionals

1. Find opportunities to acknowledge, express, and work through your experience in a supportive environment. Debrief yourself regularly, and build healthy support groups.
2. Seek assistance from other colleagues and caregivers who have had experience with trauma and have remained healthy and hopeful or have learned from their experience. Take their advice.
3. Delegate responsibilities and get help from others for routine work, when appropriate.
4. Develop a healthy support system to protect yourself from further fatigue and emotional exhaustion.
5. Remember that most survivors of trauma do grow and learn from their experiences and so can their helpers.

Live a Healthy, Balanced Life

1. Eat nutritious food, exercise, rest, meditate or pray, and take care of yourself as a whole being.
2. Set and keep healthy boundaries for work. Ask yourself, "Would the world fall apart if I stepped away from my work for a day or a week?"
3. Think about the idea that if you never say "no," what is your "yes" worth?
4. Find professional activities that provide opportunities for growth and renewal.
5. Take an honest look at your life before a crisis strikes. Find help in identifying your obvious risks, and work to correct or minimize them.
6. Find ways to provide yourself with emotional and spiritual strength for the future.
7. Develop and reward a sense of humor. Expose yourself to humorous situations. Learn to laugh, enjoy life, have healthy personal relationships, and breathe deeply.
8. Avoid chaotic situations and learn simplicity.
9. Regularly, take time to return to normal activities.
10. Avoid additional stressful situations.
11. Spend plenty of quiet time alone. Learning mindfulness meditation is an excellent way to ground yourself in the moment and keep your thoughts from pulling you in different directions. The ability to reconnect with a spiritual source will also help you achieve inner balance

and can produce an almost miraculous turnaround, even when your world seems its blackest.

12. Recharge your batteries daily. Something as simple as committing to eat better and stopping all other activities while eating can have an exponential benefit on both your psyche and your physical body. A regular exercise regimen can reduce stress, help you to achieve outer balance, and reenergize you for when you spend time with family and friends.
13. Hold one focused, connected, and meaningful conversation each day. This will jump-start even the most depleted batteries. Time with family and close friends feeds the soul like nothing else and, sadly, seems to be the first thing to go when time is scarce.
14. Depersonalize the process when it is appropriate by recognizing countertransference reactions and the signs of secondary traumatic stress.
15. Learn the art of a taking 15-minute vacation and taking time to be silent and very still every day.
16. Set aside at least one 2 to 4 hour period of time each week for self-care, relaxation, play, exercise, and rest.
17. Triage daily events, and prioritize tasks to avoid the tyranny of the urgent.
18. Have realistic expectations of self at the personal level and in terms of potential therapeutic outcomes with clients.
19. Resolve those things that can be attended to easily and quickly, and focus most of your available resources in those directions.
20. Learn to manage the clock, the calendar, and the appointment book by saying "no" when necessary and without feeling guilty about it.
21. Delegate to others whenever, wherever, and however it is appropriate.
22. Schedule a personal retreat at least once a year for a time of renewal, reflection, and refocusing.
23. Find two or three key people in your life as part of a personal support system and as accountability partners who have permission to offer objective feedback (Scalise, 2003). Reprinted with permission.

Compassion Fatigue Can Impair Your Functioning in Ways That You Need to Keep in Mind, So It Comes With Its Own List of "Don'ts"

1. Don't make big decisions. We advise our compassion-fatigued clients not to make any major life decisions until they've recovered physically, emotionally, and spiritually. This is perhaps the most important advice we can give. Don't quit your job, get a divorce, have an affair, or spend your money on a lavish trip or a new sports car. It may feel great at the time, but a few days or weeks later you'll find yourself waking up to the same set of problems.

2. Don't blame others. Similarly, blaming the administration, the staff, colleagues, or the "system" will do you no good. Being adversarial will only exhaust you further and will prevent the deeper healing that needs to take place.

3. Don't spend your energy complaining. We also advise that you avoid commiserating with discontented colleagues. You've heard the old saying "Misery loves company." It's easy to fall into the habit of complaining when you're consumed by compassion fatigue, but it will only make you feel worse. There are other, more constructive environments to share your feelings.

4. Don't try a quick fix. Compassion fatigue can make you vulnerable to addictive behaviors and substance abuse. We've seen many clients try to deal with compassion fatigue by working longer and harder. Others may self-medicate with alcohol and prescription drugs. A whole host of other addictive behaviors, including sex, are often used to relieve personal pain. Don't let yourself abuse work, alcohol, or drugs, and don't fall prey to a quick fix. Just as drugs can be addictive and eventually cause a whole different set of problems, the quick fix almost always ends up complicating an already overburdened life, escalating the downward spiral.

Self-Care Strategies

- **If you experience self-blame and guilt:** Distinguish between events that can be controlled and those that are uncontrollable. Be positive and focus on the positive things that are happening, one day at a time
- **If you feel helpless and hopeless:** Write down current thoughts or share your experiences with others. Try to participate in school and community events, in memorial services, and in future initiatives to prevent violence or self-destructive behavior among children and adolescents.
- **If you lose interest and feel down:** Try to arrange an interesting or positive experience each day, plan for future special events, discuss enjoyable topics; and focus on the future.
- **If you lose or gain weight (with stress, people often seek comfort food):** Cook your favorite foods and make mealtime a pleasant occasion.
- **If you have sleep difficulties:** Keep regular bedtime hours; do relaxing and calming activities 1 hour before bedtime, such as reading or listening to soft music; end the day with a positive experience.
- **If you can't concentrate and feel restless:** Change activities that may increase restlessness, participate in activities that promote relaxation, and increase physical exercise and recreational activities.
- **If you feel scared and fearful:** Participate in planned activities with friends or family; keep active and busy.

- **If you have feelings of anger and revenge (which are normal):** Express your feelings in appropriate ways, such as talking to friends, to family, and to other trusted adults; work out frustration and anger with physical exercise; or organize a living memorial for those lost with memory books, poems, letters, mementos, and so on. Public mourning has become an acceptable and meaningful way of acknowledging loss within the last decade.

The Precurser to Compassion Fatigue: Burnout

Due to the stress of helping others with trauma, counselors, teachers, and other helping professionals often experience anger, rage, or despair; feelings of powerlessness, guilt, or terror; and cynicism. After a prolonged period on the job, helping professionals may experience burnout. Take a self-inventory:

- Listen to the warning signs illuminated in the body. Rapid heartbeat, stomach pains, tightness in the chest, trembling, feeling tired all the time, headaches, and other aches and pains may be signs of stress.
- Survey your mental well-being. Difficulty in concentrating, in difficulty remembering, finding oneself more "disorganized than usual, feeling overwhelmed, or feeling fearful are all signs of stress.
- Get in touch with your emotions. Constantly feeling angry, sad, fearful, or hopeless may be signs of stress. Symptoms of burnout are listed in the following section (Ehrenreich, 2002; Schaufeli & Bunnk, 1996).

There is also the risk of experiencing *vicarious traumatization* when one is exposed to many heartrending scenes, powerful emotions, and horrifying stories. One can identify with the survivors and experience the same emotions, therefore having same traumatic reaction vicariously.

Signs of Compassion Fatigue

What used to be called *burnout* is now also labeled *compassion fatigue, secondary traumatization,* and *nervous exhaustion.* People can become prey to this insidious form of emotional exhaustion. Those who constantly and conscientiously care for others, in whatever capacity, are the most vulnerable. Compassion fatigue is a state of emotional, physical, and mental exhaustion, where one feels depleted, chronically tired, helpless, hopeless, and bad, even cynical, about oneself, work, life, and the state of the world.

The Germans have a very precise word for this "feeling the pain of the world," which they call *weltschmertz.* Caregivers are often elevated to some special status, by themselves or by others, and this only adds to the problem. Frustration is common, and one's usual sense of humor is often stretched beyond limits. Workers become exhausted, and anger comes easily to the surface. The anger of others—workers, survivors, and media—becomes difficult to deal with and may be seen as a personal attack on the worker, rather than as a normal response to exhaustion. Survivor's guilt may emerge, as workers see the losses of others when they have suffered none themselves.

Compassion fatigue is marked by a gradual disengagement, emotions are blunted, and exhaustion affects motivation and drive. The grief engendered by a loss of ideals and hope may lead to a deepening depression, a sense of helplessness and hopelessness, and a feeling that life is just not worth living. Substance abuse can arise as a form of self-medication. Although symptoms vary, the following red flags might indicate that you may have compassion fatigue:

- Abusing drugs, alcohol, or food
- Anger
- Blaming
- Chronic lateness
- Depression
- Diminished sense of personal accomplishment
- Exhaustion (physical or emotional)
- Frequent headaches
- Gastrointestinal complaints
- High expectations
- Hopelessness
- Hypertension
- Inability to maintain a balance of empathy and objectivity
- Increased irritability
- Less ability to feel joy
- Low self-esteem
- Sleep disturbances
- Workaholism

MORE SPECIFIC COPING SKILLS FOR HELPING PROFESSIONALS DURING A CRITICAL INCIDENT

With the increased incidence of violence in our society, helping professionals will continue to be called upon to process emotionally stressful events. Holaday and Smith (1995) conclude that to protect their emotional well-being, helping professionals would benefit from five categories of coping strategies: social support, task-focused behaviors, emotional distancing, cognitive self-talk, and altruism (p. 360).

To Increase Social Support

☑

❑ Work in pairs, or always be within speaking distance of another helping professional to ask for assistance or for additional emotional support.
❑ Smile and make eye contact with peers.
❑ Talk to peers about the situation, especially in terms of how they are handling the stress.
❑ Use humor to relieve tension and anxiety.
❑ Give comfort through physical contact (e.g., touch, hold, or hug people who are distraught).
❑ Take breaks with peers; share food, if available, to revitalize yourselves.

To Maintain Task-Focused Behaviors

☑

❑ Use problem-solving skills (i.e., think and plan about what needs to be done, and take an active approach to helping).
❑ Generate solutions, and quickly think of ways to resolve problems.
❑ Evaluate potential solutions. Ask: What is the most efficient thing you can do? Does it minimize harm? Identify and establish task-related priorities.
❑ Take action and request help if needed.
❑ Focus on the task at hand. Do not be distracted by what is happening.
❑ Avoid thinking about the consequences or the long-term implications of the stressful event by focusing on what has to be done now.

To Increase Emotional Distancing

☑

❑ Think of the experience as a temporary event that will be over soon.
❑ Protect yourselve from being overwhelmed. Block emotions during the event and utilize relaxation techniques.
❑ Pretend that the event is not really happening, that it is merely a dream.
❑ Think about other things that are more pleasant.
❑ Talk about unrelated topics with other helping professionals or talk to the person who is being helped about everyday, mundane things, to avoid thinking about pain, loss, and other issues.
❑ Try not to think of survivors as people, as having children or families who will be affected. Do not look at their faces.

❑ Distance yourself from the experience by singing or whistling; keep moving; look off into the distance and imagine being somewhere else.

To Manage Emotions Through Cognitive Self-Talk

☑

❑ Be mentally prepared; think about what will happen at the scene. Focus on the positive aspects of your work. Acknowledge that bad things happen to good people.
❑ Prepare physically. Take a deep breath, stand straight, and focus on staying in control.
❑ Use positive self-talk by focusing on self-competence, resourcefulness, and unique training experiences. Focus on your strengths, maintain an "optimistic perseverance," and become aware of self-defeating thoughts.
❑ Reframe interpersonal language to reduce negative impact. Change statements such as "This is horrible" to "This is challenging."
❑ Translate arduous tasks into meaningful ones; find a deeper meaning in the tasks at hand. Do not just revive someone—"Help someone get well." Celebrate with the survivors.

To Feel Better Using Altruism

☑

❑ Spare others by doing more work, so that others are relieved.
❑ Work for those who may not be as "strong," or work for those who "cannot take it as well."
❑ Remember that it is a good thing to sacrifice for others; it feels good to help others. Be thankful for the opportunity to help.
❑ Put the needs of others as paramount. Persevere and draw strength from adversity.

Stress-relieving activities are not as difficult or time-consuming as one might think. A 15-minute walk during a lunch or coffee break; talking to a coworker, a supervisor, or a mental health worker; going out to dinner or a movie; or just learning and using deep breathing exercises can significantly reduce stress. During the crisis or the critical incident, it's important to eat nutritious foods, avoid drinking large amounts of caffeine and alcohol, get some exercise whenever possible, and get as much sleep as you can, in order to continue meeting the challenges of your job. To reduce the inevitable stress response learn some stress management and other coping skills for emotional protection:

- Visualize a pleasant image (e.g., a tropical island or a natural outdoor setting) to avoid ruminating about the trauma and the impossibility of doing all that has to be done. Try to visualize the scene in some detail. For example, if you choose a beach, imagine the waves rolling up the sand, the sea gulls overhead, and the clouds in the sky. Imagine the roar of the waves, the cries of the sea gulls. Imagine feeling the sand on your feet and the warm breeze across your face.
- Take a few deep breaths. Focus your attention on feeling the air moving in and out of your body. Continue to breathe deeply. Now imagine that the tension in the muscles of your forehead is flowing out of your body with each exhalation. Do the same thing, breath by breath, with the muscle groups of your jaw, shoulders, arms, and legs.
- Press your thumbs and forefingers together tightly. Take a slow, deep breath and hold it for 2 or 3 seconds. Then slowly release your breath, while you simultaneously relax the pressure of your fingers, and slowly say to yourself "relax" (Ehrenreich, 2002, p. 30).

Working in the area of trauma response takes its toll on the helping teams, in much the same way that the event overpowered the people in it. Counseling after a crisis is a time filled with heavy emotion. It is a time of opportunity, as well as of turmoil. It demands much of counselors. Knowing what to expect can make the experience both positive and productive. Inherently, the previously mentioned coping skills reduce the negative effects of a stressful event. Helping professionals must be able to cope with their own post-traumatic stress.

Daily Crisis Response Team debriefings should be held to review and modify plans and communication, in order to promote accountability. A workable referral system, using resources within a school (school counselors, social workers, school psychologists) and within the community (mental health counselors, agency personnel), becomes very important in achieving a positive resolution of the crisis that develops when a sudden death or a suicide occurs. When managing a crisis, helping professionals need to know what to do and must have the mechanisms to restore the school and community to their precrisis equilibrium.

FIGURE 10.1
Compassion Satisfaction and Fatigue (CSF) Test

Helping others puts you in direct contact with other people's lives. As you probably have experienced, your compassion for those you help has both positive and
negative aspects. This self-test helps you to estimate your compassion status: how
much you are at risk of burnout and compassion fatigue and also your degree of
satisfaction with helping others. Consider each of the following characteristics about
you and your **current** situation. Write in the number that honestly reflects how
frequently you experienced these characteristics in the last week. Then follow the
scoring directions at the end of the self-test.

0 = Never	1 = Rarely	2 = A Few Times
3 = Somewhat Often	4 = Often	5 = Very Often

Items About You

_____ 1. I am happy.
_____ 2. I find my life satisfying.
_____ 3. I have beliefs that sustain me.
_____ 4. I feel estranged from others.
_____ 5. I find that I learn new things from those I care for.
_____ 6. I force myself to avoid certain thoughts or feelings that remind me of a
frightening experience.
_____ 7. I find myself avoiding certain activities or situations because they remind
me of a frightening experience.
_____ 8. I have gaps in my memory about frightening events.
_____ 9. I feel connected to others.
_____10. I feel calm.
_____11. I believe that I have a good balance between my work and my free time.
_____12. I have difficulty falling or staying asleep.
_____13. I have outbursts of anger or irritability with little provocation.
_____14. I am the person I always wanted to be.
_____15. I startle easily.
_____16. While working with a survivor, I think about violence against the perpetrator.
_____17. I am a sensitive person.
_____18. I have flashbacks connected to those I help.
_____19. I have good peer support when I need to work through a highly stressful
experience.
_____20. I have had firsthand experience with traumatic events in my adult life.
_____21. I have had firsthand experience with traumatic events in my childhood.
_____22. I think that I need to "work through" a traumatic experience in my life.
_____23. I think that I need more close friends.
_____24. I think that there is no one to talk with about highly stressful experiences.
_____25. I have concluded that I work too hard for my own good.
_____26. Working with those whom I help brings me a great deal of satisfaction.
_____27. I feel invigorated after working with those whom I help.

_____28. I am frightened of things a person whom I helped has said or done to me.

_____29. I experience troubling dreams similar to those of people whom I help.

_____30. I have happy thoughts about those whom I help and how I can help them.

_____31. I have experienced intrusive thoughts of times with especially difficult people whom I helped.

_____32. I have suddenly and involuntarily recalled a frightening experience while working with a person whom I helped.

_____33. I am preoccupied with more than one person whom I help.

_____34. I am losing sleep over the traumatic experiences experienced by a person whom I help.

_____35. I have joyful feelings about how I can help the survivors I work with.

_____36. I think that I might have been "infected" by the traumatic stress of those whom I help.

_____37. I think that I might be positively "inoculated" by the traumatic stress of those whom I help.

_____38. I remind myself to be less concerned about the well-being of those whom I help.

_____39. I have felt trapped by my work as a helper.

_____40. I have a sense of hopelessness associated with working with those whom I help.

_____41. I have felt "on edge" about various things, and I attribute this to working with certain people whom I help.

_____42. I wish that I could avoid working with certain people whom I help.

_____43. Some people whom I help are particularly enjoyable to work with.

_____44. I have been in danger working with people whom I help.

_____45. I feel that some people whom I help dislike me personally.

Items About Being a Helper and Your Helping Environment

_____46. I like my work as a helper.

_____47. I feel like I have the tools and resources that I need to do my work as a helper.

_____48. I have felt weak, tired, and run down as a result of my work as helper.

_____49. I have felt depressed as a result of my work as a helper.

_____50. I have thoughts that I am a "success" as a helper.

_____51. I am unsuccessful at separating helping from my personal life.

_____52. I enjoy my coworkers.

_____53. I depend on my coworkers to help me when I need it.

_____54. My coworkers can depend on me for help when they need it.

_____55. I trust my coworkers.

_____56. I feel little compassion toward most of my coworkers.

_____57. I am pleased with how I am able to keep up with helping technologird.

_____58. I feel that I am working more for the money/prestige than for personal fulfillment.

_____59. Although I have to do paperwork that I don't like, I still have time to work with those whom I help.

_____60. I find it difficult separating my personal life from my helper life.

____61. I am pleased with how I am able to keep up with helping techniques and protocols.

____62. I have a sense of worthlessness/disillusionment/resentment associated with my role as a helper.

____63. I have thoughts that I am a "failure" as a helper.

____64. I have thoughts that I am not succeeding at achieving my life goals.

____65. I have to deal with bureaucratic, unimportant tasks in my work as a helper.

____66. I plan to be a helper for a long time.

© B. Hudnall Stamm, TSRG (1995–2000). http://www.isu.edu/~bhstamm. This form may be freely copied as long as (a) authors are credited, (b) no changes are made, and (c) it is not sold.

Last updated 3/12/2002, 11:21 P.M.

Suggested reference: Stamm, B. H., & Figley, C. R. (1996). *Compassion satisfaction and fatigue test.* Available on the World Wide Web: http://www.isu.edu/~bhstamm/tests.htm. Reprinted with permission.

Scoring Instructions

Please note that research is ongoing on this scale, and the following scores should be used as a guide, not as confirmatory information.

1. Be certain that you respond to all items.
2. Mark the items for scoring:
   a. Put an x by the following 26 items: 1–3, 5, 9–11, 14, 19, 26–27, 30, 35, 37, 43, 46–47, 50, 52–55, 57, 59, 61, 66.
   b. Put a check by the following 16 items: 17, 23–25, 41, 42, 45, 48, 49, 51, 56, 58, 60, 62-65.
   c. Circle the following 23 items: 4, 6–8, 12, 13, 15, 16, 18, 20-22, 28, 29, 31-34, 36, 38–40, 44.
3. Add the numbers you wrote next to the items for each set of items and note:
   a. *Your potential for compassion satisfaction (x):*
   b. 118 and above = extremely high potential;
   c. 100–117 = high potential;
   d. 82–99 = good potential;
   e. 64–81 = modest potential;
   f. below 63 = low potential.
   g. *Your risk for burnout (check):*
   h. 36 or less = extremely low risk;
   i. 37–50 = moderate risk;
   j. 51–75 = high risk;
   k. 76–85 = extremely high risk.
   l. *Your risk for compassion fatigue (circle):*
   m. 26 or less = extremely low risk,
   n. 27–30 = low risk;
   o. 31–35 = moderate risk;
   p. 36–40 = high risk;
   q. 41 or more = extremely high risk.

The psychometric information reported here is based on a pooled sample of 370 people. Multivariate analysis of variance did not provide evidence of differences based on country of origin, type of work, or sex when age was used as a control variable.

Age	Sex	Type of Work	Country of Origin
Mean 35.4	Males n = 121 (33%)	Trauma Professional n = 58 (16%)	U.S.A. Rural-Urban mix n = 160 (43%)
Median 36	Females n = 207 (56%)	Business volunteer n = 130 (35%)	Canada-Urban n = 30 (8%)
SD 12.16	Unknown n = 42 (11%)	Red Cross n = 30 (8%)	South Africa-Urban n = 130 (35%)
		Caregivers in training n = 102 (27%)	Internet (unknown origin) n = 50 (13%)

Scale	Alpha	Mean	Standard Deviation	Interpretation
Compassion Satisfaction	.87	92.10	16.04	Higher is better satisfaction with ability to caregiver (e.g. feel it is a pleasure to help, like colleagues, feel good about ability to help and make contribution, etc.)
Burnout	.90	24.18	10.78	Higher is higher risk for burnout (feel hopeless and unwilling to deal with work, onset gradual as a result of feeling one's efforts make no difference or having very high workload)
Compassion Fatigue	.87	28.78	13.15	Higher is higher risk for compassion fatigue (symptoms of work-related PTSD, onset rapid as a result of exposure to highly stressful caregiving)

Additional information: Lay Mental Health Caregivers in Rural Africa (n = 16) (*Note:* Compassion Satisfaction Subscale was not given).

First assessment (min. 3 months' work) CF Mean 45 (SD 14.4) BO Mean 32 (SD 11.3)

Second assessment (3 months later)   CF Mean 44 (SD 13.6) BO Mean 28.86 (SD 9.6)

Here is the SPSS Scoring Code.

COMPUTE Comsat = SUM(1, 2, 3, 5, 9, 10, 11, 14, 19, 26, 27, 30, 35, 37, 43, 46, 47, 50, 52, 53, 54, 55, 57, 59, 61, 66)

COMPUTE Burnout = SUM(17, 23,24, 25, 41, 42, 45, 48, 49, 51, 56, 58, 60, 62, 63, 64, 65)

COMPUTE Compassion Fatigue = SUM(4, 6, 7, 8, 12, 13, 15, 16, 18, 20, 21, 22, 28, 29, 31, 32, 33, 34, 36, 38, 39, 40, 44)

CONCLUSION

School counselors who work in schools and have experienced multiple traumatic incidents are more susceptible to "secondary traumatic stress" or "vicarious trauma." The school counselors are more vulnerable if they knew the young person and if there was insufficient recovery time between the incidents. A growing body of research has revealed that secondary traumatic stress or vicarious trauma is associated with secondary traumatic stress disorder (Figley, 1995, 1998, 1999), as well as compassion fatigue, stress, and burnout. Figley (1995) maintained that compassion fatigue defines secondary traumatic stress as "the natural consequent behaviors and emotions resulting from knowing about a traumatizing event experienced by a significant other—the stress resulting from helping or wanting to help a traumatized or suffering person." Figley (1995, 1998, 1999) suggested that compassion stress and compassion fatigue are appropriate substitutes for secondary traumatic stress.

School counselors and related helping professionals who regularly work with trauma that affects all those who interact with the school (students, parents, teachers, and support personnel) require an ongoing support system to assist them in managing these intense normal reactions to abnormal events. Such support systems could include a peer support network, an individual colleague who provides shadow support at the time of the next incident, and supervision either in a peer supervision group or with a clinical supervisor. Just as no survivor can recover alone, no school counselor can work with trauma alone.

References

American Psychiatric Association. (2000). *Diagnostic and statistical manual of mental disorders, DSM-IV-TR*. Washington, DC: Author.

Balk, D. (1983). How teenagers cope with sibling death: Some implications for school counselors. *The School Counselor, 31*(2), 150–158.

Bereavement Association, The. (2003). *After the death by suicide* (2003). St. John's, Newfoundland, Canada: Author.

Bisson, J. I., McFarlane, A. C., & Rose, S. (2000). Psychological debriefing. In E. B. Foe, T. M. Keane, & M. J. Friedman (Eds.), *Effective treatment for PSTD*. New York: Guilford Press.

Brewin, C. R., Andrews, B., Rose, S., & Kirk, M. (1999). Acute stress disorder and post-traumatic stress disorder in victims of violent crime. *American Journal of Psychiatry, 156*(32), 360–365.

Brooks, R. (1987). Storytelling and the therapeutic process for children with learning disabilities. *Journal of Learning Disabilities, 20,* 546–550.

Bryant, R. A., Harvey, A. G., Guthrie, R., & Moulds, M. (2000). A prospective study of acute psychophysiological arousal, acute stress disorder, and post-traumatic stress disorder. *Journal of Abnormal Psychology, 109*(36), 341–344.

Cann, A. C. (1972). *Survivors of suicide.* Springfield, IL: Thomas.

Davis, J. A. (1992, May). *Graduate seminar in the forensic sciences: Mass disaster preparation and psychological trauma.* Unpublished Lecture Notes, San Diego, CA.

Davis, J. A. (1993, March). *On-site critical incident stress debriefing field interviewing techniques utilized in the aftermath of mass disaster.* Training Seminar to Emergency Responders and Police Personnel, San Diego, CA.

DeWolfe, D. (2001). *Mental health response to mass violence and terrorism.* A Training Manual for Mental Health Workers and Human Service Workers.

Dwyer, K., Osher, D., & Warger, C. (1998). *Early warning, timely response: A guide to safe schools.* Washington, DC: U.S. Department of Education.

Dyer, K. A. (2002). *Physical reactions: Acute traumatic response.* www.journeyofthe hearts.org.

Dyer, K. A. (2002). *Emotional reactions: Acute traumatic response.* www.journeyofthe hearts.org.

Dyer, K. A. (2002). *Cognitive reactions: Acute traumatic response.* www.journeyofthe hearts.org.

Dyer, K. A. (2002). *Behavioral reactions: Acute traumatic response.* www.journeyofthe hearts.org.

Dyer, K.A. (2002). *Physical responses: Acute traumatic response.* www.journeyofthe hearts.org.

Dyer, K. A. (2002). *Emotional symptoms: Acute grief response.* www.journeyofthe hearts.org.

Dyer, K. A. (2002). *Social symptoms for acute grief response.* www.journeyofthe hearts.org.

Dyer, K.A. (2002). *Behavioral symptoms for acute grief response.* www.journeyofthe hearts.org.

Dyregrov, A. (1997). The process of psychological debriefing. *Journal of Traumatic Stress, 10,* 589-604.

Ehrenreich, J. H. (2002). *A guide for humanitarian, health care, and human rights workers.* Center for Psychology and Society, State University of New York: Old Westbury.

Ehrenreich, J. H. (2001). *Coping with disasters: A guidebook to psychosocial intervention.* Center for Psychology and Society, State University of New York: Old Westbury.

Everly, G. S., & Boyle, S. (1997, April). *CISD: A meta-analysis.* Paper presented to the 4th World Congress on Stress, Trauma, and Coping in the Emergency Services Professions. Baltimore, MD.

Everly, G., Flannery, R. B., & Mitchell, J.T. (2000). Critical incident stress management (CISM): A review of the literature. *Aggression and Violent Behavior, 5*(11), 23-40.

Everly, G. S., & Mitchell, J.T. (1997). *Critical Incident Stress Management (CISM): A new era and standard of care in crisis intervention.* Ellicott City, MD: Chevron.

Fassler, D. G., & Dumas, L. S. (1998). *Help me, I'm sad: Recognizing, treating and preventing childhood and adolescent depression.* New York: Viking Press.

Figley, C. R. (1999). Compassion fatigue. In B. H. Stamm (Ed.), *Secondary traumatic stress: Self-care issues for clinicians, researchers and educators* (2nd ed.). Lutherville, MD: Sidran Press. http://www.sidran.org/digicart/products/stss.html.

Figley, C. R. (1998). Burnout as systemic traumatic stress: A model for helping traumatized family members. In C. R. Figley (Ed.), *Burnout in families: The systemic costs of caring* (pp. 15-28). Boca Raton, FL: CRC Press.

Figley, C. R. (1995). *Compassion fatigue: Coping with secondary traumatic stress disorder in those who treat the traumatized.* New York: Brunner Mazel. http://www.opengroup.com/open/dfbooks/087/0876307594.shtml.

Flannery, R. B. (1998). *The Assaulted Staff Action Program: Coping with the psychological aftermath of violence.* Ellicott City, MD: Chevron.

Foa, E., Terence, K., & Friedman, M. (2000), *Effective Treatment of PSTD.* New York: Guilford Press.

Fullerton, C. S., Ursano, R. J., Vance, K., & Wang, L. (2000). Debriefing following trauma. *Psychiatric Quarterly, 71*(23), 259-276.

Goldman, L. (2000). *Life and loss: A guide to help children with complicated grief.* New York: Taylor & Francis.

Greenstone, J. L., & Leviton, S. C. (1993). *Elements of crisis intervention: Crises and how to respond to them.* Pacific Grove, CA: Brooks/Cole.

Grinspoon, L. (1991, September). Dual diagnosis: Part II. *The Harvard Mental Health Letter, 8,* 1.

Hawton, K. (1986). *Suicide and attempted suicide among children and adolescents.* Beverly Hills, CA: Sage.

Hodgkinson, P., & Stewart, M. (1998). *Coping with catastrophe: A handbook of post-disaster psychosocial after care.* London: Taylor and Francis.

Holaday, M., & Smith, A. (1995). Coping skills training: Evaluating a training model. *Journal of Mental Health Counseling, 17*(3), 360–367.

Homeland security: The role of schools in a post 9/11 environment. (2003). Westlake Village, CA: Author. www.nssccl.org.

Kalafat, J. (1990). Adolescent suicide and the implications for school response programs. *The School Counselor, 37*(5), 11–17.

Kubler-Ross, E. (1969). *On death and dying.* San Francisco, CA: Groth House.

Kottman, T. (1990). Counseling middle school students: Techniques that work. *Elementary School Guidance and Counseling, 25,* 2.

Learner, M. D., & Shelton, R. D. (2001). *How do people respond during traumatic exposure?* Commack, NY: American Academy of Experts in Trauma Stress.

McFarlane, A. C. (1988). The longitudinal course of post-traumatic morbidity: The range of outcomes and their predictors. *Journal of Nervous and Mental Disease, 76*(42), 30–39.

McKee, P. W., Jones, R. W., & Barbe, R. H. (1993). *Suicide and the school: A practical guide to suicide prevention.* Horsham, PA: LRP Productions.

Mitchell, J. T. (1983). When disaster strikes: The critical incident stress debriefing process. *Journal of Emergency Services, 8,* 36–39.

Mitchell, J. T. (1988a). The history, status and future of critical incident stress debriefing process. *Journal of Emergency Medical Services, 8*(1), 36–39.

Mitchell, J. T. (1988b). Development and functions of a critical incident stress debriefing. *Journal of Emergency Medical Services, 13*(12), 43–46.

Mitchell, J. T., & Everly, G. S. (1996). *Critical Incident Stress Debriefing: An operations manual.* Ellicott City, MD: Chevron.

Nader, K., Pynoos, R., Fairbanks, L., & Frederick, C. (1990). Children's PTSD reactions one year after a sniper attack in their school. *American Journal of Psychiatry, 147*(36), 1526–1530.

National Association of School Psychologists. (2001). *Helping children and youth cope with this crisis.* (2001). Bethesda, MD: Author.

National Organization for Victims Assistance. (2001). *Crisis management/crisis intervention.* Washington, DC: Author.

Perrone, P. A. (1987). Counselor response to adolescent suicide. *The School Counselor, 35*(19), 12–16.

Pfefferbaum, B., & Doughty, D. (2001). Increased alcohol use in a treatment sample of Oklahoma City bombing victims. *Psychiatry, 63*(22), 296–303.

Pfefferbaum, B., Seale, T., McDonald, N., Brandt, E., Rainwater, S., Maynard, B., & Miller, P. (2001). Posttraumatic stress two years after the Oklahoma City bombing in youths geographically distant from the explosion. *Psychiatry, 63*(22), 358–370.

Pynoos, R., Goenjian, A., Tashjian, M., Karakashian, M., Manjikian, R., & Manoukian, G. (1993). Post-traumatic stress reactions in children after the 1988 Armenian earthquake. *British Journal of Psychiatry, 163*(46), 239–247.

Pynoos, R., & Nader, K. (1993). Issues in the treatment of posttraumatic stress in children and adolescents. In J. P. Wilson & B. Rapheal (Eds.), *International handbook of traumatic stress syndromes* (pp. 535–549). New York: Plenum.

Quinnett, P. (2002). *The many paths and the wall to suicide*. Spokane, WA: QPR Institute, QPRInstitute.com.

Rando, T. (1993). *Grief, dying and death*. Champaign, IL: Research Press.

Rose, S., Brewin, C. R., Andrews, B., & Kirk, M. (1999). A randomized controlled trial of individual psychological debriefing of victims of violent crime. *Psychological Medicine, 29*(16), 793–799.

Rustemli, A., & Karanci, A. (1996). Distress reactions and earthquake-related cognitions of parents and their adolescent children in a victimized population. *Journal of Social Behavior, 38*(11), 767–780.

Sandoval, J. (1985). Crisis counseling: Conceptualizations and general principals. *School Psychology Review, 14*, 257–265.

Scalise, E. (2003). Compassion fatigue: Managing yourself. *Newslink*. Richmond, VA: Board of Professional Counselors and Marriage and Family Therapists.

Schaufeli, W., & Buunk, B. (1996). Professional burnout. In M. Schabracq, J. Winnubst, & C. Cooper (Eds.), *Handbook of work and health psychology* (pp. 311–346). New York: Wiley.

Sheeley, V. L., & Herily, B. (1989). Counseling suicidal teens: A duty to warn and protect. *The School Counselor, 37*, 89–101.

Slaikeu, K. A. (1984). *Crisis intervention: A handbook for practice and research*. Boston: Allyn & Bacon.

Smead, V. S. (1988). Best practices in crisis intervention. In A. Thomas & J. Grimes (Eds.), *Best practices in school psychology* (pp. 674–693). Washington, DC: National Association of School Psychologists.

Steele, W., & Raider, M. (2002). *Structured sensory interventions for traumatized children, adolescents and parents: Strategies to alleviate trauma (SITCAP)*. New York: Edwin Mellen Press.

Stephens, R. (2003). *Homeland security: The role of schools in a post 9/11 environment*. Westlake Village, CA: National School Safety Center.

Stramm, B. H., & Figley, C. R. (1996). Compassion satisfaction and fatigue test. www.isu.edu/bstramm/tests.htm.

Thompson, R. A. (1990, February). Strategies for crisis management in the schools. National Association of Secondary School Principals. *Bulletin, 74*(523), 54–58.

Thompson, R.A. (1993). Post-traumatic stress and post-traumatic loss debriefing: Brief strategic intervention for survivors of sudden loss. *The School Counselor, 41*, 16–21.

Thompson, R.A. (1995). Being prepared for suicide or sudden death in schools: Tools to restore equilibrium. *Journal of Mental Health Counseling, 17*(3), 264–277.

Unsafe School Choice Option (USCO). http://www.ed.gov/offices/OESE/SDFS/unsafeschoolchoice.doc

United States Secret Service and United States Department of Education. (2002). *The final report and findings of the safe school initiative: Implications for the prevention of school attacks in the United States*. Washington, DC: Author.

U.S. Public Health Service (1999). *The Surgeon General's Call To Action To Prevent Suicide*. Washington, DC: Author.

Wilson, D., & Sigman, P. (1996). *Guide to disaster recovery program design and implication: The Missouri Model—putting the pieces back together*. Jefferson City, MO: Missouri Department of Mental Health.

Index